# Killing
# Lincoln

# Killing Lincoln

### THE
### SHOCKING ASSASSINATION
### THAT CHANGED AMERICA
### FOREVER

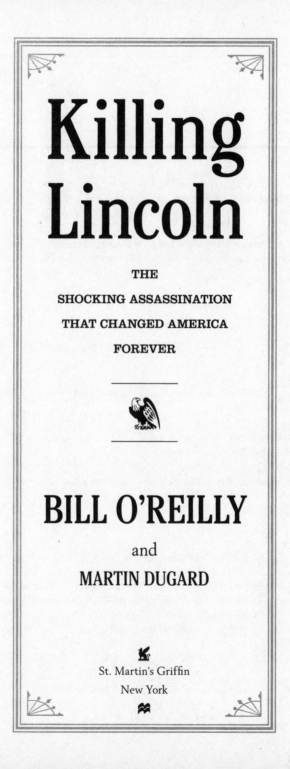

## BILL O'REILLY

### and

### MARTIN DUGARD

St. Martin's Griffin
New York

www.stmartins.com

Designed by Meryl Sussman Levavi
Maps by Gene Thorp

The Library of Congress has cataloged the Henry Holt edition as follows:

O'Reilly, Bill.
  Killing Lincoln : the shocking assassination that changed America forever / Bill O'Reilly and Martin Dugard.—1st ed.
    p. cm.
  Includes bibliographical references and index.
  ISBN 978-0-8050-9307-0 (hardcover)
  ISBN 978-1-4299-9687-7 (e-book)
  1. Lincoln, Abraham, 1809–1865—Assassination. I. Dugard, Martin. II. Title.
  E457.5.O74 2011
  973.7092—dc22

                                                                    2011014342

ISBN 978-1-250-01216-6 (trade paperback)

St. Martin's Griffin books may be purchased for educational, business, or promotional use. For information on bulk purchases, please contact the Macmillan Corporate and Premium Sales Department at 1-800-221-7945, extension 5442, or write to specialmarkets@macmillan.com.

First published by Henry Holt, an imprint of Henry Holt and Company, LLC

First St. Martin's Griffin Edition: September 2015

1  3  5  7  9  10  8  6  4  2

For Makeda Wubneh,
who makes the world a better place

# Killing
# Lincoln

# A NOTE TO READERS

The story you are about to read is true and truly shocking. It has been 150 years since the beginning of the Civil War, the bloodiest war in our nation's history, a conflict so full of horror it is almost impossible to describe. The assassination of President Abraham Lincoln, only days after the end of the war, was a terrible tragedy. Much has been speculated about the events leading up to the murder and immediately afterward, but few people know what *really* happened.

Before historian Martin Dugard and I began writing this book, I *thought* I understood the facts and implications of the assassination. But even though I am a former teacher of history, I had no clue. The ferocious assassination plan itself still has elements that have not been clarified. This is a saga of courage, cowardice, and betrayal. There are layers of proven conspiracy and alleged conspiracy that will disturb you. You will learn much in these pages, and the experience, I believe, will advance your understanding of our country, and how Lincoln's murder changed it forever.

This book is a departure from the

contemporary nonfiction I have written for more than a decade and from the daily news analysis that I do on television. But the lessons you will learn within these pages are relevant to all our lives. For those of us who want to improve the United States and keep it the greatest nation in the world, we must be aware of the true heroes who have made the country great as well as the villains who have besmirched it.

Finally, this book is written as a thriller. But don't let the style fool you. What you are about to read is unsanitized and uncompromising. It is a no spin American story, and I am proud of it.

BILL O'REILLY
*April 3, 2011*
*Long Island, New York*

# PROLOGUE

SATURDAY, MARCH 4, 1865
WASHINGTON, D.C.

The man with six weeks to live is anxious.

He furls his brow, as he does countless times each day, and walks out of the Capitol Building, which is nearing completion. He is exhausted, almost numb.

Fifty thousand men and women stand in pouring rain and ankle-deep mud to watch Abraham Lincoln take the oath of office to begin his second term. His new vice president, Andrew Johnson, has just delivered a red-faced, drunken, twenty-minute ramble vilifying the South that has left the crowd squirming, embarrassed by Johnson's inebriation.

So when Lincoln steps up to the podium and delivers an eloquent appeal for reunification, the spiritual message of his second inaugural address is all the more uplifting. "With malice toward none, with charity for all, with firmness in the right as God gives us to see the right, let us strive on to finish the work we are in, to bind up the nation's wounds, to care for him who shall have borne the battle and for his widow and his orphan, to do all which may achieve and cherish a just and lasting peace among ourselves and with all nations," the president intones humbly.

Despite his exhaustion, Lincoln is charismatic. And momentarily energized.

Suddenly, the sun bursts through the clouds as he speaks, its light enveloping the tall and outwardly serene Lincoln. But 120 miles away in the Virginia railroad junction of Petersburg, any thought of serenity is a fantasy. The Confederate army, under the command of General Robert E. Lee, has been pinned inside the city for more than 250 days by Union forces under the command of General Ulysses S. Grant. Though living in trenches and reduced to eating rats and raw bacon, Lee's men will not surrender. Instead, Lee is making plans to slip out of Petersburg and escape south to the Carolinas. If he succeeds, Lincoln's prayer for a reunified United States of America may never be answered. America will continue to be divided into a North and a South, a United States of America and a Confederate States of America.

∽

Lincoln's inaugural speech is a performance worthy of a great dramatic actor. And indeed, one of America's most famous thespians stands just a few feet away as Lincoln raises his right hand. John Wilkes Booth is galvanized by the president's words—though not in the way Lincoln intends.

Booth, twenty-six, raised in Maryland, is an exceptional young man. Blessed with a rakish smile and a debonair gaze, he is handsome, brilliant, witty, charismatic, tender, and able to bed almost any woman he wants—and he has bedded quite a few. It's no wonder that the actor has known success on the Broadway stage.

His fiancée stands at his side, a sensual young woman whose senator father has no idea that his daughter is secretly engaged to a man of Booth's lowly theatrical calling. Lucy Hale and John Wilkes Booth are a beautiful young couple quite used to the adoration of high society and the opposite sex. Yet not even she knows that Booth is a Confederate sympathizer, one who nurses a pathological hatred for Lincoln and the North. Lucy has no idea that her lover has assembled a crack team of conspirators to help him bring down the president. They have guns, financing, and a precise plan. At this point, patience is their watchword.

Standing in the cold Washington drizzle in the shadow of the Capitol dome, Booth feels nothing but hot rage and injustice. The

*John Wilkes Booth: celebrity, Confederate
sympathizer, assassin*

actor is impulsive and prone to the melodramatic. Just before Lincoln's speech, as the president stepped out onto the East Portico, Booth's carefully crafted conspiracy was instantly forgotten.

Though he had no gun or knife, Booth lunged at Lincoln. An officer from Washington's Metropolitan Police, a force known to be heavily infiltrated by Confederate sympathizers, grabbed him hard by the arm and pulled him back. Booth struggles, which only made Officer John William Westfall grasp him tighter. Like everyone else in the city, Westfall is well aware that there are plots against Lincoln's life. Some say it's not a matter of if but when the president will die. Yet rather than arrest Booth, or even pull him aside for questioning, Westfall accepted Booth's excuse that he merely stumbled. Arresting a celebrity like Booth might have caused the policeman problems.

But Booth is definitely not finished. He seethes as he listens to Lincoln's speech. The grace and poetry of the words ignite his rage. The sight of so many black faces beaming up at Lincoln from the crowd makes him want to vomit. No, Booth is most definitely not finished. If anything, his determination to knock Lincoln off his "throne" becomes more intense.

Lincoln isn't finished, either. The president has epic plans for his second term in office. It will take every one of those four years, and maybe longer, to heal the war-torn nation. Healing is Lincoln's one overriding ambition, and he will use every last bit of his trademark determination to see it realized. Nothing must stand in his way.

But evil knows no boundaries. And it is a most powerful evil that is now bearing down on Abraham Lincoln.

# Part One

❧

# TOTAL WAR

*Lincoln with Union troops at Antietam*

# CHAPTER ONE

The man with fourteen days to live is himself witnessing death. Lincoln (he prefers to go by just his last name. No one calls him "Abe," which he loathes. Few call him "Mr. President." His wife actually calls him "Mr. Lincoln," and his two personal secretaries playfully refer to him as "the Tycoon") paces the upper deck of the steamboat *River Queen*, his face lit now and again by distant artillery. The night air smells of the early spring, damp with a hint of floral fragrance. The *River Queen* is docked at City Point, a bustling Virginia port that was infiltrated by Confederate spies last August. Yet Lincoln strides purposefully back and forth, unprotected and unafraid, as vulnerable as a man can be to sniper fire, the bombardment serving as the perfect distraction from his considerable worries. When will this war ever end?

As one Confederate soldier will put it, "the rolling thunder of the heavy metal" began at nine P.M. Once the big guns destroy the Confederate defenses around Petersburg, the Union army—*Lincoln's* army—will swarm from their positions and race across no-man's-land into the enemy trenches, hell-bent on capturing the city that has eluded them for ten long months.

What happens after that is anyone's guess.

In a best-case scenario, Lincoln's general in chief, Ulysses S. Grant,

*Federal supply boats in the harbor of City Point, Virginia, 1865*

will trap Confederate general Robert E. Lee and his army inside Petersburg, forcing their surrender. This is a long shot. But if it happens, the four-year-old American Civil War will be over, and the United States will be divided no more. And this is why Abraham Lincoln is watching the battlefield.

But Marse Robert—"master" as rendered in southern parlance—has proven himself a formidable opponent time and again. Lee plans to escape and sprint for the North Carolina border to link up with another large rebel force. Lee boasts that his Army of Northern Virginia can hold out forever in the Blue Ridge Mountains, where his men will conceal themselves among the ridges and thickets. There are even bold whispers among the hardcore Confederates about shedding their gray uniforms for plain civilian clothing as they sink undercover to fight guerrilla-style. The Civil War will then drag on for years, a nightmare that torments the president.

Lincoln knows that many citizens of the North have lost their stomach for this war, with its modern technology like repeating rifles and long-range artillery that have brought about staggering losses of life. Anti-Lincoln protests have become more common than the battles themselves. Lee's escape could guarantee that the northern states rise up and demand that Lincoln fight no more. The Confederates, by default, will win, making the chances of future reunification virtually nonexistent.

Nothing scares Lincoln more. He is so eager to see America healed that he has instructed Grant to offer Lee the most lenient surrender terms possible. There will be no punishment of Confederate soldiers. No confiscation of their horses or personal effects. Just the promise of a hasty return to their families, farms, and stores, where they can once again work in peace.

∽

In his youth on the western frontier, Lincoln was famous for his amazing feats of strength. He once lifted an entire keg of whiskey off the ground, drank from the bung, and then, being a teetotaler, spit the whiskey right back out. An eyewitness swore he saw Lincoln drag a thousand-pound box of stones all by himself. So astonishing was his physique that another man unabashedly described young Abraham Lincoln as "a cross between Venus and Hercules."

But now Lincoln's youth has aged into a landscape of fissures and contours, his forehead and sunken cheeks a road map of despair and brooding. Lincoln's strength, however, is still there, manifested in his passionate belief that the nation must and can be healed. He alone has the power to get it done, if fate will allow him.

Lincoln's top advisers tell him assassination is not the American way, but he knows he's a candidate for martyrdom. His guts churn as he stares out into the night and rehashes and second-guesses his thoughts and actions and plans. Last August, Confederate spies had killed forty-three people at City Point by exploding an ammunition barge. Now, at a rail-thin six foot four, with a bearded chin and a nose only a caricaturist could love, Lincoln's unmistakable silhouette makes him an easy target, should spies once again lurk nearby. But Lincoln is not afraid. He is a man of faith. God will guide him one way or another.

On this night Lincoln calms himself with blunt reality: right now, the most important thing is for Grant to defeat Lee. Surrounded by darkness, alone in the cold, he knows that Grant surrounding Lee and crushing the will of the Confederate army is all that matters.

Lincoln heads to bed long after midnight, once the shelling stops and the night is quiet enough to allow him some peace. He walks belowdecks to his stateroom. He lies down. As so often happens when he stretches out his frame in a normal-sized bed, his feet hang over the end, so he sleeps diagonally.

Lincoln is normally an insomniac on the eve of battle, but he is so tired from the mental strain of what has passed and what is still to come that he falls into a deep dream state. What he sees is so vivid and painful that when he tells his wife and friends about it, ten days later, the description shocks them beyond words.

∽

The dream finally ends as day breaks. Lincoln stretches as he rises from bed, missing his wife back in Washington but also loving the thrill of being so close to the front. He enters a small bathroom, where he stands before a mirror and water basin to shave and wash his hands and face. Lincoln next dons his trademark black suit and scarfs a quick breakfast of hot coffee and a single hard-boiled egg, which he eats while reading a thicket of telegrams from his commanders, including Grant, and from politicians back in Washington.

Then Lincoln walks back up to the top deck of the *River Queen* and stares off into the distance. With a sigh, he recognizes that there is nothing more he can do right now.

It is April 2, 1865. The man with thirteen days left on earth is pacing.

# CHAPTER TWO

Sunday, April 2, 1865
Petersburg, Virginia

There is no North versus South in Petersburg right now. Only Grant versus Lee—and Grant has the upper hand. Lee is the tall, rugged Virginian with the silver beard and regal air. Grant, forty-two, is sixteen years younger, a small, introspective man who possesses a fondness for cigars and a whisperer's way with horses. For eleven long months they have tried to outwit one another. But as this Sunday morning descends further and further into chaos, it becomes almost impossible to remember the rationale that has defined their rivalry for so long.

At the heart of it all is Petersburg, a two-hundred-year-old city with rail lines spoking outward in five directions. The Confederate capital at Richmond lies twenty-three miles north—or, in the military definition, based upon the current location of Lee's army, to the rear.

The standoff began last June, when Grant abruptly abandoned the battlefield at Cold Harbor and wheeled toward Petersburg. In what would go down as one of history's greatest acts of stealth and logistics, Grant withdrew 115,000 men from their breastworks under cover of darkness and marched them south, crossed the James River without a single loss of life, and then pressed due west to Petersburg. The city was unprotected. A brisk Union attack would have taken the city within hours. It never happened.

*Robert E. Lee and Ulysses S. Grant*

Grant's commanders dawdled. Lee raced in reinforcements. The Confederates dug in around Petersburg just in time, building the trenches and fortifications they would call home through the blazing heat of summer, the cool of autumn, and the snow and bitter freezing rain of the long Virginia winter.

Under normal circumstances, Grant's next move would be to surround the city, cutting off those rail lines. He could then effect a proper siege, his encircled troops denying Lee's army and the inhabitants of Petersburg all access to food, ammunition, and other supplies vital to life itself—or, in more graphic terms, Grant's men would be the hangman's noose choking the life out of Petersburg. Winning the siege would be as simple as cinching the noose tighter and tighter with each passing day, until the rebels died of starvation or surrendered, whichever came first.

∽

But the stalemate at Petersburg is not a proper siege, even though the press is fond of calling it that. Grant has Lee pinned down on three sides but has not surrounded his entire force. The Appomattox River

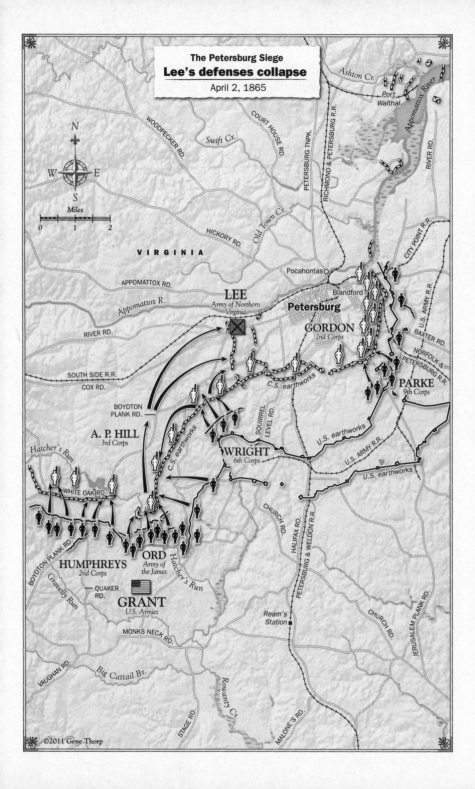

The Petersburg Siege
**Lee's defenses collapse**
April 2, 1865

makes that impossible. Broad and deep, it flows through the heart of Petersburg. The Confederates control all land north of the river and use it as a natural barrier against Union attack from the rear. This allows resupply trains to chug down from Richmond on a regular basis, keeping the Confederates armed and fed.

In this way there is normalcy, allowing men like Lee to attend church on Sundays, as he would in peacetime. Or a young general like A. P. Hill to live on a nearby estate with his pregnant wife and two small daughters, enjoying parenthood and romance. The men on both sides of the trenches live in squalor and mud, enduring rats and deprivation. But there is order there, too, as they read their newspapers and letters from home and cook their meager breakfast, lunch, and dinner.

The Confederate lines are arranged in a jagged horseshoe, facing south—thirty-seven miles of trenches and fortifications in all. The outer edges of the horseshoe are two miles from the city center, under the commands of A. P. Hill on the Confederate right and John B. Gordon on the left. Both are among Lee's favorite and most courageous generals, so it is natural that he has entrusted Petersburg's defenses to them.

The cold, hard truth, however, is that Robert E. Lee's dwindling army is reduced to just 50,000 men—only 35,000 of them ready to fight. String them out along thirty-seven miles and they are spread very thin indeed. But they are tough. Time and again over the past 293 days, Grant has attacked. And time and again, Lee's men have held fast.

Lee cannot win at Petersburg. He knows this. Grant has almost four times as many soldiers and a thousand more cannon. The steam whistles of approaching trains have grown less and less frequent in the past few months, and Lee's men have begun to starve. Confederate rations were once a pound of meal and a quarter pound of bacon a day, with an occasional tin of peas. Now such a meal would be considered a fantasy. "Starvation, literal starvation, was doing its deadly work. So depleted and poisoned was the blood of many of Lee's men from insufficient and unsound food that a slight wound which would probably not have been reported at the beginning of the war would often cause blood poison, gangrene, and death," one Confederate general will later write.

Many Confederate soldiers slide out of their trenches on moonless nights and sprint over to the Union lines to surrender—anything to fill their aching bellies. Those that remain are at their breaking point. The best Lee can hope for is to escape. For months and months, this has meant one of two options: abandon the city under cover of darkness and pull back toward Richmond or punch a hole in the Union lines and march south. In both cases, the goal is to reach the Carolinas and the waiting Confederate reinforcements.

∞

On the afternoon of April 1, Grant removes the second option. At the decisive Battle of Five Forks, General Phil Sheridan and 45,000 men capture a pivotal crossing, cutting off the main road to North Carolina, handing General George Pickett his second disastrous loss of the war—the first coming at Gettysburg, and the infamous ill-fated charge that bears his name. Five Forks is the most lopsided Union victory of the war. More than 2,900 southern troops are lost.

It is long after dark when word of the great victory reaches Grant. He is sitting before a campfire, smoking one of the cigars he came to cherish long ago in the Mexican War. Without pausing, Grant pushes his advantage. He orders another attack along twelve miles of Confederate line. He hopes this will be the crushing blow, the one that will vanquish Lee and his army once and for all. His soldiers will attack just before dawn, but the artillery barrage will commence immediately. This is the bombardment Lincoln watches from eight miles away in City Point—the president well understanding that the massive barrage will cause devastating casualties and panic in the Confederate ranks.

The infantry opens fire at four A.M., per Grant's orders, with a small diversionary attack to the east of Petersburg—cannon and musket fire mainly, just enough to distract the Confederates.

Forty-five minutes later, as soon there is enough light to see across to the enemy lines, Grant launches hell. Some 100,000 men pour into the Confederate trenches, screaming curses, throwing themselves on the overmatched rebels. The fighting is often hand to hand, and at such close range that the soldiers can clearly see and smell the men they're killing. And, of course, they hear the screams of the dying.

The Union attack is divided into two waves. Just a few hours earlier, Major General John G. Parke was so sure that the assault would fail that he requested permission to call it off. But now Parke obeys orders and leads the bluecoats to the right flank. Major General Horatio Wright, employing a revolutionary wedge-shaped attack column, charges from the left flank. Wright is a West Point–trained engineer and will later have a hand in building the Brooklyn Bridge and completing the Washington Monument. He has spent months scrutinizing the Confederate defenses, searching for the perfect location to smash the rebels. Wright is far beyond ready for this day—and so are his men.

General Wright's army shatters Lee's right flank, spins around to obliterate A. P. Hill's Third Corps, then makes a U-turn and marches on Petersburg—all within two hours. The attack is so well choreographed that many of his soldiers are literally miles in front of the main Union force. The first rays of morning sunshine have not even settled upon the Virginia countryside when, lacking leadership and orders, Wright's army is stymied because no other Union divisions have stepped up to assist him. Wright's army must stop its advance.

∽

Meanwhile, Lee and his assistants, Generals Pete Longstreet and A. P. Hill, gape at Wright's army from the front porch of Lee's Confederate headquarters. They can see the destruction right in front of them. At first, as Longstreet will later write, "it was hardly light enough to distinguish the blue from the gray." The three of them stand there, Lee with his wrap against the chill, as the sun rises high enough to confirm their worst fears: every soldier they can see wears blue.

A horrified A. P. Hill realizes that his army has been decimated. Lee faces the sobering fact that Union soldiers are just a few short steps from controlling the main road he plans to use for his personal retreat. Lee will be cut off if the bluecoats in the pasture continue their advance. The next logical step will be his own surrender.

Which is why, as he rushes back into the house and dresses quickly, Lee selects his finest gray uniform, a polished pair of riding boots, and then takes the unusual precaution of buckling a gleaming ceremonial sword around his waist—just in case he must offer it to his captors.

It is Sunday, and normally Lee would be riding his great gray gelding, Traveller, into Petersburg for services. Instead, he must accomplish three things immediately: the first is to escape back into the city; the second is to send orders to his generals, telling them to fall back to the city's innermost defenses and hold until the last man or nightfall, whichever comes first. The third is to evacuate Petersburg and retreat back across the Petersburg bridges, wheel left, and race south toward the Carolinas.

There, Lee believes, he can regain the upper hand. The Confederate army is a nimble fighting force, at its best on open ground, able to feint and parry. Once he regains that open ground, Lee can keep Grant's army off balance and gain the offensive.

If any of those three events do not take place, however, he will be forced to surrender—most likely before dusk.

Fortune, however, is smiling on Lee. Those Union soldiers have no idea that Marse Robert himself is right in front of them, for if they did, they would attack without ceasing. Lee is the most wanted man in America. The soldier who captures him will become a legend.

The Union scouts can clearly see the small artillery battery outside Lee's headquarters, the Turnbull house, and assume that it is part of a much larger rebel force hiding out of sight. Too many times, on too many battlefields, soldiers who failed to observe such discretion have been shot through like Swiss cheese. Rather than rush forward, the Union scouts hesitate, looking fearfully at Lee's headquarters.

Seizing the moment, Lee escapes. By nightfall, sword still buckled firmly around his waist, Lee crosses the Appomattox River and then orders his army to do the same.

The final chase has begun.

# CHAPTER THREE

Monday, April 3, 1865
Petersburg, Virginia

Lee's retreat is unruly and time-consuming, despite the sense of urgency. So it is, more than eight hours after Lee ordered his army to pull out of Petersburg, that General U. S. Grant can still see long lines of Confederate troops marching across the Appomattox River to the relative safety of the opposite bank. The bridges are packed. A cannon barrage could kill hundreds instantly, and Grant's batteries are certainly close enough to do the job. All he has to do is give the command. Yes, it would be slaughter, but there is still a war to be won. Killing those enemy soldiers makes perfect tactical sense.

But Grant hesitates.

The war's end is in sight. Killing those husbands and fathers and sons will impede the nation's healing. So now Grant, the man so often labeled a butcher, indulges in a rare act of military compassion and simply lets them go. He will soon come to regret it.

For now, his plan is to capture the Confederates, not to kill them. Grant has already taken plenty of prisoners. Even as he watches these rebels escape, Grant is scheming to find a way to capture even more.

The obvious strategy is to give chase, sending the Union army across the Appomattox in hot pursuit. Lee certainly expects that.

But Grant has something different in mind. He aims to get ahead

of Lee and cut him off. He will allow the Confederates their unmolested thirty-six-hour, forty-mile slog down muddy roads to Amelia
Court House, where the rebels believe food is waiting. He will let
them unpack their rail cars and gulp rations to their hearts' content.
And he will even allow them to continue their march to the Carolinas—
but only for a while. A few short miles after leaving Amelia Court
House, Lee's army will run headlong into a 100,000-man Union roadblock. This time there will be no river to guard Lee's rear. Grant will
slip that noose around the Confederate army, then yank on its neck
until it can breathe no more.

∞

Grant hands a courier the orders. Then he telegraphs President Lincoln at City Point, asking for a meeting. Long columns of rebels still
clog the bridges, but the rest of Petersburg is completely empty, its
homes shuttered, the civilians having long ago given them over to the
soldiers, and soldiers from both sides are now racing across the countryside toward the inevitable but unknown point on the map where they
will fight to the death in a last great battle. Abandoned parapets, tents,
and cannons add to the eerie landscape. "There was not a soul to be
seen, not even an animal in the streets," Grant will later write. "There
was absolutely no one there."

The five-foot-eight General Grant, an introspective man whom
Abraham Lincoln calls "the quietest little man" he's ever met, has
Petersburg completely to himself. He lights a cigar and basks in the still
morning air, surrounded by the ruined city that eluded him for 293
miserable days.

He is Lee's exact opposite: dark-haired and sloppy in dress. His
friends call him Sam. "He had," noted a friend from West Point, "a
total absence of elegance." But like Marse Robert, Grant possesses a
savant's aptitude for warfare—indeed, he is capable of little else.
When the Civil War began he was a washed-up, barely employed
West Point graduate who had been forced out of military service,
done in by lonely western outposts and an inability to hold his liquor.
It was only through luck and connections that Grant secured a commission in an Illinois regiment. But it was tactical brilliance, courage
under fire, and steadfast leadership that saw him rise to the top.

THE REISSUE OF

# HARPER'S WEEKLY.

## A JOURNAL OF CIVILIZATION.

VOL. VII.—No. 343.] NEW YORK, SATURDAY, JULY 25, 1863. [SINGLE COPIES SIX CENTS. $3.00 PER YEAR IN ADVANCE.

Entered according to Act of Congress, in the Year 1863, by Harper & Brothers, in the Clerk's Office of the District Court for the Southern District of New York.

MAJOR-GENERAL ULYSSES S. GRANT ("UNCONDITIONAL SURRENDER" GRANT).—FROM A NEW PHOTOGRAPH JUST RECEIVED FROM VICKSBURG.—[SEE PAGE 472.]

*General Grant, "Sam" to his friends*

The one and only time he met Lee was during the Mexican War. Robert E. Lee was already a highly decorated war hero, while Grant was a lieutenant and company quartermaster. He despised being in charge of supplies, but it taught him invaluable lessons about logistics and the way an army could live off the land through foraging when cut off from its supply column. It was after one such scrounge in the Mexican countryside that the young Grant returned to headquarters in a dirty, unbuttoned uniform. The regal Lee, Virginian gentleman, was appalled when he caught sight of Grant and loudly chastised him for his appearance. It was an embarrassing rebuke, one the thin-skinned, deeply competitive Grant would never forget.

∞

Lee isn't the only Confederate general Grant knows from the Mexican War. James "Pete" Longstreet, now galloping toward Amelia Court House, is a close friend who served as Grant's best man at his wedding. At Monterrey, Grant rode into battle alongside future Confederate president Jefferson Davis. There are scores of others. And while he'd known many at West Point, it was in Mexico that Grant learned how they fought under fire—their strengths, weaknesses, tendencies. As with the nuggets of information he'd learned as a quartermaster, Grant tucked these observations away and then made keen tactical use of them during the Civil War—just as he is doing right now, sitting alone in Petersburg, thinking of how to defeat Robert E. Lee once and for all.

Grant lights another cigar—a habit that will eventually kill him—and continues his wait for Lincoln. He hopes to hear about the battle for Richmond before the president arrives. Capturing Lee's army is of the utmost importance, but both men also believe that a Confederacy without a capital is a doomsday scenario for the rebels. Delivering the news that Richmond has fallen will be a delightful way to kick off their meeting.

The sound of horseshoes on cobblestones echoes down the quiet street. It's Lincoln. Once again the president has courted peril by traveling with just his eleven-year-old son, a lone bodyguard, and a handful of governmental officials. Lincoln knows that, historically, assassination is common during the final days of any war. The victors are jubilant, but the vanquished are furious, more than capable of venting their rage on the man they hold responsible for their defeat.

A single musket shot during that horseback ride from City Point could have ended Lincoln's life. Despite his profound anxieties about all other aspects of the nation's future, Lincoln chooses to shrug off the risk. At the edge of Petersburg he trots past "the houses of negroes," in the words of one Union colonel, "and here and there a squalid family of poor whites"—but no one else. No one, at least, with enough guts to shoot the president. And while the former slaves grin broadly, the whites gaze down with "an air of lazy dislike," disgusted that this tall, bearded man is once again their president.

Stepping down off his horse, Lincoln walks through the main gate of the house Grant has chosen for their meeting. He takes the walkway in long, eager strides, a smile suddenly stretching across his face, his deep fatigue vanishing at the sight of his favorite general. When he shakes Grant's hand in congratulation, it is with great gusto. And Lincoln holds on to Grant for a very long time. The president appears so happy that Grant's aides doubt he's ever had a more carefree moment in his life.

The air is chilly. The two men sit on the veranda, taking no notice of the cold. They have become a team during the war. Or, as Lincoln puts it, "Grant is my man, and I am his." One is tall and the other quite small. One is a storyteller, the other a listener. One is a politician; the other thinks that politics is a sordid form of show business. But both are men of action, and their conversation shows deep mutual respect.

Former slaves begin to fill the yard, drawn back into Petersburg by the news that Lincoln himself is somewhere in the city. They stand quietly in front of the house, watching as the general and the president proceed with their private talk. Lincoln is a hero to the slaves— "Father Abraham"—guiding them to the promised land with the Emancipation Proclamation.

∞

Lincoln and Grant talk for ninety minutes, then shake hands goodbye. Their parting has a bittersweet feel, the two great men perhaps sensing that they are marching toward two vastly different destinies. Grant is off to finish an epic war and subsequently to become president himself. Lincoln is off to heal a nation, a noble goal he will not live to see realized.

Now, as the president looks on, Grant saddles up his charger and gallops off to join his army.

Before leaving himself, Lincoln shakes hands with some people in the crowd gathered in front of the meeting place. He then rides back to City Point, once again exposing himself to possible violence. The way is littered with hundreds of dead soldiers, their unburied bodies swollen by death and sometimes stripped bare by scavengers. Lincoln doesn't look away, absorbing the sober knowledge that these men died because of him. Outrage about Lincoln's pursuit of the war has many calling for his death—even in the North. "Let us also remind Lincoln, that Caesar had his Brutus," one speaker cried at a New York rally. And even in Congress, one senator recently asked the simple question "How much more are we going to take?" before going on to allude to the possibility of Lincoln's murder.

Lincoln endures all this because he must, just as he endures the slow trot through the battlefield. But there is a purpose to all he does, and upon his return to City Point he receives a great reward when he is handed the telegram informing him that Richmond has fallen. Confederate troops have abandoned the city to link up with Lee's forces trying to get to the Carolinas.

"Thank God that I have lived to see this," Lincoln cries. "It seems to me that I have been dreaming a horrid dream for four years, and now the nightmare is gone."

But it's not really gone. President Lincoln has just twelve days to live.

# CHAPTER FOUR

Tuesday, April 4, 1865
Newport, Rhode Island

As blood flows in Virginia, wine flows in Rhode Island, far removed from the horrors of the Civil War. It is here that John Wilkes Booth has traveled by train for a romantic getaway with his fiancée. Since the Revolutionary War, Newport has been a retreat for high society, known for yachting and mansions and gaiety.

John Wilkes Booth is one of eight children born to his flamboyant actor father, Junius Brutus Booth, a rogue if there ever was one. Booth's father abandoned his first wife and two children in England and fled to America with an eighteen-year-old London girl, who became Booth's mother. Booth was often lost in the confusion of the chaotic household. His father and brother eclipsed him as actors, and his upbringing was hectic, to say the least. Now anger has become a way of life for him. Throughout his journey to Rhode Island he has been barraged by news of the southern demise. Northern newspapers are reporting that Richmond has fallen and that Confederate president Jefferson Davis and his entire cabinet fled the city just hours before Union troops entered. In cities like New York, Boston, and Washington, people are dancing in the streets as the rebel collapse appears to be imminent. It is becoming clear to Booth that he is a man with a destiny—the only man in America who can end the

North's oppression. Something drastic must be done to preserve slavery, the southern way of life, and the Confederacy itself. If Robert E. Lee can't get the job done, then Booth will have to do it for him.

Booth's hatred for Lincoln, and his deep belief in the institution of slavery, coalesced into a silent rage after the Emancipation Proclamation. It was only in August 1864, when a bacterial infection known as erysipelas sidelined him from the stage, that Booth began using his downtime to recruit a gang that would help him kidnap Lincoln. First he contacted his old friends Michael O'Laughlen and Samuel Arnold. They met at Barnum's City Hotel in Baltimore, and after several drinks Booth asked them if they would join his conspiracy. Both men agreed. From there, Booth began adding others, selecting them based on expertise with weapons, physical fitness, and knowledge of southern Maryland's back roads and waterways.

In October, Booth traveled to Montreal, where he met with agents of Jefferson Davis's. The Confederate president had set aside more than $1 million in gold to pay for acts of espionage and intrigue against the Union and housed a portion of the money in Canada. Booth's meeting with Davis's men not only provided funding for his conspiracy, it forged a direct bond between himself and the Confederacy. He returned with a check for $1,500, along with a letter of introduction that would allow him to meet the more prominent southern sympathizers in Maryland, such as Samuel Mudd and John Surratt, who would become key players in his evil plan. Without their help, Booth's chances of successfully smuggling Lincoln out of Washington and into the Deep South would have been nonexistent.

∽

After recovering from his illness, Booth immersed himself deeper into the Confederate movement, traveling with a new circle of friends that considered the kidnapping of Lincoln to be of vital national importance. He met with secret agents and sympathizers in taverns, churches, and hotels throughout the Northeast and down through Maryland, always expanding his web of contacts, making his plans more concise and his chances of success that much greater. What started as an almost abstract hatred of Lincoln has now transformed itself into the actor's life's work.

Yet Booth is such a skilled actor and charismatic liar that no one outside the secessionist movement—not even his fiancée—has known the depth of his rage.

Until today.

Booth's betrothed, Lucy Lambert Hale, is the daughter of John Parker Hale, a staunchly pro-war senator from New Hampshire. She is dark-haired and full-figured, with blue eyes that have ignited a spark in the heart of many a man. Like Booth, she is used to having her way with the opposite sex, attracting beaus with a methodical mix of flattery and teasing. But Lucy is no soft touch. She can quickly turn indifferent and even cruel toward her suitors if the mood strikes her.

Among those enraptured with Miss Hale is a future Supreme Court justice, Oliver Wendell Holmes Jr., now a twenty-four-year-old Union officer. Also John Hay, one of Lincoln's personal secretaries. And, finally, none other than Robert Todd Lincoln, the president's twenty-one-year-old son, also a Union officer. Despite her engagement to Booth, Lucy still keeps in touch with both Hay and young Lincoln, among many others.

Strikingly pretty, Lucy appeals to Booth's vanity. When they are together, heads turn. The couple's initial passion was enough to overcome societal obstacles—at least in their minds. By March 1865 their engagement isn't much of a secret anymore, and they are even seen together at the second inaugural.

But in the past month, with Lucy possibly accompanying her father to Spain, and Booth secretly plotting against the president, their relationship has become strained. They have begun to quarrel. It doesn't help that Booth flies into a jealous rage whenever Lucy so much as looks at another man. One night, in particular, he went mad at the sight of her dancing with Robert Lincoln. Whether or not this has anything to do with his pathological hatred for the president will never be determined.

Booth has told her nothing about the conspiracy or his part in it. She doesn't know that his hiatus from the stage was extended by his maniacal commitment to kidnapping Lincoln. She doesn't know about the secret trips to Montreal and New York to meet with other conspirators, nor about the hidden caches of guns or the buggy that

Booth purchased specifically to ferry the kidnapped president out of Washington, nor about the money transfers that fund his entire operation. She doesn't know that his head is filled with countless crazy scenarios concerning the Lincoln kidnapping. And she surely doesn't realize that her beloved has a passion for New York City prostitutes and a sizzling young Boston teenager named Isabel Sumner, just seventeen years old. Lucy knows none of that. All she knows is that the man she loves is mysterious and passionate and fearless in the bedroom.

∞

Perhaps, with all of Booth's subterfuge, it is not surprising that their lovers' getaway to Newport is turning into a fiasco.

Booth checked them into the Aquidneck House hotel, simply signing the register as "J. W. Booth and Lady." He made no attempt whatsoever to pretend they are already married. It's as if the couple is daring the innkeeper to question their propriety. There is no question that Booth is spoiling for a fight. He is sick of what he sees as the gross imbalance between the poverty of the war-torn South and the prosperity of the North. Other than the uniformed soldiers milling about the railway platforms, he saw no evidence, during the train ride from Washington to Newport, via Boston, that the war had touched the North in any way.

After checking into the hotel, he and Lucy walk the waterfront all morning. He wants to tell her about his plans, but the conspiracy is so vast and so deep that he would be a fool to sabotage it with a careless outburst. Instead, he rambles on about the fate of the Confederacy and about Lincoln, the despot. He's shared his pro-southern leanings with Lucy in the past, but never to this extent. He rants endlessly about the fall of Richmond and the injustice of Lincoln having his way. Lucy knows her politics well, and she argues right back, until at some point in their walk along the picturesque harbor, with its sailboats and magnificent seaside homes, it becomes clear that they will never reach a common ground.

Toward evening, they stop their fighting and walk back to the Aquidneck House. Despite John Wilkes Booth's many infidelities, Lucy Hale is the love of his life. She is the only anchor that might keep him from committing a heinous crime, effectively throwing his life away in the process. In her eyes he sees a happy future replete with marriage, children, and increased prosperity as he refocuses on his career. They can travel the world together, mingling with high society wherever they go, thanks to her father's considerable connections. All he has to do is to choose that love over his insane desire to harm the president.

Booth tells the desk clerk that Lucy isn't feeling well and that they will take their evening meal in the bedroom. Upstairs, there is ample time for lovemaking before their food is delivered. But the acts of intimacy that made this trip such an exotic idea have been undone by the news about Richmond. They will never make love again after tonight, and both of them sense it. Rather than spend the night together, Booth and Lucy pack their bags and catch the evening train back to Boston, where she leaves him to be with friends.

Booth is actually relieved. He has made his choice. Now no one stands in his way.

# CHAPTER FIVE

TUESDAY, APRIL 4, 1865
AMELIA COURT HOUSE, VIRGINIA

As Booth and Lucy depart Newport long before their supper can be delivered, Robert E. Lee's soldiers are marching forty long miles to dine on anything they can find, all the while looking over their shoulders, fearful that Grant and the Union army will catch them from behind.

Lee has an eight-hour head start after leaving Petersburg. He figures that if he can make it to Amelia Court House before Grant catches him, he and his men will be amply fed by the waiting 350,000 rations of smoked meat, bacon, biscuits, coffee, sugar, flour, and tea that are stockpiled there. Then, after that brief stop to fill their bellies, they will resume their march to North Carolina.

And march they must. Even though Jefferson Davis and his cabinet have already fled Richmond and traveled to the Carolinas on the very same rail line that is delivering the food to Lee's forces, there is no chance of the army using the railway as an escape route. There simply isn't enough time to load and transport all of Lee's 30,000 men.

The day-and-a-half trudge to Amelia Court House begins optimistically enough, with Lee's men happy to finally be away from Petersburg and looking forward to their first real meal in months. But forty miles on foot is a long way, and mile by mile the march turns into a death pageant. The line of retreating rebels and supply wagons stretches for twenty miles. The men are in wretched physical condition after months in the trenches. Their feet have lost their calluses and their muscles the firm tone they knew earlier in the war, when the Army of Northern Virginia was constantly on the march. Even worse, each painful step is a reminder that, of the two things vital to an army on the move—food and sleep—they lack one and have no chance of getting the other.

Lee's army is in total disarray. There is no longer military discipline, or any attempt to enforce it. The men swear under their breaths, grumbling and swearing a thousand other oaths about wanting to go home and quit this crazy war. The loose columns of Confederate soldiers resemble a mob of hollow-eyed zombies instead of a highly skilled fighting force. The men "rumbled like persons in a dream," one captain will later write. "It all seemed to me like a troubled vision. I was consumed by fever, and when I attempted to walk I staggered like a drunken man."

The unlucky are barefoot, their leather boots and laces rotted away from the rains and mud of winter. Others wear ankle-high Confederate brogans with holes in the soles and uppers. The only men sporting new boots are those who stripped them off dead Union soldiers. The southerners resent it that everything the Union soldiers wear seems to be newer, better, and in limitless supply. A standing order has been issued for Confederate soldiers not to dress in confiscated woolen Union overcoats, but given a choice between being accidentally shot by a fellow southerner or surviving the bitter nightly chill, the rebels pick warmth every time. A glance up and down the retreat shows the long gray line speckled everywhere with blue.

∽

Bellies rumble. No one sings. No one bawls orders. A Confederate officer later sets the scene: there is "no regular column, no regular pace. When a soldier became weary he fell out, ate his scanty rations—if indeed, he had any to eat—rested, rose, and resumed the march when the inclination dictated. There were not many words spoken. An indescribable sadness weighed upon us."

It is even harder for the troops evacuating Richmond, on their way to link up with Lee at Amelia Court House. Many are not soldiers at all—they are sailors who burned their ships rather than let them fall into Union hands. Marching is new to them. Mere hours into the journey, many have fallen out of the ranks from blisters and exhaustion.

Making matters worse is the very real fear of Union troops launching a surprise attack. "The nervousness," a Confederate major will remember, "resulting from this constant strain of starvation, fatigue and lack of sleep was a dangerous thing, sometimes producing lamentable results." On several occasions bewildered Confederate troops open fire on one another, thinking they're firing at Yankees. In another instance, a massive black stallion lashed to a wooden fence "reared back, pulling the rail out of the fence and dragging it after him full gallop down the road crowded with troops, mowing them down like the scythe of a war chariot."

It's no wonder that men begin to desert. Whenever and wherever the column pauses, men slip into the woods, never to return. The war is clearly over. No sense dying for nothing.

Lee has long craved the freedom of open ground, but now his objective is to retreat and regroup, not to fight. His strategy that his army "must endeavor to harass them if we cannot destroy them" depends upon motivated troops and favorable terrain. These are essential to any chance of Lee snatching victory from the jaws of defeat. But the fight will have to wait until they get food.

To lighten his army's load and move faster, Lee orders that all unnecessary guns and wagons be left behind. The pack animals pulling them are hitched to more essential loads. A few days from now, as bone thin and weary as the soldiers themselves, these animals will be butchered to feed Lee's men.

Everything about the retreat—starvation, poor morale, desertion—speaks of failure. And yet when messengers arrive saying that the Petersburg bridges were blown by his sappers once the last man was across, making it impossible for Grant to follow, Lee is optimistic. Even happy. He has escaped once again. "I have got my army safely out of its breastworks, and in order to follow me the enemy must abandon his lines and can derive no further benefits from his railroads or James River," he notes with relief.

Grant's army is sliding west en masse, racing to block the road, even as Lee feels relief in the morning air. Lee suspects this. But his confidence in his army and in his own generalship is such that he firmly believes he can defeat Grant on open ground.

Everything depends on getting to Amelia Court House. Without food Lee's men cannot march. Without food they cannot fight. Without food, they might as well have surrendered in Petersburg.

Lee's newfound optimism slowly filters down into the ranks. Against all odds, his men regain their confidence as the trenches of Petersburg recede further and further into memory and distance. By the time they reach Amelia Court House, on April 4, after almost two consecutive days on the march, electricity sizzles through the ranks. The men speak of hope and are confident of victory as they wonder where and when they will fight the Yankees once again.

It's just before noon. The long hours in the saddle are hard on the fifty-eight-year-old general. Lee has long struggled with rheumatism and all its crippling agonies. Now it flares anew. Yet he presses on, knowing that any sign of personal weakness will be immediately noticed by his men. As much as any soldier, he looks forward to a good meal and a few hours of sleep. He can see the waiting railroad cars, neatly parked on a siding. He quietly gives the order to unload the food and distribute it in an organized fashion. The last thing Lee wants is for his army to give in to their hunger and rush the train. Composure and propriety are crucial for any effective fighting force.

The train doors are yanked open. Inside, great wooden crates are stacked floor to ceiling. Lee's excited men hurriedly jerk the boxes down onto the ground and pry them open.

Then, horror!

This is what those boxes contain: 200 crates of ammunition, 164 cartons of artillery harnesses, and 96 carts to carry ammunition.

There is no food.

# CHAPTER SIX

TUESDAY, APRIL 4, 1865
RICHMOND, VIRGINIA

While John Wilkes Booth is still in Newport, a hungry Robert E. Lee is in Amelia Court House, Ulysses S. Grant is racing to block Lee's path, and Abraham Lincoln stands on the deck of USS *Malvern* as the warship chugs slowly and cautiously up the James River toward Richmond. The channel is choked with burning warships and the floating corpses of dead draft horses. Deadly anti-ship mines known as "torpedoes" bob on the surface, drifting with the current, ready to explode the instant they come into contact with a vessel. If just one torpedo bounces against the *Malvern*'s hull, ship and precious cargo alike will be reduced to fragments of varnished wood and human tissue.

Again Lincoln sets aside his concerns. For the *Malvern* is sailing into Richmond, of all places. The Confederate capital is now in Union hands. The president has waited an eternity for this moment. Lincoln can clearly see that Richmond—or what's left of it—hardly resembles a genteel southern bastion. The sunken ships and torpedoes in the harbor tell only part of the story. Richmond is gone, burned to the ground. And it was not a Union artillery bombardment that did the job, but the people of Richmond themselves.

When it becomes too dangerous for the *Malvern* to go any farther, Lincoln is rowed to shore. "We passed so close to torpedoes that we could have put out our hands and touched them," bodyguard William Crook will later write. His affection for Lincoln is enormous, and of all the bodyguards, Crook fusses most over the president, treating him like a child who must be protected.

It is Crook who is fearful, while Lincoln bursts with amazement and joy that this day has finally come. Finally, he steps from the barge and up onto the landing.

But what Lincoln sees now can only be described as appalling.

Richmond's Confederate leaders have had months to prepare for the city's eventual surrender. They had plenty of time to come up with a logical plan for a handover of power without loss of life. But such was their faith in Marse Robert that the people of Richmond thought that day would never come. When it did, they behaved like fools.

∽

Their first reaction was to destroy the one thing that could make the Yankees lose control and vent their rage on the populace: whiskey. Union troops had gone on a drunken rampage after taking Columbia, South Carolina, two months earlier, and had then burned the city to the ground.

Out came the axes. Teams of men roamed through the city, hacking open barrel after barrel of fine sour mash. Thousands of gallons of spirits were poured into the gutters. But the citizens of Richmond were not about to see all that whiskey go to waste. Some got down on their hands and knees and lapped it from the gutter. Others filled their hats and boots. The streetlamps were black, because Richmond's gas lines had been shut off to prevent explosions. Perfectly respectable men and women, in a moment of amazing distress, found a salve for their woes by falling to their knees and quenching their thirst with alcohol flowing in the gutter.

Many took more than just a drink. Everyone from escaped prisoners to indigent laborers and war deserters drank their share. Great drunken mobs soon roamed the city. Just as in Amelia Court House, food was first and foremost on everyone's minds. The city had suffered such scarcity that "starvation balls" had replaced the standard debutante and charity galas. But black market profiteers had filled entire warehouses with staples like flour, coffee, sugar, and delicious smoked meats. And, of course, there were Robert E. Lee's 350,000 missing rations, neatly stacked in a Richmond railway siding instead of being packed on the train that Lee expected in Amelia Court House.

Little did the general know that Confederate looters had stolen all the food.

The worst was still to come. Having destroyed and consumed a potential supply of alcohol for the Union army, Richmond's city fathers now turned their attention to their most profitable commodity: tobacco. The rebel leadership knew that President Lincoln wanted to capture tobacco stores in order to sell them to England, thereby raising much-needed money for the nearly bankrupt U.S. Treasury.

In their panic, the city fathers ignored an obvious problem: lighting tinder-dry bales of tobacco on fire would also burn the great old wooden warehouses in which they were stacked.

Soon, spires of flame illuminated the entire city of Richmond. The warehouse flames spread to other buildings. The rivers of whiskey caught fire and inferno ensued.

The true nature of a firestorm involves not only flame but also wind and heat and crackling and popping and explosion, just like war. Soon residents mistakenly believed the Yankees were laying Richmond to waste with an artillery barrage.

And still things got worse.

The Confederate navy chose this moment to set the entire James River arsenal ablaze, preferring to destroy their ships and ammunition rather than see them fall into Union hands.

But the effect of this impulsive tactical decision was far worse than anything the northerners would have inflicted. Flaming steel particles were launched into the air as more than 100,000 artillery rounds exploded over the next four hours. Everything burned. Even the most respectable citizens were now penniless refugees, their homes smoldering ruins and Confederate money now mere scraps of paper. The dead and dying were everywhere, felled by the random whistling shells. The air smelled of wood smoke, gunpowder, and burning flesh. Hundreds of citizens lost their lives on that terrible night.

∽

Richmond was a proud city and perhaps more distinctly American than even Washington, D.C. It could even be said that the United States of America was born in Richmond, for it was there, in 1775, in Richmond's St. John's Episcopal Church, that Patrick Henry looked out on a congregation that included George Washington and Thomas Jefferson and delivered the famous "Give me liberty or give me death" speech, which fomented American rebellion, the Revolutionary War, and independence itself. As the capital of Virginia since 1780, it was where Jefferson had served as governor; he'd also designed its capitol building. It was in Richmond that Jefferson and James Madison crafted the statute separating church and state that would later inform the First Amendment of the Constitution.

And now it was devastated by its own sons.

Soldiers of the Confederate Army of Northern Virginia sowed land mines in their wake as they abandoned the city. Such was their haste that they forgot to remove the small rows of red flags denoting the narrow but safe path through the minefields, a mistake that saved hundreds of Union lives as soldiers entered the city.

Richmond was still in flames on the morning of April 3 when the Union troops, following those red flags, arrived. Brick facades and chimneys still stood, but wooden frames and roofs had been incinerated. "The barbarous south had consigned it to flames," one Union officer wrote of Richmond. And even after a night of explosions, "the roar of bursting shells was terrific." Smoldering ruins and the sporadic whistle of artillery greeted the Twenty-fourth and Twenty-fifth Corps of the Union army.

The instant the long blue line marched into town, the slaves of Richmond were free. They were stunned to see that the Twenty-fifth contained black soldiers from a new branch of the army known as the USCT—the United States Colored Troops.

Lieutenant Johnston Livingston de Peyster, a member of General Wetzel's staff, galloped his horse straight to the capitol building. "I sprang from my horse," he wrote proudly, and "rushed up to the roof." In his hand was an American flag. Dashing to the flagpole, he hoisted the Stars and Stripes over Richmond. The capital was Confederate no more.

That particular flag was poignant for two reasons. It had thirty-six stars, a new number owing to Nevada's recent admission to the Union. Per tradition, this new flag would not become official until the Fourth of July. It was the flag of the America to come—the postwar America, united and expanding. It was, in other words, the flag of Abraham Lincoln's dreams.

So it is fitting when, eleven short days later, a thirty-six-star flag will be folded into a pillow and placed beneath Abraham Lincoln's head after a gunman puts a bullet in his brain. But for now President Lincoln is alive and well, walking the ruined streets of the conquered Confederate capital.

## CHAPTER SEVEN

TUESDAY, APRIL 4, 1865
RICHMOND, VIRGINIA

Abraham Lincoln has never fought in battle. During his short three-month enlistment during the Black Hawk War in 1832, he was, somewhat oddly, both a captain and a private—but never a fighter. He is a politician, and politicians are seldom given the chance to play the role of conquering hero. It could be said that General Grant deserved the honor more than President Lincoln, for it was his strategy and concentrated movements of manpower that brought down the Confederate government. But it is Lincoln's war. It always has been. To Lincoln goes the honor of conquering hero—and the hatred of those who have been conquered.

No one knows this more than the freed slaves of Richmond. They throng to Lincoln's side, so alarming the sailors who rowed him ashore that they form a protective ring around the president, using their bayonets to push the slaves away. The sailors maintain this ring around Lincoln as he marches through the city, even as his admiring entourage grows from mere dozens to hundreds.

The white citizens of Richmond, tight-lipped and hollow-eyed, take it all in. Abraham Lincoln is their enemy no more. As the citizens of Petersburg came to realize yesterday, he is something even more despicable: their president. These people never thought they'd see the day Abraham Lincoln would be strolling down the streets of

Richmond as if it were his home. They make no move, no gesture, no cry, no sound to welcome him. "Every window was crowded with heads," one sailor will remember. "But it was a silent crowd. There was something oppressive in those thousands of watchers without a sound, either of welcome or hatred. I think we would have welcomed a yell of defiance."

Lincoln's extraordinary height means that he towers over the crowd, providing an ideal moment for an outraged southerner to make an attempt on his life.

∽

But no one takes a shot. No drunken, saddened, addled, enraged citizens of Richmond so much as attacks Lincoln with their fists. Instead, Lincoln receives the jubilant welcome of former slaves reveling in their first moments of freedom.

The president keeps walking until he is a mile from the wharf. Soon Lincoln finds himself on the corner of Twelfth and Clay Streets, staring at the former home of Jefferson Davis.

When first built, in 1818, the house was owned by the president of the Bank of Virginia, John Brockenbrough. But Brockenbrough is now long dead. A merchant by the name of Lewis Crenshaw owned the property when war broke out, and he had just added a third floor and redecorated the interior with all the "modern conveniences," including gaslights and a flush toilet, when he was persuaded to sell it, furnished, to Richmond authorities for the generous sum of $43,000—in Confederate dollars, of course.

The authorities, in turn, rented it to the Confederate government, which was in need of an executive mansion. It was August 1861 when Jefferson Davis, his much younger second wife, Varina, and their three young children moved in. Now they have all fled, and Lincoln steps past the sentry boxes, grasps the wrought iron railing, and marches up the steps into the Confederate White House.

He is shown into a small room with floor-to-ceiling windows and crossed cavalry swords over the door. "This was President Davis's office," a housekeeper says respectfully.

Lincoln's eyes roam over the elegant dark wood desk, which Davis had so thoughtfully tidied before running off two days earlier. "Then this must be President Davis's chair," he says with a grin, sinking into its burgundy padding. He crosses his legs and leans back.

That's when the weight of the moment hits him. Lincoln asks for a glass of water, which is promptly delivered by Davis's former butler—a slave—along with a bottle of whiskey.

Where Davis has gone, Lincoln does not know. He has no plans to hunt him down. Reunification, however painful it might be to southerners, is within Lincoln's grasp. There will be no manhunt for the Confederate president, nor a trial for war crimes. As for the people of Richmond, many of whom actively conspired against Lincoln and the United States, Lincoln has ordered that the Union army command the citizenry with a gentle hand. Or, in Lincoln's typically folksy parlance: "Let 'em up easy."

He can afford to relax. Lincoln has Richmond. The Confederacy is doomed. All the president needs now is for Grant to finish the rest of the job, and then he can get to work. Lincoln still has miles to go before he sleeps.

# CHAPTER EIGHT

---

Wednesday, April 5, 1865
Amelia Court House, Virginia
Noon to Midnight

Wave after wave of retreating Confederate soldiers arrive in Amelia Court House throughout the day of April 4. They have marched long and hard, yanked forward on an invisible rope by the promise of a long sleep and a full belly. But it was a lie, a broken promise, and a nightmare, all at once. Without food they have no hope. Like the sailors who quit the march from Richmond because their feet hurt, many Confederate soldiers now find their own way to surrender. Saying they are going into the woods to hunt for dinner, they simply walk away from the war. And they keep on walking until they reach their homes weeks and months later—or lie down to die as they desert, too weak to take another step.

Lee's optimism has been replaced by the heavy pall of defeat. "His face was still calm, as it always was," wrote one enlisted man. "But his carriage was no longer erect, as his soldiers had been used to seeing it. The troubles of these last days had already plowed great furrows in his forehead. His eyes were red as if with weeping, his cheeks sunken and haggard, his face colorless. No one who looked upon him then, as he stood there in full view of the disastrous end, can ever forget the intense agony written on his features."

His hope rests on forage wagons now out scouring the countryside in search of food. He anxiously awaits their return, praying they will be overflowing with grains and smoked meats and leading calves and pigs to be slaughtered.

The wagons come back empty.

The countryside is bare. There are no rations for Lee and his men. The soldiers become frantic, eating anything they can find: cow hooves, tree bark, rancid raw bacon, and hog and cattle feed. Some have taken to secreting packhorses or mules away from the main group, then quietly slaughtering and eating them. Making matters worse, word now reaches Lee that Union cavalry intercepted a column of supply wagons that raced out of Richmond just before the fall. The wagons were burned and the teamsters taken prisoner.

Lee and his army are in the great noose of Grant's making, which is squeezing tighter and tighter with every passing hour.

*❧*

Lee must move before Grant finds him. His fallback plan is yet another forced march, this one to the city of Danville, where more than a million rations allegedly await. Danville, however, is a hundred miles south. As impossible as it is to think of marching an army that far on empty stomachs, it is Lee's only hope.

Lee could surrender right then and there. But it isn't in his character. He is willing to demand incredible sacrifice to avoid the disgrace of defeat.

A cold rain falls on the morning of April 5. Lee gives the order to move out. It is, in the minds of one Confederate, "the cruelest marching order the commanders had ever given the men in four years of fighting." Units of infantry, cavalry, and artillery begin slogging down the road. Danville is a four-day march—if they have the energy to make it. "It is now," one soldier writes in his diary, "a race of life or death."

They get only seven miles before coming to a dead halt at a Union roadblock outside Jetersville. At first it appears to be no more than a small cavalry force. But a quick look through Lee's field glasses tells him differently. Soldiers are digging trenches and fortifications along the road, building the berms and breastworks that will protect them from rebel bullets, and then fortifying them with fallen trees and fence rails.

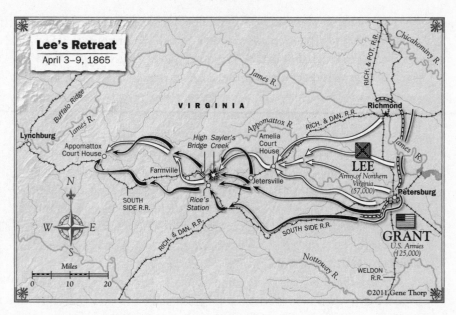

**Lee's Retreat**
April 3–9, 1865

©2011 Gene Thorp

Lee gallops Traveller to the front and assesses the situation. Part of him wants to make a bold statement by charging into the Union works in a last grand suicidal hurrah, but Lee's army has followed him so loyally because of not only his brilliance but also his discretion. Sometimes knowing when *not* to fight is just as important to a general's success as knowing *how* to fight.

And this is not a time to engage.

Lee quickly swings his army west in a grand loop toward the town of Paineville. The men don't travel down one single road but follow a series of parallel arteries connecting the hamlets and burgs of rural Virginia. The countryside is rolling and open in some places, in some forested and in others swampy. Creeks and rivers overflowing their banks from the recent rains drench the troops at every crossing. On any other day, the Army of Northern Virginia might not have minded. But with so many miles to march, soaking shoes and socks will eventually mean the further agony of walking on blistered, frozen feet.

The topography favors an army lying in wait, ready to spring a surprise attack. But they are an army in flight, at the mercy of any force hidden in the woods. And, indeed, Union cavalry repeatedly harass the rear of Lee's exhausted column. The horsemen are not bold or dumb enough to attack Lee's main force, which outnumbers them by thousands. Instead they attack the defenseless supply wagons in a series of lightning-quick charges. On narrow, swampy roads, the Union cavalry burn more than 200 Confederate supply wagons, capture eleven battle flags, and take more than 600 prisoners, spreading confusion and panic.

Sensing disaster, Lee springs to the offensive, ordering cavalry under the command of his nephew Major General Fitzhugh Lee and Major General Thomas Rosser to catch and kill the Union cavalry before they can gallop back to the safety of their Jetersville line. In the running battle that follows, rebel cavalry kill 30 and wound another 150 near the resort town of Amelia Springs. If the Union needs proof that there is still fight in Lee's army, it now has it.

Lee marches his men all day, and then all night. At a time when every fiber of their beings cries out for sleep and food, they press forward over muddy rutted roads, enduring rain and chill and the constant harassment of Union cavalry. The roads are shoulder to shoulder with exhausted men, starving pack animals, and wagons sinking up to their axles in the thick Virginia mud. Dead and dying mules and horses are shoved to the side of the road so as not to slow the march. Dead men litter the ground, too, and are just as quickly tossed to the shoulder—or merely stepped over. There is no time for proper burials. Nothing can slow the march to Danville.

Men drop their bedrolls because they lack the strength to carry them. Many more thrust their guns bayonet-first into the earth and leave them behind. On the rare occasions when the army stops to rest, men simply crumple to the ground and sleep. When it is time to march again, officers move from man to man, shaking them awake and ordering them to their feet. Some men refuse to rise and are left sleeping, soon to become Union prisoners. Others can't rise because they're simply too weak, in the early phases of dying from starvation. These men, too, are left behind. In this way, Lee's army dwindles. The 30,000 who retreated from Petersburg just three days ago have been reduced by half. As the long night march takes a greater toll, even those hardy men stagger like drunks, and some lose the power of speech. And yet, when it comes time to fight, they will find a way to lift their rifle to their shoulder, aim at their target, and squeeze the trigger.

∞

"My shoes are gone," a veteran soldier laments during the march. "My clothes are almost gone. I'm weary, I'm sick, I'm hungry. My family has been killed or scattered, and may be wandering helpless and unprotected. I would die, yes I would die willingly, because I love my country. But if this war is ever over, I'll be damned if I ever love another country."

His is the voice of a South that wants no part of Lincoln and the United States of America—and for whom there can be no country but the Confederacy. Just as the Union officer in Richmond spoke of the "barbarous south," so these soldiers and men like John Wilkes Booth view the North as an evil empire. This is the divisiveness Lincoln will face if he manages to win the war.

Now, in the darkness after midnight, a courier approaches the marching soldiers and hands Lee a captured Union message from Grant to his generals, giving orders to attack at first light.

But at last Lee gets good news, in the form of a report from his commissary general, I. M. St. John: 80,000 rations have been rushed to the town of Farmville, just nineteen miles away. Lee can be there in a day.

He swings his army toward Farmville. It is Lee's final chance to keep the Confederate struggle alive.

# CHAPTER NINE

General Sam Grant is also on a midnight ride. The great hooves of his horse beat a tattoo on the bad roads and forest trails of central Virginia. Speed is of the essence. Scouts report that Lee is escaping, marching his men through the night in a bold attempt to reach rations at Farmville. From there it's just a short march to High Bridge, a stone-and-wood structure wide enough to handle an army. Once Lee crosses and burns the bridge behind him, his escape will be complete, and the dreadful war will continue.

Tonight decides everything. Grant is so close to stopping Lee. So very close. Grant digs his spurs into his horse, named Jeff Davis after the Confederate president, in a gesture uncharacteristically vindictive of Grant, who is usually polite and respectful even to his enemies. Grant knows that he must ride hard. Lee must be captured now. And Grant must capture him personally.

As always, his battle plan is simple: Get in front of Lee. Block his path. How many times has he explained this to Generals Sheridan and Meade? Block Lee's path, stop him in his tracks, then attack and crush the Army of Northern Virginia. So how is it that Lee came within spitting distance of the Jetersville roadblock and escaped?

It confounds Grant that his top generals are so terrified of Lee, holding back when they should rush in. The Union soldiers are better armed, better fed, and far more rested than Lee's men. The generals must be relentless, pressing forward without ceasing until the war is won. But they are not.

So it is up to Grant to lead the way.

∞

The culprit, Grant decides, is not General Phil Sheridan. He and the cavalry are more than doing their part, charging far and wide over the Virginia countryside, harassing Lee's wagons and skirmishing with Confederate cavalry. Sheridan is Grant's eyes and ears, sending scouts to track Lee's movements and ensuring that Marse Robert doesn't disappear into the Blue Ridge Mountains. Grant would be lost without Sheridan.

The same cannot be said of General George Meade. His force reached Jetersville at dusk on April 5, after a dreary day of pursuit. But rather than launch an immediate assault on Lee's rear, as Grant ordered, Meade halted for the night, claiming that his men were too tired to fight.

Grant knows there's more to it than that. The problem, in a nutshell, is the unspoken rivalry between infantry and cavalry—between the unglamorous and the swashbuckling. Meade's refusal to fight is his way of pouting about the cavalry divisions sharing the roads with his men, slowing their march. "Behold, the whole of Merritt's division of cavalry filing in from a side road and completely closing the way," one of Meade's aides wrote home. "That's the way it is with those cavalry bucks: they bother and howl about infantry not being up to support them, and they are precisely the people who are always blocking the way . . . they are arrant boasters.

"To hear Sheridan's staff talk, you would suppose ten-thousand mounted carbineers had crushed the entire Rebellion. . . . The plain truth is, they are useful and energetic fellows, but commit the error of thinking they can do everything and that no one else does anything."

So Meade made his point by refusing to attack.

Sheridan was furious. "I wish you were here," he wired Grant. "We can capture the Army of Northern Virginia if enough force be thrown to this point."

Grant reads between the lines. Rather than wait until morning, and the chance that Meade will find another excuse for not fighting, he orders his staff to mount up for the sixteen-mile midnight ride to Jetersville. Never mind that it is a cold, pitch-black night. There is purpose in the journey. They travel carefully, lest they surprise Union troops and be mistakenly shot as southern scouts.

Grant is always one to keep his emotions in check. But as he guides his horse from the village of Nottoway Court House to Jetersville, from the sandy soils west of Petersburg to the quartz and red soil of the Blue Ridge foothills, Grant fears that Lee is on the verge of out-foxing him again.

Grant knows that the Confederates are beatable. His spies captured a note from one of Lee's aides, detailing the poor morale and horrible conditions the Confederates are experiencing. Grant is also aware of the massive desertions. He has heard about the roads littered with rifles and bedrolls, abandoned wagons and broken horses. He knows that an astronomic number of Confederate men have been taken prisoner. But all this means nothing if he cannot get ahead of Lee and block the Confederate escape to the Carolinas. And not just that: he must win what he calls the "life and death struggle for Lee to get south to his provisions."

Once a second-rate fighting force, the Union soldiers have gained remarkable strength since the assault on Petersburg. "Nothing seemed to fatigue them," Grant marvels. "They were ready to move without rations and travel without rest until the end." Unlike Lee's bedraggled force, Grant's men march with a bounce in their step. Bands play. Nobody straggles or falls out of ranks. They walk the unheard-of distance of thirty miles in one day.

∽

Now Grant and the cavalry detail that guards his life walk their horses through a forest to Sheridan's camp. Sentries cry out, ordering them to stop. Grant steps forward to show himself. Within seconds the sentries allow them to pass and usher Grant to Sheridan's headquarters.

Grant speaks briefly with "Little Phil," the short and fiery dynamo who makes no secret that he wants his cavalry "to be there at the death" of the Confederate insurrection. Then the two men saddle up and ride through the darkness to Meade's headquarters in Jetersville. The lanky Pennsylvanian is in bed with what he claims to be a fever. Grant chalks it up to fear and orders Meade to get his army ready to attack.

Meade was a hero of Gettysburg, outwitting Lee on the battlefield despite having a reputation for being timid and temperamental. At forty-nine, the "Old Snapping Turtle" is the oldest and most experienced man in the room. Grant bears him a grudging respect, but respect isn't enough right now. Grant needs a man who will press the attack, day and night, fresh or exhausted, ill or in good health.

Meade is not that man. He never has been. Furthermore, it is not merely a question of heart anymore but of logistics: it is simply impossible for Meade's infantry to outrace Lee to Farmville. Marse Robert had a good head start, and Meade's halt for the night only increased the distance. Grant now thinks of Lee, somewhere out there in the darkness, sitting tall astride Traveller, not letting his men stop their all-night march for any reason. Lee has cavalry, artillery, and infantry at his disposal, should it come to a fight.

It will take a fast and mobile fighting force to beat the rebels. In other words: Sheridan's cavalry.

∽

Grant delivers his orders.

There will be no more waiting, he decrees, proposing a pincer movement, Sheridan in front and Meade from the rear. At first light Meade's infantry will chase and find Lee's army, then harass them and slow their forward movement. Sheridan, meanwhile, will "put himself south of the enemy and follow him to his death." In this way, the Confederate race to North Carolina will stop dead in its tracks. As Sheridan revels in the glory to come, Meade bites his tongue and accepts Grant's decision. He has to.

There is nothing more Sam Grant can do. His midnight ride has produced exactly the results he was hoping for. Promptly at six A.M., the earth shakes with the clip-clop of thousands of hooves as

Sheridan's cavalry trot west in their quest to get in front of Lee. Meade's army, meanwhile, marches north to get behind Lee, the two armies forming Grant's lethal pincers.

Meade's men march past Grant as he sits down at sunrise, lighting a cigar. Grant is confident. Finally, the Black Thursday of the Confederacy has arrived.

# CHAPTER TEN

General Robert E. Lee has been up all night yet still looks crisp and composed as he rides, backlit by the rising sun, into Rice's Station. The Army of Northern Virginia, looking for all the world like the most beaten-down fighting force in history, cheers as the beloved general glides past on Traveller. Marse Robert is stately and rugged, six feet tall and afraid of no man. He is almost asleep in the saddle, thanks to the all-night march. But his broad gray hat remains firmly in place as he acknowledges the adulation of his suffering men. Many don't have shoes; those that do can put two fingers through the rotting leather soles. Half of Lee's force has quit the war between Petersburg and this tiny depot, slinking into the woods to search for the slightest morsel of a meal and then not coming back. Those who remain are so crazed from lack of sleep and belly-hollowing hunger that their cheers resemble frantic drunken slurs.

Many are too weak even to shoulder a musket, but Lee knows that somehow they will fight when called to do so. The roads of central Virginia are now littered with the detritus of Lee's retreating army: guns, blankets, broken wagons, artillery limbers, dead horses, and dead men.

It has now been four days since the Confederate army began retreating from Petersburg. The soldiers have endured the betrayal at Amelia Court House, where boxcars full of food had been stolen by Confederate scavengers. Still, Lee's men marched on, nerves frazzled by the threat of Union attack, but never stopping for more than five or ten minutes to sleep in the mud and rain before resuming their march. The general understands their suffering. Still, he orders them to push on.

Now they see that he was right all along. For the Army of Northern Virginia has eluded the army of General Ulysses S. Grant. Better yet, there are rations waiting just a few miles away, in Farmville.

Which is why Lee's crazed soldiers cheer him on this dawn as they march into Rice's Station. Lee is all they believe in right now—not Confederate president Jefferson Davis, not the Army of Northern Virginia, not even terms like "states' rights" or "pro-slavery," which spurred many men to enlist in the Confederate cause. Now those things mean nothing. Only Marse Robert matters.

They would follow him into hell.

∞

Ahead of General Lee is his trusted point man General Pete Longstreet. Behind Lee is the rear guard under the command of General John B. Gordon, the fearless Georgian. In between is a ten-mile-long supply column, supervised by General Richard "Fighting Dick" Anderson and General Richard Ewell, a veteran soldier with just one leg who oversees a scrappy band of bureaucrats, frontline veterans, and land-locked sailors who escaped from Richmond just days earlier.

The tiny hamlet of Rice's Station is a crossroads. One way leads to the Carolinas and safety; the other direction leads back to Petersburg. Longstreet orders cannons pointed down the Petersburg road, to scare off any Union force that might be stalking them. The tired men dig trenches and earthworks to protect themselves from bullets. The woods serve as latrines, the newly dug trenches as beds. Longstreet's mandate is to remain in Rice's Station until Lee's entire army has passed through. Only then will he and his men evacuate.

Incredibly, a bleary-eyed Robert E. Lee is reveling in the moment. The air is fresh, scrubbed clean by the night's rain. Birds are singing to greet this fine spring morning. He knows that Farmville is less than an hour away, with its boxcars filled with smoked meat, cornmeal, and all the makings of a great military feast. Advance scouts have confirmed that the food is actually there this time. Looters have not touched it.

The plan is for Lee's men to fill their empty bellies in Farmville this morning, then march over the great span known as High Bridge, which towers over the Appomattox River, separating central and western Virginia. Lee will order the bridge burned immediately after they cross, preventing the Union from following. The Carolinas will be reached in days.

Lee's escape is so close.

But then grim news arrives. A flying column of Union cavalry galloped through Rice an hour ago. They are now ahead of the Confederates. Longstreet's scouts report that 800 bluecoats on foot and on horseback are headed for High Bridge. Their goal, obviously, is to burn the bridge and close Lee's escape route.

General Lee quietly ponders Longstreet's information. He knows he has no way of stopping this Union advance.

For one of the few times in his adult life, Robert E. Lee is stymied.

∾

Lee hears the thunder of approaching hooves. General Thomas Lafayette Rosser, a gregarious twenty-eight-year-old Texan, gallops his cavalry into Rice's Station. Rosser's classmate at West Point was the equally audacious George Armstrong Custer, now a Union general involved on the other side of this very fight.

Longstreet approaches Rosser and, warning him about the Union plan, screams, "Go after the bridge burners. Capture or destroy the detachment, even if it takes the last man of your command to do it."

Rosser salutes, his face stolid. Only afterward does he grin, then bark the order. His cavalry, enlisted men and officers alike, gallop toward High Bridge. The quiet morning air explodes with noise as hundreds of hooves pound into the narrow dirt road.

When the war first broke out, Thomas Lafayette Rosser was so eager to take up arms for the Confederacy that he dropped out of West Point two weeks before graduation. Starting as a lieutenant, he distinguished himself at more than a dozen key battles, among them Manassas, Bull Run, and Gettysburg. Though wounded several times, Rosser never altered his daring approach to combat. In January 1865, as the Army of Northern Virginia huddled in its Petersburg defenses, Rosser selected 300 of his toughest riders for an impossible mission. They crossed the Allegheny Mountains in the dead of winter, seeking to destroy the Union infantry headquartered in the town of Beverly, West Virginia. Thunderstorms drenched them their second day on the march; then the temperature plummeted below zero, freezing their overcoats stiff. But those hardships actually helped Rosser, making the attack a complete surprise. The daring nighttime raid yielded 800 Union prisoners.

So Longstreet knows that Rosser is the sort of man who will not be afraid of the "kill or be killed" order. Rosser will not let him down.

After Rosser departs, there is nothing to do but wait. As Longstreet directs his men to strengthen their impromptu defenses in Rice's Station, Lee can only wonder how long it will take the rest of his army and its wagon train to catch up. With every passing second, the danger of Grant's scouts finding his army grows. Lee cannot let this happen. He must get over High Bridge by the end of the day.

Overcome with exhaustion, at last the fifty-eight-year-old general instructs his orderly to find someplace for him to nap. It is midmorning. Lee will close his eyes just long enough to feel rejuvenated. Then he will begin perhaps his last campaign. If he doesn't get over High Bridge, Lee knows, he will be defeated.

# CHAPTER ELEVEN

Thursday, April 6, 1865
Farmville, Virginia
Midmorning

The Union force racing to burn High Bridge consists of the Fourth Massachusetts Cavalry, the Fifty-fourth Pennsylvania Infantry, and the 123rd Ohio Infantry. The cavalry comprise 79 soldiers on horseback, who can fight either in the saddle or as dismounted foot soldiers. The two infantry regiments comprise almost 800 fighters who can wage war only on foot.

If the entire Union force were cavalry, the fearless General Rosser and his men would never catch them. A fast-walking soldier, even one on a mission of the utmost military importance, is obviously no match for a cavalry horse.

Colonel Francis Washburn of the Fourth Massachusetts knows this, which is why he orders his cavalry to gallop ahead of the foot soldiers. His men will burn the bridge while the infantry covers the rear.

High Bridge is an engineering marvel, considered by some to be the finest bridge in the world. The architects of the Brooklyn Bridge will steal liberally from its design. And yet High Bridge is situated not in one of the world's great cities but in a quiet, wooded corner of Virginia. Made of stone and felled trees, it stretches a half mile, from the bluff outside Farmville marking the southern shore of the Appomattox River floodplain to the Prince Edward Court House bluff at the opposite end. Twenty 125-foot-tall brick columns support the wooden superstructure. That two great armies, at the most pivotal point in their histories, have descended upon High Bridge at the same time is one of those random acts of fate that so often decide a war.

As Colonel Washburn and his men ride within three miles of High Bridge, they are joined by Union general Theodore Read, who has undertaken a daring mission to warn Washburn that the Confederates are hot on his trail, and that a small force of rebels who have been at High Bridge for months are dug in around the span. Read has full authority to cancel Washburn's mission if he thinks it too risky.

Washburn and Read hold a council of war at a hilltop plantation known as Chatham, roughly halfway between Rice's Station and High Bridge. They can see the bridge in the distance, and the two earthen forts defending it. There are just a few dozen Confederates dug in at the bridge, but they have a clear field of fire. A direct frontal assault would leave Washburn's men badly battered.

Another concern is that the ground between the Chatham plateau and High Bridge is a swampy morass of small creeks, sand, and hills, taking away any advantage of speed—and adding the very real potential of getting caught in a kill zone. Nevertheless, General Read orders Washburn to proceed to the bridge. Read will stay behind, with the infantry, to cover the cavalry's rear. This is a gamble, and both of these brave officers know it—a gamble with their own lives and those of their men.

It is also a gamble that could end the war by sundown.

∞

Washburn leads his cavalry toward High Bridge. He has a reputation for recklessness and impatient courage and shares the commonly held Union belief that the rebels are too demoralized to fight back. He will burn the bridge at any cost.

Washburn's cavalry ride for an hour, taking in the countryside as they prepare for battle. But then, seemingly out of nowhere, they are ambushed by rebel cavalry. It is a scene out of Lexington and Concord, as Confederate sharpshooters take aim. Again and again, and without warning, rebel cavalry charge. Washburn, fearing nothing, gives chase. But it's a clever trap, the rebels drawing the bluecoats in as they link up with the other Confederate force defending the bridge. Suddenly, Confederate artillery rains down on Washburn and his men, putting an instant halt to the Union pursuit. These cannonballs are the slap in the face that Washburn needs, making him realize that the rebels are hardly too demoralized to fight back. He also knows this: Colonel Francis Washburn of the Fourth Massachusetts is right now the one man in America who can end the Civil War this very day. He will go down in history. All he has to do is burn High Bridge.

Washburn is within a quarter mile of the bridge, his force largely intact. But then comes the crackle of gunfire from behind him. Three years of combat experience tells Washburn that he is in deep trouble; Confederate cavalrymen have found his infantry. High Bridge must wait.

The Fourth Massachusetts has been in the saddle since four A.M. It is now almost noon. The men are exhausted, as are their horses. The soldiers gallop their weary animals back across the floodplain, over the Sandy River and on up to the Chatham plateau. Men and horses are breathless from the race and the midday heat, the riders' blue uniforms and gloved hands bathed in sweat. Their stomachs rumble from lack of food, and their lips are chapped from thirst. They expect only a minor battle, because the main Confederate force is still miles away. But that expectation turns out to be brutally wrong.

Some 1,200 Confederate horsemen wait to attack Washburn's cavalry and infantry, which together number just slightly more than 800. Rebel horses and riders hold in a long line, awaiting the inevitable order to charge forth and crush the tiny Union force.

Colonel Washburn remains cool, surveying what could be a hopeless situation. Infantry is no match against the speed and agility of cavalry. His infantry lie on their bellies and peer across at Confederate cavalry. They have had no time to dig trenches or build fortifications, so hugging the ground is their only defense. Washburn is cut off from the rest of Grant's army, with no hope of rescue. How can 79 Union riders possibly hold off 1,200 Confederate horsemen?

∞

Washburn decides that his only hope is to be bold—a quality this Harvard man possesses in abundance.

After conferring with General Read, Washburn orders his cavalry to assemble. They are now on the brow of the hill, just out of rifle range, in columns of four. Washburn addresses the ranks. He barks out his plan, then reminds the infantry to get their butts up off the ground and follow right behind the Union riders to punch a hole through the rebel lines.

On Washburn's command, the Fourth Massachusetts trot their mounts forward. While the Confederates purchased their own horses or brought them from home, the Union horses are government-issue. Each trooper has ridden mile upon mile with the same horse, in the same saddle. As they arrive at this fateful moment, animal and rider alike know each other's moods and movements—the nudge of a knee, the gathering of the haunch muscles, the forward lean to intimate danger or the need for speed—so that they work as one.

Passing the infantry's far right flank, Washburn's cavalry wheels left. The colonel's accent is Brahmin and his tone is fearless. The precision of his cavalry is something that Washburn takes for granted, for they have practiced time and again on the parade ground. And the show of force stuns the enemy. The Confederates see what is coming, even if they don't believe it.

Counting Read and Washburn, there are now 80 Union horsemen. Outnumbered by more than fifteen to one, they shut out all thoughts of this being the last battle of their young lives. They ride hard. Their fate comes down to one simple word: "Charge!"

Washburn screams the command. Spurs dig into horses. Sabers clank as they are withdrawn from their sheaths. Some men fire their Spencer carbines as they gallop within rifle range, clutching the gun in their right hand and the reins in their left. Others wield pistols. Still others prefer the killing blade of a cavalry sword. The audacity of their charge and succeed-at-all-costs desperation ignites panic in the rebel army. The battlefield splits in two as Washburn's men punch through the first wave of the rebel line. The Union charge at Chatham, for a brief instant, is a triumph.

∞

But, stunningly, after the cavalry charges, Washburn's infantry does not move. Not a muscle. Even as the Confederate defenses crumble, and as Washburn organizes his men for the secondary attack that will smash an escape route through the rebel lines, the foot soldiers are still on their bellies, sealing their own doom.

General Rosser senses exactly what's happening. He doesn't waste a second. The Texan yells for his Confederate cavalry to prepare for a counterattack.

The Confederate general James Dearing, just twenty-four years old, leads the way. Both sides race toward each other at top speed before pulling back on the reins in the center of the plain. The fight becomes a brutal test of courage and horsemanship. Men and horses wheel about the battlefield, fighting hand to hand, saddle to saddle. Each man wages his own individual battle with a ferocity only a life-and-death situation can bring. Bullets pierce eyes. Screams and curses fill the air. The grassy plain runs blood-red.

A rifle is too unwieldy in such tight quarters, so men use the butt end rather than the barrel. Pistols and sabers are even more lethal. "I have been many a day in hot fights," the unflappable Rosser will marvel later, "but I never saw anything approaching that at High Bridge."

Rosser's gaze drifts over to the amazing sight of his enemy. Washburn, in the thick of the action, is a frenzied dervish, slaying everything in his path. Men fall and die all around as Washburn rides tall in the saddle, his saber slashing at any man who steps forward to challenge him.

Suddenly, the young Confederate general Dearing shoots the Union general Theodore Read, at point-blank pistol range. Read falls from his saddle to the ground. Seeing this, Colonel Washburn takes his revenge. He engages Dearing in an intense saber duel, brought to a sudden end when a Union soldier fires two bullets into Dearing's chest. His sword falls to the ground, as does he.

Washburn is still sitting tall in the saddle—but not for long. As he turns his head, he is shot through the mouth at point-blank range. The bullet lodges in his lungs. His jaw hangs slack as blood pours from the hole in his face, down onto his sweaty, dusty blue uniform.

The force of the gunshot does not kill Washburn, nor even render him unconscious. It is, however, strong enough to knock him out of the saddle for the first time all day. As the colonel falls, a Confederate flails at his toppling body with a thirty-four-inch saber, burying the blade deep in Washburn's skull. Incredibly, one day later, as a burial detail cleans the battlefield, Washburn will be found alive.

There are many, many casualties.

The Confederates lose 100 men.

The Union loses everyone.

Every single one of the 847 Union soldiers sent to burn High Bridge is either captured or killed. Those who try to fight their way out are slaughtered, one by one. The failure of the Union infantry to obey Washburn's orders to attack sealed their fate.

Rosser leads his weary men back toward Rice's Station, content in the knowledge that he has single-handedly saved the Confederacy.

Lee will now have his escape. Or at least it appears that way.

# CHAPTER TWELVE

As the battle for High Bridge commences, Union general George Meade's infantry finally finds the tail end of the Confederate column about ten miles away from the High Bridge fight. A hard rain falls. In the first of what will be many firefights on this day, small bands of Union soldiers begin shooting at the Confederate rear guard. The movement is like a ballet, with skirmishers pushing forward through the trees and craggy ground to engage the rebels. The instant they run out of ammunition, these skirmishers pull back and another group races forward to take their place. And all the while, other infantrymen capture artillery pieces, burn wagons, and force the rebels to turn and fight—and sometimes even dig in, separating them further from Lee's main force.

Confederate general John Gordon's force falls behind first. The ferocious Georgian understands that he is being cut off. In fact, Lee's entire Confederate army is being separated. No longer is it a single force; it has been broken into four separate corps. Under normal conditions, the cavalry would plug these gaps or, at the very least, chase away the Union skirmishers, but the cavalry have their hands full at High Bridge.

Meanwhile, in Rice's Station, Lee rises from his nap and assesses the situation. Hearing the ferocity of the firing from High Bridge, he assumes that the Union force is much bigger than the 800 men who galloped past him a few hours ago. If Lee had any cavalry at his disposal, they would act as his eyes and ears, scouting ahead and returning with the truth. But he doesn't. Lee can only guess at what's happening—and he guesses wrong.

Fearing that the Union general Sheridan has already leapfrogged out in front, Lee holds his entire corps in Rice's Station. At a time when it is crucial to be on the move, Lee chooses to remain in place.

∽

As Lee waits, Sheridan's three divisions of cavalry are searching high and low for the Army of Northern Virginia. His three commanders are Generals George Armstrong Custer, Thomas Devin, and George Crook. Custer is the youngest and most aggressive, the blond-haired dynamo who roomed with Thomas Rosser at West Point. Custer has a flair for the dramatic. He is the sort of man who rides into battle wearing a flamboyant red kerchief around his neck and accompanied by a brass band.

That kind of display will make George Custer famous. Eleven years later, it will also kill him. As Sheridan holds back to plot strategy, it is Custer who leads the Union cavalry on their search-and-destroy mission against the Confederate column. At midmorning he discovers the heart of the column, perhaps six miles from High Bridge. Custer does not hesitate. His division attacks. But upon meeting resistance, the young general stalls, allowing another cavalry division to attack. In this way, Custer slowly works his way up the Confederate line, riding closer and closer to the very front, toward Sam Grant's objective of getting out in front of Lee.

The pace is cruel. By noon Custer's horses are thirsty and in need of rest. They stop at a small stream. Custer's aide approaches, bringing news that scouts have found a gap in the Confederate line. Now Custer sets aside all thoughts of getting out in front of Lee. He excitedly gives the command to mount up. Without waiting for the other two divisions (a habit that will seal his doom at the Little Bighorn), his cavalry race toward the gap, hoping to drive a permanent wedge between the Confederate divisions.

*General George Armstrong Custer*

Custer succeeds. By two P.M. Custer's division pours into the small town of Marshall's Crossroads, where they are met by a lone artillery battalion. The Confederate cannons are no match for Custer's horsemen. He captures the small force and sets the rebel guns ablaze. But then another Confederate force counterattacks, pushing Custer out of the town. The Confederates dig in immediately, knowing that more fighting is imminent. The rebels hope to hold on long enough for Lee's main army to reinforce them.

George Custer, however, is not to be denied. He dismounts his men and orders them to assume an infantry posture. Then he scribbles a message to Crook and Devin, requesting help. Within an hour, their divisions are on the scene.

All afternoon, the three Union divisions initiate mounted and dismounted cavalry charges against the dug-in rebels. In the absence of artillery, the bluecoats boldly ride their horses up and over the Confederate breastworks. The Confederates cower in their trenches to avoid being trampled to death. The alternative is to run. Those who do are chased and cut down with sabers.

Even so, the rebels hold fast, repelling each and every charge. The general in charge, "Fighting Dick" Anderson, is a brilliant tactician, placing his limited resources in just the right place to repel the cavalry.

Finally, as daylight turns to evening, Custer assembles his men for one final charge. He orders the regimental band to play, hoping to strike fear in the enemy. Seeing the assembled cavalry, Confederate officers call an immediate retreat. Their goal is to reach Lee at Rice's Station.

Custer and the Union cavalry ride fast and hard into Anderson's lines before they can retreat. By now Sheridan has sent word, saying, "Go right through them. They're demoralized as hell"—an order that the Union cavalry take to heart. Anderson's Confederate corps breaks, the men dropping their weapons and running for their lives.

Of about 3,000 rebels, only 600 escape Custer. But the general is still not satisfied. He orders three Union cavalry divisions to give chase, cutting men down as they run. In a rare act of lenience, those who make it into the woods are allowed to live. Later they will be rounded up as prisoners of war. For now their confinement is the woods itself; those who try to fight their way out are promptly driven back inside.

More than 2,600 Confederates are captured, among them the one-legged General Richard Ewell. As he surrenders to Custer, he knows that a portion of his men are trapped on a grassy hillside a few miles up the road, above a swollen stream known as Sayler's Creek. These men are spoiling for another fight, a battle that will go down as the most barbaric and ferocious of the entire war.

General George Custer has seen much ferocious fighting in his young life, but he has never seen anything like Sayler's Creek.

# CHAPTER THIRTEEN

In 1865, the Sayler's Creek area of central Virginia is a place of outstanding beauty. Verdant rolling hills compete with virgin forest to present a countryside that is uniquely American, a place where families can grow amid the splendors of nature. But the beauty of the area will soon be defiled by the ugliness of war. Grant's Union army has finally arrived to confront Lee's forces. Lee's men are tired and hungry. Many have fought the north from the beginning, seeing action at Manassas, at Fredericksburg, and at Gettysburg. One group, in particular, the Stonewall Brigade, marched into battle under Stonewall Jackson, who, next to Lee, was the greatest of all southern generals. These same hardened fighters wept tears of grief when Jackson fell from his horse, the victim of friendly fire. Years of battle have reduced the numbers of the Stonewall Brigade from 6,000 soldiers to just a few hundred battle-tested veterans.

These men know the meaning of war. They also know the meaning, if not the precise military definition, of terms like "enfilade" and "field of fire" and "reverse-slope defense," for they can execute them in their sleep. The Stonewall Brigade and the rest of Lee's men, depleted as they are, are practiced experts at warfare.

Lee knows that his fighting force is splintered. Near a bucolic estate called Lockett's Farm, the Jamestown Road crosses over Big Sayler's Creek and Little Sayler's Creek at a place called Double Bridges. There are, as the name implies, two narrow bridges. The wagons must all funnel into a narrow line and cross one at a time. Lee is miles away from his supply train and cannot protect it. His only hope is that the Union army will be too slow in catching up to the wagons.

Grant's army is now in sight. The soldiers' blue uniforms and the glint of their steel bayonets strike fear into the hearts of the teamsters, causing the wagons to attempt to cross Double Bridges two and three at a time. Wheels become tangled. Horses and mules balk in their traces, confused by the noise and smelling the panic. Their pace grows slower and slower, until one of the bridges actually collapses from the weight, and the Confederate advance comes to an abrupt halt.

Within minutes, the Union attacks. Sweeping down from the high ground, General Meade's infantry pounces on the terrified Confederates, who abandon their wagons and race into the woods on foot.

The Confederate infantry waits a few hundred yards ahead of the chaos, watching. They stand shoulder to shoulder, their line of battle almost two miles wide. Thus are 4,000 of Lee's troops poised to meet the Union attack.

Behind them, rebel wagons are burning on the double bridges above Sayler's Creek. To the left of the Confederate force is the Appomattox River. Straight in front of them are thousands of advancing blue-clad Yankees. At first, the Confederate infantry line holds. But under withering artillery fire the men begin to fall back.

It is a mile-long retreat over open ground that offers almost no cover. The rebel infantry topple the wagons that have made it across the double bridges, using them as an impromptu breastworks, hiding behind a spoked wheel or a tilted axle. The sun cannot set quickly enough for these men. With 10,000 Union troops almost on top of them, darkness is the rebels' only hope.

∞

Night does not come soon enough, and the fight begins. Almost immediately, the Confederates take incredible losses. Artillery and bullets level any man who dares to stand still. Many soldiers quit the war right then and there, convinced that this endless wave of blue is unbeatable. They see the wagons afire, and hear the explosions of the ammunition inside, and know in an instant that of the three things a soldier needs to survive in wartime—bullets, sleep, and food—they have none.

Others, however, are more game. They abandon the cover of the wagons and begin to splash across Sayler's Creek. They are rewarded.

Just as the North surges forward, hope arrives. It comes in the form of Robert E. Lee, who has spent the afternoon on horseback, trying to find his own army. He sits astride Traveller, looking down from a nearby ridgeline. "The disaster which had overtaken the army was in full view," one of his officers will later write. "Teamsters with their teams and dangling traces, retreating infantry without guns, many without hats, a harmless mob, with massive columns of the enemy moving orderly on."

This "harmless mob," Lee realizes, is his own Army of Northern Virginia.

"My God," says a horrified Lee, staring down at the columns of smoke and tongues of flames and stacks of bodies—so many that the ground along both branches of Sayler's Creek is a carpet of gray and blue. "Has the army been dissolved?"

∽

Two miles south of Lee's viewpoint, and a half mile north of where General Custer still has a Confederate force pinned down, perhaps the most ferocious battle ever seen on American soil is unfolding.

"At three o'clock in the afternoon," one Confederate soldier will remember, "we reached Sayler's Creek, a small creek that at the time had overflowed its banks from the continuous rains of the past few days, giving the appearance of a small river. We halted a few minutes then waded across this stream and took our positions on the rising ground one hundred yards beyond."

The hill is grassy, but the site of the Confederate stand is toward the back of the rise, under the cover of broom sedge and pine shrubs. Now the rebels hold the high ground. Any force attacking Lee's army of almost 4,000 will have to expose themselves to fire while wading the four-foot-deep morass of Sayler's Creek. If they get across safely, they will then have to fight their way uphill to the rebel positions.

"We threw ourselves prone upon the ground. Our battle line was long drawn out, exceedingly thin. Here we rested awaiting the attack, as the enemy had been following closely behind us," a Confederate major will later chronicle.

At five-thirty, the Union artillery opens fire on the grassy hill, lobbing shells at the Confederate positions from just four hundred yards away. The rebels have no artillery of their own and cannot fire back. The screams of the wounded are soon drowned out by the whistle and explosion of shells. All the Confederates can do is hug the ground and pray as the Union gunners take "their artillery practice without let or hindrance."

The shelling lasts twenty minutes. Under cover of that heavy fire, long blue lines of Union infantry wade the creek, separated into two battle lines, and slowly march up the hill. The Confederates are devastated by the precision artillery, but do not retreat. Instead, they lie flat on the ground, muskets pointed at the stream of blue uniforms picking their way up the grassy slope. A Confederate major steps boldly in front of the line and walks the entire length, exposing himself to fire as he reminds the rebels that no one is allowed to shoot until ordered to do so. He later recalls the instruction: "That when I said 'ready' they must all rise, kneeling on the right knee; that when I said 'aim' they must all aim about the knees of the advancing line; and that when I said 'fire' they must all fire together."

⁂

Everything, as one officer notes, is as "still as the grave." The advancing line of blue moves forward in a giant scrum, slowly ascending the hill. Some of the men wave white handkerchiefs, mocking the Confederates, jeering that they should surrender. But the rebels say nothing, letting the Union soldiers believe that the South is already beaten. The bluecoats refrain from charging, preferring to plod, letting the notion of surrender sink in, for the rebels surely know there is no way they can get off this hill alive.

"Ready!" comes the cry from the Confederate lines. They are low on ammunition and may get only a shot or two. Even then, reloading a musket takes time. Better to make each shot count.

"The men rose, all together, like a piece of mechanism, kneeling on their right knees and their faces set with an expression that meant—everything," a Confederate officer will write.

On the cry of "Aim!" a line of horizontal musket barrels points directly at the blue wall. Then: "Fire!"

"I have never seen such an effect, physical and moral, produced by the utterance of one word," marvels the Confederate major. "The enemy seemed to have been totally unprepared for it."

The entire front row of Union soldiers falls in bloody chaos. The second line turns and runs down the hill.

This is Grant's vaunted army, a force better rested, better fed, and better equipped than the half-dressed Confederates. And yet the blue-coats flee in terror, their white handkerchiefs littering the ground. It is a triumph, and in that instant the Confederate force is overcome by righteous indignation. The memory of that hard overnight march in the rain, the starvation, the delirious craziness born of exhaustion—all of it blends into a single moment of fury. The rebels leap to their feet and chase after the bluecoats. Down the hill they run, caps flying off, curses streaming from their mouths. Dead men are everywhere, on both sides, and the Confederates have to hop and jump over bodies. But the rebels never stop running.

The Union soldiers finally gather themselves. They stop, turn, and fire. Knowing they are outgunned, the Confederates retreat back to their positions, only to be surrounded as the Union force quickly counterattacks the hill.

And this time the bluecoats aren't plodding. Union soldiers sprint up the hill, overrunning the Confederate positions. Out of ammunition, and heavily outnumbered, the Army of Northern Virginia still refuses to surrender. The fighting becomes hand to hand. Soldiers claw at each other, swinging fists, kicking. "The battle degenerated into a butchery and a confused melee of personal conflicts. I saw numbers of men kill each other with bayonets and the butts of muskets, and even bite each other's throats and ears and noses, rolling on the ground like wild beasts," one Confederate officer will write. "I had cautioned my men against wearing Yankee overcoats, especially in battle, but had not been able to enforce the order perfectly—and almost at my side I saw a young fellow of one of my companies jam the muzzle of his musket against the back of the head of his most intimate friend, clad in a Yankee overcoat, and blow his brains out."

Although the battle is little remembered in history, witnesses will swear they have never seen more suffering, or a fight as desperate, as during the final moments of Sayler's Creek.

∽

And still it grows more vicious. None other than General George Armstrong Custer, who has been killing Confederates since breakfast, has broken off from his former position and races his cavalry through the pine thickets behind the rebel lines. His horsemen ride into the action behind him, sabers swinging. Custer is impervious to personal injury, his savagery today adding to his growing legend for fearlessness. Custer slashes his sword, showing no mercy. He spurs his men to do the same. Rebel troops on foot are cut to pieces by bullets and steel blades.

The Union artillerymen, not wanting to be left out, pull their guns to the edge of Sayler's Creek and take aim into those stray bands of Confederate soldiers on the fringes of the fighting. Firing rounds of canister and grape—lethal small balls and bits of sharpened metal designed to maim and disfigure—the artillery adds to the chaos. On the ground, bodies missing heads, legs, and arms are sprawled in absurd contortions, a gruesome reminder of what close-quarter combat will yield.

Soon, one by one, the rebels raise their musket butts in the air as a signal of surrender. Union soldiers round up these men, whom they have fought so savagely for the previous hour. Then, shocked by the sunken eyes and gaunt Confederate faces, some of the bluecoats open their rucksacks and share their food.

The last rebels to surrender are the sailors and marines recently converted to infantry. Surrounded in a grove of trees, with no hope of escape, they lay down their rifles.

∽

One Confederate corps has managed to escape from the confusion of Sayler's Creek, and now it reaches General Lee at the top of the ridge. Seeing his forces trudging back toward him, Lee grabs a battle flag and holds it aloft. The Confederate Stars and Bars snaps in the wind, the flag's bright red color a compass beacon guiding the weary surviving soldiers to safety. Union forces try to give chase but abandon the effort when the darkness makes it impossible to tell whether they are shooting at friend or foe.

A day that started so well for the Confederates at Rice's Station, then saw triumph at High Bridge, is now finished. In the morning, Lee will continue his escape, but without 13 battle flags, 300 wagons, 70 ambulances, and almost 8,000 men, either killed or taken prisoner. Ten of Lee's top officers are either dead or captured. Among the captured is his eldest son, Custis Lee.

The Union army, on the other hand, suffers 1,200 casualties. So fierce is the fighting, and so courageous the actions of the fighters, that 56 Union soldiers will receive the Congressional Medal of Honor for their actions on the field that day.

Night falls, and so ends what will come to be known as the Black Thursday of the Confederacy. Half of Lee's army is gone. Except for General Longstreet, his remaining generals think the situation is hopeless. Lee continues to improvise, still looking for a way to save his army and get to the Carolinas. Yet even he is devastated. "A few more Sayler's Creeks and it will all be over," sighs Marse Robert.

But Lee cannot bring himself to utter the one word he dreads most: "surrender."

# CHAPTER FOURTEEN

FRIDAY, APRIL 7, 1865
CITY POINT, VIRGINIA
DAWN

Lincoln is desperate for news from the front. The time away from Washington was meant to be a working vacation, and it has clearly revived the president. The "incredible sadness" he has carried for so long is gone, replaced by "serene joy." Mary Lincoln has joined her husband at City Point, bringing with her a small complement of guests from Washington. The mood in the nation's capital has turned festive since the fall of Richmond. Mary and her guests plan to visit Richmond in the morning, as if the burned-out husk of a city has become a tourist attraction. Lincoln will stay behind on the riverboat and tend to the war. Still, he is glad for the company. He tells jokes and makes small talk, all the while wondering when the next telegram from General Grant will arrive.

Early on the morning of April 7, just hours after Sayler's Creek, Lincoln receives the news for which he's been waiting. Grant's telegram states that Sheridan has ridden over the battlefield, counting Confederate dead and captured, particularly the many top Confederate generals now in Union custody. "If the thing is pressed," Grant quotes Sheridan as saying, "I think Lee will surrender."

Lincoln telegraphs his heartfelt reply: "Let the thing be pressed."

# CHAPTER FIFTEEN

---

PALM SUNDAY, APRIL 9, 1865
APPOMATTOX COURT HOUSE

The end has come. General Robert E. Lee rides forth from the Confederate lines, into the no-man's-land separating his dwindling force from the vast Union forces. The Army of Northern Virginia is cornered in a sedate little village called Appomattox Court House—Lee's 8,000 men surrounded on three sides by Grant's 60,000. After escaping Sayler's Creek the rebels reached Farmville, only to be attacked again and forced to flee before they could finish eating their rations. They raced across High Bridge, only to find that mortar wouldn't burn. The Union army crossed right behind them. Grant was then able to get ahead and block Lee's path to the Carolinas.

Lee's final great hope for a breakout came the previous night. He had entrusted his toughest general, John Gordon from Georgia, with punching a hole in the Union lines. The attack began at five P.M. Three hours later, after Gordon encountered wave after never-ending wave of blue-clad soldiers—too many for his men to beat down—he sent word back to Lee that he had "fought my corps to a frazzle."

In other words: Gordon could not break through.

Lee's proud shoulders slumped as he received the news. "There is nothing left for me to do but go and see General Grant," he said aloud. Lee was surrounded by his staff but was talking to himself. The man

who had succeeded his entire life, excelling at everything and failing at
nothing, was beaten. "I would rather die a thousand deaths," he said.

∽

Dressed in an impeccable formal gray uniform, polished black boots,
and clean red sash, Lee now rides forth. A spectacular ceremonial
sword is buckled around his waist. He expects to meet Grant once he
crosses over into the Union lines, there to surrender his sword and
be taken prisoner.

But before Grant's soldiers march him off to the penitentiary, Lee
plans to argue on behalf of his men, seeking the best possible terms
of surrender for the Army of Northern Virginia. He has written to
Grant repeatedly on this subject. Grant's evasive replies have given
little evidence as to which way he leans on the issue.

Lee and a small group of aides ride to a spot between the Union
and Confederate lines. They halt their horses in the middle of the
country lane and wait for Grant to meet them.

And they wait. And they wait some more. All the while it becomes
more obvious that the Union forces are not just enjoying a quiet Sunday morning—cleaning rifles, filling cartridge cases, putting out the
breakfast fires. No, they are preparing for battle. Lee can see it in the
way the gun crews have unlimbered the cannons and howitzers and
are now sighting them toward his lines. The big guns—those M1857
Napoleons—can drop a twelve-pound projectile on top of a man's
head from a mile away, and those howitzers can lob an eighteen-
pound shell nearly as far. Looking at the Union lines, Lee sees dozens
of these guns, capable of inflicting catastrophic damage.

If this is a display of force by Grant to hasten Lee's surrender, it is
working.

But Grant does not show himself. In fact, he is miles away, suffering
from a severe migraine headache. Lee sits astride Traveller, painfully
vulnerable to a sniper's bullet despite his flag of truce. After about two
hours with no response, Lee sees a Union soldier riding out. The soldier informs Lee that the attack will be launched in a few moments.
For his own safety, Lee must return to the Confederate lines.

∽

The boom of artillery breaks the morning quiet. Lee jots a quick note intended for Grant and hands it to an orderly, who gallops toward the Union lines under a white flag. He also requests that the attack be postponed until Grant can be located.

With the irrefutable logic of a man conditioned to follow orders, the Union colonel in charge tells Lee's courier that he does not have the authority to halt the attack. It will go forward as planned.

As the courier gallops back to Lee, Union skirmishers march to the front and prepare to probe the Confederate lines for vulnerability.

Lee writes another letter to Grant, asking for "a suspension of the hostilities pending the adjustment of the terms of the surrender of this army."

Even as fighting threatens to break out all around him, Lee is unruffled. He sits astride Traveller, whose flanks are flecked with mud, waiting for permission to surrender. But when the first wave of skirmishers is just a hundred yards away, Lee has no choice but to find safety. With a reluctant tug on Traveller's reins, he turns back toward his men.

∞

Moments later he is stopped. A Union courier tells Lee that his letter has not found Grant, but it has found General George Meade, whom Lee knew long before the war. Meade has ordered a sixty-minute truce, hoping that Grant can be located in the meantime.

Lee turns Traveller once again. He rides back toward the front and dismounts. It's been four hours since he first sought the surrender meeting. The sun is now directly overhead. Lee sits on a pile of fence rails, in the meager shade of an apple tree bearing the first buds of spring. There, he writes yet another letter to Grant, hoping to impress upon the Union general the seriousness of his intentions. This, too, is sent off under a white flag through the Union lines. Finally, at twelve-fifteen, a lone Union officer and his Confederate escort arrive to see Lee. The officer, a colonel named Babcock, delivers a letter into Lee's hands:

GENERAL R. E. LEE
COMMANDING C.S. ARMIES:
Your note of this date is of but this moment (11:50 a.m.) received. In consequence of my having passed from the

Richmond and Lynchburg road to the Farmville and Richmond road, I am at this writing about four miles west of
Walker's church, and will push forward to the front for
the purpose of meeting you. Notice sent on this road
where you wish the interview to take place will meet me.

Very respectfully, your obedient servant

U. S. Grant

Lieutenant-General

With a mixture of sadness and relief, Lee and his three aides ride
past the Union lines. These troops do not cheer him, as the Army of
Northern Virginia is in the habit of doing. Instead, the Sunday afternoon is preternaturally quiet after so many days and years of war.
There is no thunder of artillery or jingle of a cavalry limber. Just
those miles-long lines of men in blue, staring up at Lee as he rides
past, dressed so impeccably and riding so tall and straight-backed in
the saddle. Not even his eyes give away his mourning, nor the
dilemma that he has endured since Sayler's Creek, when it became
clear that his army was no longer able to acquit itself.

Per Grant's letter, Lee sends his aide Colonel Charles Marshall up
the road to find a meeting place. Marshall settles on a simple home.
By a great twist of fate, the house belongs to a grocer named Wilmer
McLean, who moved to Appomattox Court House to escape the war.
A cannonball had landed in his fireplace during the first Battle of Bull
Run, at the very start of the conflict. Fleeing to a quieter corner of
Virginia was his way of protecting his family from harm.

But the Civil War once again finds Wilmer McLean. He and his
family are asked to leave the house. Soon, Lee marches up the front
steps and takes a seat in the parlor. Again, he waits.

∞

At one-thirty, after a half hour, Lee hears a large group of horsemen
galloping up to the house. Moments later, General U. S. Grant walks
into the parlor. He wears a private's uniform; it is missing a button. He
has affixed shoulder boards bearing the three stars of a lieutenant general, but otherwise there is nothing elegant about the Union leader. He
has been wearing the same clothes since Wednesday night, and they

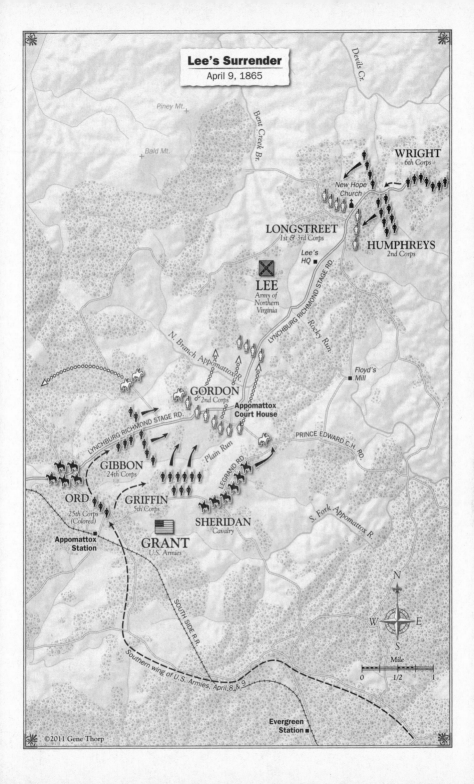

are now further spattered by mud from his thirty-five-mile ride this morning. "Grant," Colonel Amos Webster, a member of the Union general's staff, will later remember, "covered with mud in an old faded uniform, looked like a fly on a shoulder of beef."

Removing his yellow cloth riding gloves, Grant steps forward and shakes Lee's hand.

Almost twenty years earlier, during the Mexican War, he was a mere lieutenant when Lee was a major soon to be promoted to colonel. Grant well recalled how Lee had scolded him because of his slovenly appearance. While not a vindictive man, U. S. Grant does not suffer slights easily. He has an encyclopedic memory. Lee has only a minor recollection of meeting Grant prior to this moment in Wilmer McLean's parlor, but Grant remembers every single word. So while Lee sits before him, proud but fallen, resplendent in his spotless uniform, Grant looks and smells like a soldier who could not care less about appearance or ceremony.

∽

As the moment of surrender nears, however, Grant starts to feel a bit embarrassed by the prospect of asking one of history's great generals to give up his army and has second thoughts about his dress. "General Lee was dressed in a full uniform which was entirely new," he will later write in his memoirs, "and was wearing a sword of considerable value, very likely the sword that had been presented by the State of Virginia. At all events, it was an entirely different sword than the one that would ordinarily be worn in the field. In my rough traveling suit, the uniform of private with the straps of a lieutenant general, I must have contrasted very strangely with a man so handsomely dressed, six feet high and of faultless form. But this was not a matter that I thought of until afterwards."

As Grant's generals and staff—among them Custer and Sheridan—file into the room and stand to one side, Lee's aides gather behind their leader.

Grant and Lee sit at a small wooden table. An area rug covers the floor beneath them. The room's balance of power is tilted heavily toward the Union—Grant and his twelve to Lee and his two. Lee's men are staff officers, neatly dressed and strangers to the battlefield.

Grant's men, on the other hand, include staff and top generals, men who have spent the last week on horseback, harassing Lee's army. They are dressed for battle, swords clanking and spurs jangling, the heels of their cavalry boots echoing on the wooden floor. They can barely suppress smirks betraying their good fortune, for not only destroying Lee's army but to be present at the moment of Marse Robert's greatest humiliation. Sheridan, in particular, has great reason to be here. He believes that Lee's request for a cease-fire and these negotiations are yet another clever attempt to help his army escape. A shipment of rations is waiting for Lee and his army at the local railway depot, and Sheridan is convinced that Lee means to use the food to get him one step closer to the Carolinas.

What Sheridan and General Custer know, but Lee does not, is that Union cavalry has already captured that station. The food is in Union hands. Even if Lee is lying, and somehow manages to escape, his army will never make it the final hundred miles to freedom on empty stomachs.

"I met you once before, General Lee," Grant starts. His voice is calm, as if this moment is just a random occasion for small talk. "We were serving in Mexico, when you came over from General Scott's headquarters to visit Garland's brigade, to which I belonged. I have always remembered your appearance, and I think I should have recognized you anywhere."

"Yes. I know I met you on that occasion," Lee answers in the same casual tone as Grant, letting the reference sit between them, though certainly not apologizing. His face, in Grant's estimation, is "impassable." "I have often thought of it and tried to recollect how you looked, but I have never been able to recall a single feature," Lee says.

The generals speak of Mexico, recalling long-ago names like Churubusco and Veracruz. Grant finds the conversation so pleasant that he momentarily forgets the reason for their meeting. Lee is the one to take the initiative.

"I suppose, General Grant, that the object of our present meeting is fully understood," he says. "I asked to see you to ascertain upon what terms you would receive the surrender of my army."

Grant calls for his order book, a thin volume of yellow paper with carbon sheets. He lights a cigar and stares at a page, composing the sequence of words that will most amicably end the war. A cloud of smoke hovers around his head. Lee does not smoke, and he watches as Grant, after waving a distracted hand in the air to shoo the cigar smoke away, writes out his terms in pen.

When he is finished, Grant hands the book over to Lee.

Marse Robert digests the words in silence. The terms are remarkable in their lenience. Lee will not even have to surrender his sword. The gist is simple: Put down your guns and go home. Let's rebuild the nation together. This was President Lincoln's vision, to which Grant subscribed.

As if to underscore this point, members of Grant's staff tentatively ask Robert E. Lee for permission to go behind Confederate lines. They have old friends over there, friends they have seen only

*Appomattox Court House, 1865: victorious Union soldiers in front of the courthouse*

through the lens of a spyglass, across some great width of battlefield, these last four years.

Lee grants permission.

There is little else to say. Lee is humiliated but also grateful that his enemies have granted such favorable terms. He will be able to return to his army with some good news. Grant and Lee rise simultaneously and shake hands. After years of battle, hardship, strategizing, and sleeping in one impromptu lodging after another, the two great warriors and the thousands of men in their armies can now go home.

∽

As Lee rides back to his lines, the Army of Northern Virginia spontaneously gathers on both sides of the road. Lee fights back tears as his men call out to him. His dissolved army will soon turn over their guns and battle flags. This is their last chance to show their great love and respect for their leader. "Men," he calls out to them, "we have fought this war together and I have done the best I can for you."

Each group cheers as Lee rides past, only to give in to their sorrow and break down in sobs, "all along the route to his quarters."

Meanwhile, the reconciliation is beginning. Confederate and Union officers are renewing old friendships. "They went over, had a pleasant time with their old friends, and brought some of them back with them when they returned," Grant will write twenty years later, recalling that the McLean household became their de facto meeting place that night. The men swapped stories of their lives and remembrances of battles won and lost. "Here the officers of both armies came in great numbers, and seemed to enjoy the meeting as much as though they had been friends separated for a long time while fighting under the same flag.

"For the time being it looked very much as if all thought of the war had escaped their minds."

But the war is not so easily forgotten by others. Unbeknownst to all those men who risked their lives to fight those great battles—men who deservedly savor the peace—plans are being hatched throughout the South to seek revenge for the Union victory.

# Part Two

# THE IDES
# OF DEATH

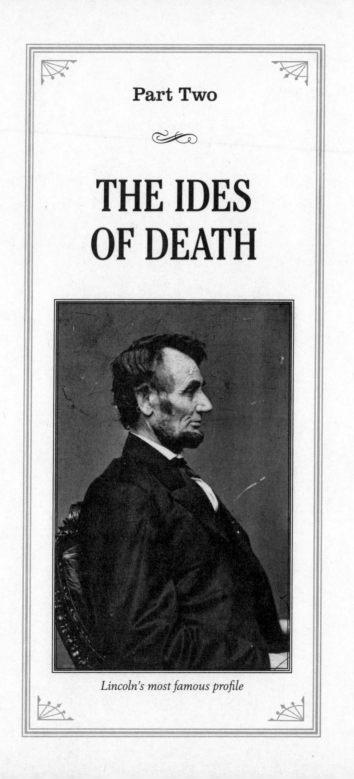

*Lincoln's most famous profile*

# CHAPTER SIXTEEN

It seems like the entire town is drunk. Lee's Confederate army has surrendered. In the Union capital whiskey is chugged straight out of the bottle, church bells toll, pistols are fired into the air, fireworks explode, newsboys hawk final editions chock-full of details from Appomattox, brass bands play, church hymns are sung, thirty-five U.S. flags are hoisted, and army howitzers launch an astonishing five-hundred-gun salute, which shatters windows for miles around the city.

The war is done! After four long years, and more than 600,000 dead altogether, euphoria now floats through the air like an opiate.

Complete strangers clasp one another's hands like long-lost friends. They rub shoulders in taverns, restaurants, cathouses, and the impromptu glow of blazing streetside bonfires. Revelers march from one place to the next, passing the flask, aimless and amazed. Sooner or later it becomes obvious that their passion needs a purpose—or, at the very least, a focus. The human mass snakes toward the White House, handheld torches lighting the way. The people of Washington, D.C., overcome by news of the war's end, hope to glimpse their president on this historic night. Perhaps, if they are very lucky, he will give one of the speeches for which he has become so famous.

The nation's capital is not yet the cosmopolitan city it will become. The streets are mostly dirt and mud. It is not uncommon for traffic to stop as farmers drive cattle to market. Open spaces have been military staging areas during the war, with the camp followers and soldiers' businesses such a designation implies. The Tiber Creek and its adjacent canal are open sewers, a breeding ground for typhus, cholera, and dysentery. The vile stench is made worse by the Central Market's butchers, fond of heaving freshly cleaved carcasses into the rancid waters each morning. This might not be a problem, were it not for the Tiber being located a stone's throw from the Capitol Building, that beautiful unfinished idea that towers above the city like an allegory for the nation itself.

∽

To Lincoln, the Capitol is the most important structure in Washington. During the war, even when resources were limited and manpower was desperately needed on the battlefields, he refused to halt construction. Its signature element, the dome, was fitted into place just over a year ago. Inside, scaffolding still climbs up the curved walls of the unfinished rotunda. Workmen mingle with the Union soldiers who have used the Capitol as a barracks, sleeping on the sandstone floors and waking each morning to the aroma of baking bread, thanks to the cadre of bakers in the basement turning out sixty thousand loaves each day for shipment to distant battlefields.

The Capitol was an obvious artillery target during the war, so the gas lamps atop the dome remained unlit for the duration. Now they blaze. The Capitol glows above the frenzied crowds like some great torch of freedom, a wondrous reminder that Lincoln's common refrain of "the Union must go on" has, indeed, come to pass.

So it is fitting that on the night the Capitol dome is lit, the crowd of more than two thousand staggers to an unruly halt on the grass outside the White House's front door, waiting for Lincoln to show himself from the windows of the second-floor residence. When Lincoln doesn't appear right away, they cry out for him. At first it's just a few random shouts. Then a consensus. Soon they roar as one: "Lincoln," the people cry. "Speech."

The crowd is crazy to touch President Lincoln, to see him, to hear his voice. They continue calling out to him, the chant getting louder until the sound is deafening.

But Lincoln is in no mood to speak. The president sends a messenger out to the people, letting them know he is not up to it tonight. That only makes the crowd cheer louder. Lincoln tries to mollify them by going to a window, pulling back a curtain, and waving. Upon seeing the president, the crowd explodes. Men hoist their caps and umbrellas and women wave their handkerchiefs.

Still, Lincoln does not give a speech.

∽

The crowd doesn't leave. He goes to the window a second time, hoping his appearance will send them on their way. To his utter amazement, twelve-year-old Tad Lincoln is now down on the grass with all those people, running through the crowd with a captured rebel battle flag. The people laugh good-naturedly at the stunned look on Lincoln's face, then cheer him as he steps alone from the front door of the White House to retrieve his young boy. It will be impossible for him to escape without saying a word or two. Lincoln has no protection as he wades into the crowd to get Tad.

The president returns inside the White House, even as the folks remain in the front yard.

Lincoln, at heart, is a showman. He reappears at the second-floor window, smiling and holding up a hand in acknowledgment. "I am very greatly rejoiced to find that an occasion has occurred so pleasurable that the people cannot restrain themselves," he jokes, knowing that the crowd will respond by cheering even louder.

They do.

The president is tired, having hardly been able to sleep, due to a series of dreadful nightmares and anxiety over the struggles still to come. He sees the bonfires and the lanterns, and basks in the ovation, feeling the fatigue slip away. He hears the hurrahs, along with again the single loud cry in unison of "Speech."

Lincoln sighs inwardly. He has waited so long for this moment, and yet he must hold back. These words cannot be delivered impulsively. Nor can he hope to be bathed in applause after they are spoken.

The people need to hear the truth, even though that's not what they want to hear. The crowd wants retribution, not reconciliation; they want grand and eloquent words. Inspirational words. Fortifying words. Even boastful words. They will tell their children's children about the night after the war was won, the night they heard the great Abraham Lincoln frame the victory in the most beautiful and poetic way possible.

They wish, in other words, to witness history.

Lincoln would like to indulge them. But the sentiments are half-formed and the words not yet written. Instead of telling the crowd what's on his mind—how the thrill about the war's end that filled his heart just yesterday is being replaced by weariness at the prospect of the hard work to come—Lincoln smiles that easy grin for which he is so well known. If you want to hear a speech, Lincoln yells to the crowd, please come back tomorrow night.

There is no malice in his tone, no undercurrent of sarcasm born of the many years of public ridicule. The veteran politician works his audience with professional ease. His unamplified voice carries powerfully through the chill night air.

Spying the Navy Yard brass band taking shelter under the White House eaves, he calls out a request: "I always thought that 'Dixie' was one of the best tunes I ever heard. Our adversaries over the way, I know, have attempted to appropriate it. But I insist that yesterday we fairly captured it.

"It is now our property," he informs the crowd, then directs the band to "favor us with a performance."

As the musicians strike up the Confederate anthem, and the crowd sings and claps to that old familiar rhythm, Lincoln slips back into the White House and starts writing the last speech he will ever give.

# CHAPTER SEVENTEEN

Monday, April 10, 1865
Washington, D.C.
Night

John Wilkes Booth picks up his gun.

One mile down Pennsylvania Avenue, so close he can almost hear the beloved strains of "Dixie" being belted out so heretically by a Yankee band, the twenty-six-year-old actor stands alone in a pistol range. The smell of gunpowder mixes with the fragrant pomade of his mustache. His feet are set slightly wider than shoulder width, his lean athletic torso is turned at a right angle to the bull's-eye, and his right arm is extended in a line perfectly parallel with the floor. In his fist he cradles the sort of pint-sized pistol favored by ladies and cardsharps.

He fires.

Booth scrutinizes the target. Satisfied, he reloads his single-shot .44-caliber Deringer. His mood is a mixture of rage and despondence. Things have gone to hell since Lee surrendered. Richmond is gone, and with it the Confederate leadership. The "secesh" community—those southern secessionist sympathizers living a secret life in the nation's capital—is in disarray. There's no one to offer guidance to Booth and the other secret agents of the Confederacy.

At this point, there are at least four Confederate groups conspiring to harm the president. Two are plotting a kidnapping, one is planning to smuggle dress shirts infected with yellow fever into his dresser drawers, and another intends to blow up the White House.

Booth is part of a kidnapping conspiracy. He prefers the term "capture." Kidnapping is a crime, but capturing an enemy during a time of war is morally correct. The Confederate government has strict rules governing its agents' behavior. If Booth does indeed get the chance, he is allowed to capture the president, truss him like a pig, subject him to a torrent of verbal and mental harassment, and even punch him in the mouth, should the opportunity present itself. The one thing he is not allowed to do is engage in "black flag warfare."

Or in a word: murder.

∽

Booth wonders if the restriction against black flag warfare still applies. And, if not, what he should do about it. That's why he's at the range. He has a major decision to make. Shooting helps him think.

Booth fires again. The split-second bang fills him with power, drowning out the celebrations and focusing his mind. Again, he tamps in a ball and a percussion cap.

There is a darkness to Booth's personality, born of the entitlement that comes with celebrity. He is a boaster and a liar, fond of embellishing stories to make himself sound daring and adventurous. He is cruel and mercurial. He is a bully, eager to punish those who don't agree with his points of view. Outside of his love for his mother, Booth is capable of doing anything to satisfy his own urges.

Booth is also a white supremacist. His most closely guarded secret is that he has temporarily given up the profession of acting to fight for the pro-slavery movement. The abolition movement, in Booth's mind, is the real cause of the Civil War, a serpent that must be crushed. Enslavement of blacks is part of the natural order, Booth believes, and central to the South's economy. Blacks, he maintains, are third-class citizens who should spend their lives working for the white man. Not only does this life fulfill them, but they are begging for correction when they step out of line. "I have been through the whole south and have marked the happiness of master and man," Booth writes. "I have seen the black man whipped. But only when he deserved much more than he received."

As a teenager, Booth was traumatized when runaway slaves killed a schoolmate's father. He is willing to swear an oath that this sort of violence will happen on a much larger scale if the South loses the war. Newly freed slaves will slaughter southern white men, rape their women and daughters, and instigate a bloodbath unlike any other in recorded history.

The only way to prevent that is to reinstate slavery by winning the Civil War.

∽

It crushes Booth to think that the South has lost. He shuts the idea out of his mind. Lee's surrender, Booth believes, was a gross error in judgment. Even the great Marse Robert is allowed an occasional lapse.

Booth takes solace in the 146,000 Confederate troops spread out from North Carolina to Texas that have refused to lay down their weapons. So long as those men are willing to fight, the Confederacy— and slavery—will live on.

And now, Booth will give them another reason to fight.

∽

That he was born just south of the Mason-Dixon Line and nearly a northerner means nothing. Booth nurtures a deep hatred for his father and the nation's father figure, Abraham Lincoln. Booth was jealous of his father, an accomplished actor who never acknowledged his young son's talent. Booth's paternal loathing has now been transferred to the president; it flared to full burn when Lincoln issued the Emancipation Proclamation.

Booth could have enlisted in the war. But soldiering, even for the Confederate cause, is far too mundane for his flamboyant personality. He cares little about battles won or lost, or battlefields hundreds of miles from the fancy hotels he calls home. Booth is fighting the Civil War on his terms, using his talents, choreographing the action like a great director. The grand finale will be a moment straight from the stage, some stunning dramatic conclusion when antagonist and protagonist meet face-to-face, settling their differences once and for all. The antagonist, of course, will win.

That antagonist will be Booth.

And what could be more dramatic than kidnapping Lincoln?

The plan is for Booth to gag and bind him, then smuggle him out of Washington, D.C., into the hands of Confederate forces. The president of the United States will rot in a rat-infested dungeon until slavery has been reinstated. Booth will sit before him and deliver a furious monologue, accusing Lincoln of stupidity and self-importance. It doesn't matter that Lincoln won't be able to talk back; Booth has no interest in anything the president has to say.

Lincoln keeps a summer residence three miles outside Washington, at a place called the Soldiers' Home. Seeking respite from the Washington humidity or just to get away from the office seekers and politicos permeating the White House year-round, the president escapes there alone on horseback most evenings. From George Washington onward, presidents of the United States have usually been comfortable traveling with an entourage. But Lincoln, who enjoys his solitude, has no patience for that.

The president thinks his getaways are secret, but men like Booth and the members of the Confederate Secret Service are always watching. Booth's original mission, as defined by his southern handlers, was to capture Lincoln while he rode on the lonely country road to the Soldiers' Home.

Booth tried and failed twice. Now he has a new plan, one that preys on Lincoln's fondness for the theater. He will grab him in midperformance, from the presidential box at a Washington playhouse.

The scheme, however, is so crazy, so downright impossible that none of his co-conspirators will go along with it.

∽

One of them has even backed out completely and taken the train home. It is as if Booth has rehearsed and rehearsed for a major performance, only to have the production canceled moments before the curtain rises. He has poured thousands of dollars into the plan. Some of that money has come from his own pocket; most has been supplied by the Confederacy. And now the scheme will never come to pass.

Booth fires at the bull's-eye.

The Deringer is less than six inches long, made of brass, with a two-inch barrel. It launches a single large-caliber ball instead of a bullet and is accurate only at close range. For this reason it is often called a "gentleman's pistol"—small and easily concealed in a pocket or boot, the Deringer is ideal for ending an argument or extracting oneself from a dangerous predicament but wholly unsuited for the battlefield. Booth has purchased other weapons for his various plots, including the cache of revolvers and long-bladed daggers now hidden in his hotel room. But the Deringer with the chocolate-colored wooden grip is his personal favorite. It is not lost on him that the pistol's primary traits—elegance, stealth, and the potential to produce mayhem—match those of its owner.

Booth is almost out of ammunition. He loads his gun for one last shot, still plotting his next course of action.

He is absolutely certain he can kidnap Lincoln.

But as Booth himself would utter while performing Hamlet, there's the rub.

If the war is over, then kidnapping Lincoln is pointless.

Yet Lincoln is still the enemy. He always will be.

So if Booth is no longer a kidnapper, then how will he wage war? This is the question that has bothered him all night.

Booth fires his last shot, slides the Deringer into his pocket, and storms out the door, only to once again find the streets full of inebriated revelers. Outraged, he steps into a tavern and knocks back a drink. John Wilkes Booth thinks hard about what comes next. "Our cause being almost lost, something decisive and great must be done," he tells himself.

Until now, Booth has taken orders from Confederate president Jefferson Davis, currently in hiding. It was Davis who, nearly a year ago, sent two agents to Montreal with a fund of $1 million in gold. That money funded various plots against Lincoln. But Davis is done, fleeing to North Carolina in a train filled with looted Confederate gold, most likely never to return. Booth alone must decide for himself what is wrong and what is right.

From this moment forward he will live and breathe and scheme in accordance with his brand-new identity, and his new mission. The time has come for black flag warfare.

# CHAPTER EIGHTEEN

MONDAY, APRIL 10, 1865
WASHINGTON, D.C.
NIGHT

Booth's Washington residence is the National Hotel, on the corner of Pennsylvania Avenue and Sixth. Just around the corner is James Pumphrey's stable, where he often rents a horse. The actor feels perfectly at home at Pumphrey's, for the owner is also known to be a Confederate sympathizer. Now, well past eight, and with no streetlights beyond the city limits, the night is far too dark for a ride into the country. But a half-drunk Booth needs to get on a horse now—right now—and gallop through Washington, D.C., reassuring himself that he has a way out of the city after putting a bullet in Abraham Lincoln.

*I am the man who will end Abraham Lincoln's life.* That thought motivates Booth as he walks. He returns to the idea over and over again. He is thrilled by the notion, not bothered in the least by his ability to make the mental jump from the passive violence of kidnapping to cold-blooded murder. *I will kill the president of the United States.*

Booth ruminates without remorse. Of course, killing a man is immoral. Even Booth knows that.

*This is wartime. Killing the enemy is no more illegal than capturing him.*

The actor thinks of Lincoln's second inaugural and how he stood so close to Lincoln on that day. *I could have shot him then, if I had wished.*

Booth regrets the lost opportunity, then sets it aside. There will be another chance—and this time he will stand even closer, so close he can't miss. So close he will see the life drain from Lincoln's eyes.

It occurs to him that no American president has ever been assassinated. *I will be the first man to ever kill a president.* He is now even more dazzled by his own violent plan.

∽

The United States is just three months shy of being eighty-nine years old. There are thirty-six states in the Union, thanks to Nevada's recent admission. Lincoln is the sixteenth president. Two have passed away from illness while in office. None of them, as Booth well knows, has died by someone else's hand. If successful in his assassination attempt, the actor will achieve the lasting recognition he has always craved.

For a nation founded by rebellion and torn open by a civil war, the citizens of the United States have been remarkably nonviolent when confronted with politicians they despise. Only one American president was the target of an assassin. And that was Andrew Jackson, the man whose politics sowed the seeds of Confederate rebellion thirty years earlier.

Jackson was leaving a funeral in the Capitol Building on January 30, 1835, when a British expatriate fired at him twice. Unfortunately for the mentally unbalanced Richard Lawrence, who believed himself to be the king of England, both his pistols misfired. The bullets never left the chamber. Congressman Davy Crockett wrestled Lawrence to the ground and disarmed him, even as Jackson beat the would-be assassin with his cane.

Jackson was also the first and only American president to suffer bodily harm at the hands of a citizen, when a sailor discharged from the navy for embezzlement punched Jackson at a public ceremony in 1833. Robert Randolph fled the scene. Jackson, ever the warrior, refused to press charges.

These are the only acts of presidential insurrection in the nation's entire history. The American people are unique in that their considerable political passion is expressed at the ballot box, not through violence directed at their leaders, whom they can vote out of office. If judged only by this yardstick, the Democratic experiment undertaken by Americans four score and nine years ago seems to be working.

Maybe this is why Lincoln rides his horse alone through Washington or stands fearlessly on the top deck of a ship in a combat zone. The president tries to convince himself that assassination is not part of the American character, saying, "I can't believe that anyone has shot, or will deliberately shoot at me with the purpose of killing me."

A wider look at human history suggests otherwise. Tribal societies murdered their leaders long before the Egyptian pharaoh Tutankhamen was slain by his advisers in 1324 B.C. Stabbing and beating were the earliest methods of assassination. The Moabite king Eglon was disemboweled in his chambers, his girth so vast that the killer lost the knife in the folds of his fat. Over time, well-known historical figures such as Philip II of Macedon (the father of Alexander the Great) and perhaps even Alexander himself were assassinated. And politically motivated killing was not limited to Europe or the Middle East—records show that assassination had long been practiced in India, Africa, and China.

And then, of course, there was Julius Caesar, the victim of the most famous assassination in history. The Roman ruler was stabbed twenty-three times by members of the Roman Senate. Of the two stab wounds to his chest, one was the blow that killed him. The killing took place during a lunar cycle known as the ides, fulfilling a prophecy by a local soothsayer.

∽

The truth is that Lincoln, despite what he says, secretly believes he will die in office. He is by far the most despised and reviled president in American history. His closest friend and security adviser, the barrel-chested Ward Hill Lamon, preaches regularly to Lincoln about the need for improved security measures. More tangibly, there is a packet nestled in a small cubby of Lincoln's upright desk. It is marked, quite simply, "Assassination." Inside are more than eighty death threats. Every morning, sitting in his office to conduct affairs of state, Lincoln's eyes cannot help but see those letters. "God damn your god damned old hellfire god damned soul to hell," reads one letter. "God damn you and your god damned family's god damned hellfired god damned soul to hell."

"The first one or two made me a little uncomfortable," Lincoln has admitted to an artist who came to paint his portrait, "but they have ceased to give me any apprehension.

"I know I am in danger, but I am not going to worry over little things like these."

Rather than dwell on death, Lincoln prefers to live life on his own terms. "If I am killed I can die but once," he is fond of saying, "but to live in constant dread is to die over and over again."

While the war still raged he told the writer Harriet Beecher Stowe, "Whichever way the war ends, I have the impression that I shall not last long after it is over."

∽

A small number of assassins are delusional or impulsive killers, but on the whole, the successful assassin stalks his target, planning every detail of the crime. This means knowing the victim's habits, schedule, nuances, and security detail. Only then can the two most complex and dangerous tasks be successfully executed.

The first involves the shooting—and in 1865 it must be a shooting, because there is little likelihood of getting close enough to stab a major political figure. The assassin must figure out the when and where (a large crowd is ideal); determine how to get in and out of the building or ceremony; and choose the perfect weapon.

Second is the escape. A successful assassin is a murderer. A perfect assassination, however, means getting away from the scene of the murder without being caught. This is even more of a long shot than the crime itself. Plenty of men in those large crowds will want to play the hero. They will tackle and subdue the assailant without fear for their own lives. And even if an assassin eludes those crowds, he must escape the city in which it takes place, and then the country, until arriving at some foreign location of true refuge.

As Booth strolls to Pumphrey's, he carries a map in his coat pocket showing the location of General Joe Johnston and his Confederate holdouts, who are hiding in North Carolina. Booth knows the map by heart. He can pinpoint the precise route Johnston must take to evade the Federal troops and reignite the war. To Booth, the map is much more than a detailed depiction of contours and boundaries. It is also a glimmer of hope, reminding him that the noble cause is alive and well, and why he must do what he must do.

His mind wanders to his buggy, of all things. Booth bought it to transport Lincoln after the kidnapping. Now it serves no purpose. Booth makes a mental note to put the buggy up for sale. But in an instant, his thoughts revert back to President Lincoln, who now has only five days to live.

# CHAPTER NINETEEN

Booth turns onto C Street and then out of the cold, wet night into James Pumphrey's stable. His clothes are damp. He smells of drink and tobacco. A quick glance around the stalls shows that most of the horses are already rented out for the evening. Pumphrey may be a Confederate sympathizer and a full-fledged member of the secessionist movement, but he has no qualms about making an honest buck off this night of Union celebration.

Pumphrey is an acquaintance of twenty-year-old John Surratt, the courier instrumental in ensuring that Booth's operation is fully funded by the Confederacy. Surratt travels frequently between Canada, the South, New York City, and Washington, brokering deals for everything from guns to medicine. Like Booth, the young man is furious that the Confederacy has lost.

∽

John Surratt is often hard to locate, but when Booth needs details about his whereabouts or simply wants to get a message to him, the task is as simple as walking to Sixth and H Streets, where his mother keeps a boardinghouse. Mary Surratt is an attractive widow in her

*Mary Surratt*

early forties whose husband died from drink, forcing her to move to Washington from the Maryland countryside to make a living. Like her son, Mary is an active Confederate sympathizer who has been involved with spying and smuggling weapons.

She also runs a pro-Confederate tavern in the Maryland town of Surrattsville, where she and her late husband once owned a tobacco farm. The Maryland countryside is untouched by war and not occupied by Union troops.

Washington, D.C., with its Federal employees and Union loyalties, is a city whose citizens are all too prone to report any conversation that suggests pro-Confederate leanings, making it a dangerous place for people like Mary Surratt and John Wilkes Booth. Her boardinghouse and Pumphrey's stable are two of the few places they can speak their minds. For Booth, a man who deeply enjoys doing just that, such locations are safe havens.

It would seem natural that Booth tell the others about his new plan. They might have insights into the best possible means of escape: roads under construction or in need of repair, overcrowded streets, bridges still under wartime guard—for the only way out of Washington, D.C., is on a boat or over a bridge.

The first exit is via the Georgetown Aqueduct, a mile and a half northwest of the White House. The second is Long Bridge, three blocks south of the White House. The third is Benning's Bridge, on the east side of town. And the last one is the Navy Yard Bridge, on Eleventh Street.

But Booth has already made up his mind: the Navy Yard Bridge. The other three lead into Virginia, with its plethora of roadblocks and Union soldiers. But the Navy Yard Bridge will take him into the quiet backcountry of Maryland, home to smugglers and back roads. Friends like Mary Surratt and Dr. Samuel Mudd can offer their homes as way stations for a man on the run, storing weapons for him and providing a place to sleep and eat before getting back on the road. The only drawback is that sentries man the bridge and no traffic is allowed in or out of Washington after ten P.M.

Booth wants to see those sentries for himself. Tonight. Which is why he's come for a horse. He doesn't tell Pumphrey, just to be on the safe side. In the end it doesn't matter: Booth's favorite horse has already been rented.

Not the least bit discouraged, Booth walks up to Ford's Theatre on Tenth Street. This converted Baptist church is Booth's touchstone. After it was burned to the ground in 1862, owner John Ford rebuilt it as a "magnificent thespian temple," replacing the pews with seats and transforming the deacons' stalls into private boxes. Upon completion, Ford's became the most state-of-the-art theater in D.C.

Booth performed one night at Ford's in mid-March, but his theater appearances are few and far between these days. (If asked, he explains that he is taking a hiatus to dabble in the oil business.) He still, however, has his mail sent to Ford's, and his buggy is parked in a space behind the theater that was specially created for him by a carpenter and sceneshifter named Ned Spangler. Booth uses Spangler often for such favors and odd jobs. Thirty-nine and described by friends as "a very good, efficient drudge," the hard-drinking Spangler often sleeps in either the theater or a nearby stable. Despite the late hour, Booth knows he will find him at Ford's.

Inside the theater, rehearsals are under way for a one-night-only performance of the farce *Our American Cousin*. Like most actors, Booth knows it well.

Booth finds Spangler backstage, befuddled, as usual. He asks the stagehand to clean up his carriage and find a buyer. Spangler is devastated—a great many hours of work have gone into modifying the theater's storage space so that the carriage will fit. It's a waste for Booth to sell the carriage, and Spangler tells him so.

"I have no further use for it," Booth replies. "And anyway, I'll soon be leaving town." Booth will not say where he's going, leaving Spangler even more befuddled.

∽

The word "assassin" comes from "Hashshashin," the name of a group of hit men who worked for Persian kings between the eighth and the fourteenth centuries. One of their jobs was to execute the Knights Templar, a legendary band of Christian warriors known for their cunning and ferocity in battle. Legend says that the reward for a successful execution was being able to visit a lush royal garden filled with milk, honey, hashish, and concubines.

None of those things await John Wilkes Booth. He is everything an effective assassin should be: methodical, passionate, determined, and an excellent strategist and planner. He is prone to depression, as many assassins are, but his ability to turn angst into rage makes him even more dangerous. He expects no reward for killing Lincoln, though infamy would be nice.

# CHAPTER TWENTY

Lee's surrender at Appomattox is just two days old, but events are moving so quickly that it might as well be two months.

The citizens of Washington have spent today sleeping off their celebratory hangover. Now, as evening falls, they again spill out into the streets and sip a drink or two. Just like that, the party starts all over. As it grows and becomes more rowdy, every guzzle and utterance has a hum, an anticipation: Abraham Lincoln is speaking tonight. Love him or hate him, the president of the United States is making a personal appearance at the White House, and everyone wants to see it.

And then, once again, the crowd is on the march. The spring air is thick with a warm mist as the sea of humanity parades down Pennsylvania Avenue. Thousands upon thousands are on their way to hear Lincoln speak, trampling the White House lawn and standing up to their ankles in the mud of once-manicured daffodil beds, pushing and straining against one another, climbing into trees, and even pressing up against the great building itself. All are desperate to be as close to Lincoln as possible. But hungover, dehydrated, and sullen, this is not the lighthearted crowd of the night before. It is something akin to a lynch mob, thirsty for Lincoln's words, and yet ready to pass judgment on them.

And this is what the mob wants to hear: the South must be punished.

These men and women of the North, who have endured the loss of their sons, brothers, and husbands, want vengeance. They want the Confederate leaders and generals hanged, they want the South to pay war reparations, and they want Lincoln's speech to be full of the same self-righteous indignation they feel so powerfully in their hearts.

∽

Booth leans against a tall tree, using it as a buffer against the crowd. He is close enough that Lincoln will be a mere pistol shot away. With him are two co-conspirators. David Herold is a former pharmacy clerk who was born and raised in Washington, D.C. Like Booth, he possesses matinee-idol good looks. But he is more educated and rugged. Herold's degree comes from Georgetown, and he is fond of spending his leisure time with a rifle in his hand, hunting animals. It was John Surratt who introduced the two, four months earlier. Since then, Herold has been an impassioned and committed member of Booth's team.

The second co-conspirator is Lewis Powell—who also goes by the name Lewis Payne—a twenty-year-old who served as a Confederate soldier and spy before joining Booth's cause. Like Herold, he has fallen under Booth's spell.

The actor hasn't told either man that the plan has changed from kidnapping to assassination. That can wait. He brought them along to hear the speech, hoping that some phrase or anticipated course of action will fill them with rage. Then, and only then, will Booth let them in on his new plan.

Soon Lincoln stands before an open second-story window, a scroll of paper in one hand. The president is wearing the same black garb he usually wears but no hat. He is somber. His speech is now written, and he is ready to give it.

Unseen by the crowd, Mary Lincoln shows her husband her support by standing next to him. She has invited Clara Harris, her dear friend and the daughter of a New York senator, to stand with her and witness this historical moment.

Outside, the mere sight of Lincoln elicits a prolonged ovation. The applause rolls on and on and on, continuing even as Lincoln tries to speak.

The crowd cannot possibly know the tremendous weight pressing down on Lincoln's shoulders. Looking out into the audience, he prepares to tell them about the daunting task ahead and how the ability to trust the southern states to peacefully rejoin the Union will be as great a challenge to the nation as the war itself. Lincoln clearly sees the faces of the crowd, with their spontaneous smiles and unabashed joy, and prepares to deliver a speech that is anything but warmhearted. It is, in fact, a heavy, ponderous, de facto State of the Union address, specifically designed to undercut the revelry and prepare America for years of more pain and struggle.

∽

The president begins gently. "We meet this evening not in sorrow, but in gladness of heart," Lincoln says. He thanks General Grant and the army for their struggle, and promises to have a national day of celebration very soon, with a great parade through Washington.

Lincoln is one of the best speakers in America, if not the world. He can read the mood of a crowd and adjust the cadence and rhythm of his voice for maximum effect, coaxing whatever emotion or response is needed to hold the audience in the palm of his hand. Lincoln's voice is clear, his pronunciation distinct. He understands the power of words and emphasizes certain phrases to make a lasting impression. The Gettysburg Address is perhaps the best example of Lincoln's oratorical genius.

But tonight there is no theatricality. No tricks. Just cold, hard facts, delivered in a somber and even depressing monotone. The speech is so long and so unexciting that people in the audience begin shifting their feet and then lowering their heads and slipping away into the night, off to search for a real celebration. Booth stays, of course. He doesn't want to miss a single word. He listens as Lincoln talks of extending suffrage to literate blacks and those who fought for the Union.

Booth seethes at the outrageous notion that slaves be considered equal citizens of the United States, able to own property, vote, run for elected office, and maybe even marry white women. Suffrage, as preposterous as it sounds, means a black man might someday become president of the United States. Booth cannot let this ever happen.

"That means nigger citizenship," he hisses, pointing to the navy revolver on Powell's hip. Fourteen inches long, with a pistol sight and a .36-caliber round, the Colt has more than enough pop to kill Lincoln from such close range. "Shoot him now," Booth commands Powell. "Put a bullet in his head right this instant."

Powell is a dangerous young man, with powerful shoulders and a psychotic temper. But he refuses to draw his weapon. He is terrified of offending Booth but even more afraid of this mob, which would surely tear him limb from limb.

Booth sizes up the situation. It would be easy enough to grab Powell's gun and squeeze off a shot or two before the crowd overpowers him. But now is not the time to be impulsive. Booth certainly doesn't tell this to Powell. Instead he lets Powell believe that he has let Booth down. Only when Powell believes that he has really and truly disappointed Booth will he begin thinking of ways to make it up to him. And that's when Booth will tell him about his amazing new plan.

"*I'll* put him through," Booth sneers, planting another seed about assassination in the minds of Powell and Herold. "By God. I'll put him through."

Then Booth spins around and fights his way back out of the crowd. Twenty-four hours ago he was still thinking of ways to kidnap the president. Now he knows just where and how and when he will shoot Abraham Lincoln dead.

The date will be Thursday, April 13.

Or, as it was known back in Julius Caesar's time, the ides.

# CHAPTER TWENTY-ONE

"It seems strange how much there is in the Bible about dreams," Lincoln says thoughtfully, basking in the afterglow of his speech. It is just after ten P.M. The people of Washington have moved their party elsewhere, and the White House lawn is nearly empty. Lincoln is having tea and cake in the Red Room with Mary, Senator James Harlan, and a few friends. Among them is Ward Hill Lamon, the close friend with the beer-barrel girth. Lamon, the United States marshal for the District of Columbia, has warned Lincoln for more than a year that someone, somewhere will try to kill him. The lawman listens to the president intently, with a veteran policeman's heightened sense of foreboding, sifting and sorting through each word.

Lincoln continues: "There are, I think, some sixteen chapters in the Old Testament and four or five in the New in which dreams are mentioned. . . . If we believe the Bible, we must accept the fact that in the old days, God and his angels came to men in their sleep and made themselves known in dreams."

Mary Lincoln smiles nervously at her husband. His melancholy tone has her fearing the worst. "Why? Do you believe in dreams?"

Yes, Lincoln believes in dreams, in dreams and in nightmares and in their power to haunt a man. Night is a time of terror for Abraham Lincoln. The bodyguards standing watch outside his bedroom hear him moan in his sleep as his worries and anxieties are unleashed by the darkness, when the distractions and the busyness of the day can no longer keep them at bay. Very often he cannot sleep at all. Lincoln collapsed from exhaustion just a month ago. He is pale, thirty-five pounds underweight, and walks with the hunched, painful gait of a man whose shoes are filled with pebbles. One look at the bags under his eyes and even hardened newspapermen write that he needs to conserve his energies—not just to heal the nation but to live out his second term. At fifty-six years old, Abraham Lincoln is spent.

∽

There have been threats against Lincoln's life ever since he was first elected.

Gift baskets laden with fruit were sent to the White House, mostly from addresses in the South. The apples and pears and peaches were very fresh—and very deadly, their insides injected with poison. Lincoln had the good sense to have them all tested before taking a chance and chomping down into a first fatal bite.

Then there was the Baltimore Plot, in 1861, in which a group known as the Knights of the Golden Circle planned to shoot Lincoln as he traveled to Washington for the inauguration. The plot was foiled, thanks to brilliant detective work by Pinkerton agents. In a strange twist, many newspapers mocked Lincoln for the way he eluded the assassins by wearing a cheap disguise as he snuck into Washington. His enemies made much of the deception, labeling Lincoln a coward and refusing to believe that such a plot existed in the first place. The president took the cheap shots to heart.

The Baltimore Plot taught Lincoln a powerful message about public perception. He adopted a veneer of unshakable courage from that day forward. Now he would never dream of traveling in disguise. He moves freely throughout Washington, D.C. Since 1862 he has enjoyed military protection beyond the walls of the White House, but it was only late in 1864, as the war wound down and the threats became more real, that Washington's Metropolitan Police assigned a select group of officers armed with .38-caliber pistols to protect Lincoln on a more personal basis. Two remain at his side from eight A.M. to four P.M. Another stays with Lincoln until midnight, when a fourth man takes the graveyard shift, posting himself outside Lincoln's bedroom or following the president through the White House on his insomniac nights.

The bodyguards are paid by the Department of the Interior, and their job description, strangely enough, specifically states that they are to protect the White House from vandals.

Protecting Lincoln is second on their list of priorities.

∞

If he were the sort of man to worry about his personal safety, Lincoln wouldn't allow such easy public access to the White House. There is no fence or gate blocking people from entering the White House at this time. The doorman is instructed to allow citizens to roam the first floor. Friends and strangers alike can congregate inside the building all day long, seeking political favors, stealing scraps of the curtains as keepsakes, or just peering in at the president while he works. Some petitioners even sleep on the floor in the hallways, hoping to gain a moment of Lincoln's time.

Lincoln's bright young secretary John Hay frets constantly about his boss's safety. "The President is so accessible that any villain can feign business, and, while talking with him, draw a razor and cut his throat," Hay worries aloud, "and some minutes might elapse after the murderer's escape before we could discover what had been done." Lincoln, however, reminds Hay that being president of the United States stipulates that he be a man of the people. "It would never do for a President to have guards with drawn sabers at his door, as if he were, or were assuming to be an emperor," he reminds them.

∞

Death is no stranger to Abraham Lincoln, and in that way it is less terrifying. The Lincolns' three-year-old son Edward died of tuberculosis in 1850. In 1862, the Lincolns lost eleven-year-old Willie to a fever. Willie was a spirited child, fond of wrestling with his father and riding his pony on the White House lawn. Mary, who already suffered from a mental disorder that made her prone to severe mood swings, was emotionally destroyed by the loss of her boys. Even as Lincoln was mired in the war and dealing with his own grief, he devoted hours to tending to Mary and the silent downward spiral that seemed to define her daily existence. He indulged her by allowing her to spend lavishly, to the point of putting him deeply in debt, though he is by nature a very simple and frugal man. Also to please Mary, he accompanied her to a night at the theater or to a party when he would much rather conserve his energies by relaxing with a book at the White House. And while this indulgence has worked to some extent, and Mary Lincoln has gotten stronger over time, Lincoln of all people knows that she is one great tragedy away from losing her mind.

Normally, their history precludes Lincoln from talking about death with Mary present. But now, surrounded by friends and empowered by the confessional tone of that night's speech, he can't help himself.

"I had a dream the other night, which has haunted me since," he admits soulfully.

"You frighten me," Mary cries.

Lincoln will not be stopped. Ten days ago, he begins, "I went to bed late."

Ten days ago he was in City Point, each man and woman in the room calculates. It was the night Lincoln stood alone on the top deck of the *River Queen*, watching Grant's big guns blow the Confederate defenders of Petersburg to hell. "I had been waiting for important dispatches from the front. I could not have been long in bed when I fell into a slumber, for I was weary. I soon began to dream."

In addition to being the consummate public speaker, Lincoln is also a master storyteller. No matter how heavy the weight of the world, he invests himself in a story, adjusting the tone and cadence of his voice and curling his lips into a smile as he weaves his tale, until the listener eventually leans in, desperate to hear more.

But now there is pain in his voice and not a hint of a smile. Lincoln isn't telling a story but reliving an agony. "There seemed to be a deathlike stillness about me. Then I heard subdued sobs, as if a number of people were weeping. I thought I left my bed and wandered downstairs. There the silence was broken by the same pitiful sobbing, but the mourners were invisible. I went from room to room. No living person was in sight, but the same mournful sounds of distress met me as I passed along. It was light in all the rooms. Every object was familiar to me. But where were all the people who were grieving as if their hearts would break? I was puzzled and alarmed. What could be the meaning of all this?"

Lincoln is lost in the world of that dream. Yet his audience, uncomfortable as it may feel, is breathless with anticipation. "Determined to find the cause of a state of things so mysterious and shocking, I kept on until I arrived in the East Room, which I entered. There I was met with a sickening surprise. Before me was a catafalque, on which rested a corpse wrapped in funeral vestments. Around it were stationed soldiers who were acting as guards. And there were a throng of people, some gazing mournfully upon the corpse, whose face was covered, others weeping pitifully. 'Who is dead in the White House?' I demanded of one of the soldiers. 'The President,' was the answer. 'He was killed by an assassin.' Then came a loud burst of grief from the crowd."

Mary can't take it anymore. "That is horrid," she wails. "I wish you had not told it."

Lincoln is pulled back to reality, no longer sound asleep on the *River Queen* but sitting with a somewhat shell-shocked gathering of dignitaries in the here and now. Young Clara Harris, in particular, looks traumatized. "Well it was only a dream, Mary," he chides. "Let us say no more about it."

A moment later, seeing the uneasiness in the room, Lincoln adds, "Don't you see how it will all turn out? In this dream it was not me, but some other fellow that was killed."

His words convince no one, especially not Mary.

# CHAPTER TWENTY-TWO

WEDNESDAY, APRIL 12, 1865
WASHINGTON, D.C.
MORNING

After a light breakfast and a night of restless sleep, Booth walks the streets of Washington, his mind filled with the disparate strands of an unfinished plan. The more he walks, the more it all comes together.

It is the morning after Lincoln's speech and the third day since Lee's surrender.

Booth frames every action through the prism of the dramatic, a trait that comes from being born and raised in an acting household. As he builds the assassination scheme in his head, layer by layer, everything from the location to its grandiosity is designed to make him the star performer in an epic scripted tale. His will be the biggest assassination plot ever, and his commanding performance will guarantee him an eternity of recognition.

He knows there will be an audience. By the morning after Lincoln's speech Booth has decided to shoot the president inside a theater, the one place in the world where Booth feels most comfortable. Lincoln is known to attend the theater frequently. In fact, he has seen Booth perform—although Lincoln's presence in the house so angered Booth that he delivered a notably poor performance.

So the theater it will be. Booth has performed at several playhouses in Washington. He knows their hallways and passages by heart. A less informed man might worry about being trapped inside a building with a limited number of exits, no windows, and a crowd of witnesses— many of them able-bodied men just back from the war. But not John Wilkes Booth.

His solitary walk takes him past many such soldiers. The army hasn't been disbanded yet, so they remain in uniform. Even someone as athletic as Booth looks far less rugged than these men who have spent so much time in the open air, their bodies lean and hard from hours on the march. If he thought about it, their familiarity with weapons and hand-to-hand combat would terrify Booth, with his choreographed stage fights and peashooter pistol.

But Booth is not scared of these men. In fact, he wants to linger for a moment at center stage. With the stage lights shining down on his handsome features, clutching a dagger with "America, Land of the Free" inscribed on the blade, he plans to spend what will surely be the last seconds of his acting career making a political statement. *"Sic semper tyrannis,"* he will bellow in his most vibrant thespian delivery: Thus always to tyrants.

∽

The dagger is useless as a stage prop. Booth has no specific plans to use it, knowing that if he fires a shot from a few feet away and it misses, there will be no chance to run at Lincoln and stab him. He has borrowed the idea from Shakespeare's *Julius Caesar*, which he performed six months earlier on Broadway with his two actor brothers, both of whom he despises. Booth, ironically, played Marc Antony, a character whose life is spared from a potential assassin.

Those performances provided Booth with his inspiration about the ides. In Roman times it was a day of reckoning.

The ides are tomorrow.

Booth walks faster, energized by the awareness that he hasn't much time.

He must find out whether Lincoln will be attending the theater tomorrow night and, if so, which one. He must find out which play is being performed, so that he can select just the right moment in the show for the execution—a moment with few actors on stage, if possible, so that when he stops to utter his immortal line there won't be a crowd to tackle him. The details of his escape are still fuzzy, but the basic plan is to gallop out of Washington on horseback and disappear into the loving arms of the South, where friends and allies and even complete strangers who have heard of his daring deed will see that he makes it safely to Mexico.

But that's not all.

There are rumors that General Grant will be in town. If he attends the theater with Lincoln, which is a very real possibility, Booth can kill the two most prominent architects of the South's demise within seconds.

And yet Booth wants even more. He has been an agent of the Confederacy for a little less than a year and has had long conversations with the leaders of the Confederate Secret Service and men like John Surratt, discussing what must be done to topple the Union. He has, at his disposal, a small cadre of like-minded men prepared to do his bidding. He personally witnessed the northern crowd's malice toward the South at Lincoln's speech last night. Rather than just kill Lincoln and Grant, he now plans to do nothing less than undertake a top-down destruction of the government of the United States of America.

∽

Vice President Andrew Johnson is an obvious target. He is first in line to the presidency, lives at a nearby hotel, and is completely unguarded. Like all Confederate sympathizers, Booth views the Tennessee politician as a turncoat for siding with Lincoln.

Secretary of State William H. Seward, whose oppressive policies toward the South have long made him a target of Confederate wrath, is on the list as well.

The deaths of Lincoln, Grant, Johnson, and Seward should be more than enough to cause anarchy.

To Lewis Powell, the former Confederate spy who watched Lincoln's speech with Booth, will go the task of killing Secretary Seward, who, at age sixty-three, is currently bedridden, after a near-fatal carriage accident. He was traveling through Washington with his son Frederick and daughter Fanny when the horses bolted. While reaching for the reins to try to stop them, Seward caught the heel of one of

*Vice President Andrew Johnson*     *Secretary of State William H. Seward*

his new shoes on the carriage step and was hurled from the cab, hitting the street so hard that bystanders thought he'd been killed. Secretary Seward has been confined to his bed for a week with severe injuries and is on an around-the-clock course of pain medication. Seward has trouble speaking; he has no chance of leaping from the bed to elude a surprise attack.

Powell's job should be as simple as sneaking into the Seward home, shooting the sleeping secretary in bed, then galloping away to join Booth for a life of sunshine and easy living in Mexico.

For the job of killing Johnson, Booth selects a simpleton drifter named George Atzerodt, a German carriage repairer with a sallow complexion and a fondness for drink. To him will go the job of assassinating the vice president at the exact same moment Booth is killing Lincoln. Atzerodt, however, still thinks the plan is to kidnap Lincoln. He was brought into the plot for his encyclopedic knowledge of the smuggling routes from Washington, D.C., into the Deep South. Booth suspects that Atzerodt may be unwilling to go along with the new plan. Should that be the case, Booth has a foolproof plan in mind to blackmail Atzerodt into going along.

Booth has seen co-conspirators come and go since last August. Right now he has three: Powell, Atzerodt, and David Herold, the Georgetown graduate who also accompanied Booth on the night of Lincoln's speech. One would imagine that each man would be assigned a murder victim. Logically, Herold's job would be to kill Secretary of War Edwin M. Stanton, the man who trampled the Constitution by helping Lincoln suspend the writ of habeas corpus and did more than any other to treat the South like a bastard child. Stanton is the second-most-powerful man in Washington, but in the end no assassin is trained on him. Instead, Herold will act as the dim-witted Powell's guide, leading his escape out of Washington in the dead of night.

Why was the secretary of war spared?

∽

The answer may come from a shadowy figure named Lafayette Baker. Early in the war, Baker distinguished himself as a Union spy. Secretary of State William Seward hired him to investigate Confederate communications that were being routed through Maryland. Baker's success in this role saw him promoted to the War Department, where Secretary of War Edwin Stanton gave him full power to create an organization known as the National Detective Police. This precursor to the Secret Service was a counterterrorism unit tasked with seeking out Confederate spy networks in Canada, New York, and Washington.

But Lafayette Baker was a shifty character, with loyalties undefined, except for his love of money and of himself, though not necessarily in that order. Secretary Stanton soon grew weary of him, so Baker returned to New York City. His movements during this time are murky, as befitting a man who thinks himself a spy, but one elaborate theory ties together his activities with those of John Wilkes Booth. This theory suggests that Baker worked as an agent for a Canadian outfit known as the J. J. Chaffey Company. Baker received payments totaling almost $150,000 from that firm, an unheard-of sum at the time. The J. J. Chaffey Company also paid John Wilkes Booth nearly $15,000 between August 24 and October 5, 1864. He was paid in gold, credited to the Bank of Montreal. In the same month the last payment was made to him, Booth traveled to Montreal to collect the

*Lafayette C. Baker*

money and rendezvous with John Surratt and other members of the Confederate Secret Service to plot the Lincoln issue.

The common thread in the several mysterious payments and missives involving Baker and Booth is the mailing address 178½ Water Street. This location, quite mysteriously, is referenced in several documents surrounding payments between the J. J. Chaffey Company, Baker, and Booth.

To this day, no one has discovered why the J. J. Chaffey Company paid Lafayette Baker and John Wilkes Booth for anything. A few clues exist, including a telegram sent on April 2, 1865, the very same day on which Lincoln stood atop the deck of the *River Queen* to watch the fall of Petersburg. A telegram was sent from 178½ Water Street to a company in Chicago. "J. W. Booth will ship oysters until Saturday 15th," it reads, intimating that Booth, a man who never worked a day in his life in the shipping or the oyster business, was involved in some kind of project that was totally inappropriate for his skills. And yet no one has been able to conclusively determine what the telegram alluded to.

Lafayette Baker freely admitted that he had tapped Secretary of War Stanton's telegraph lines, though he never explained why he did what he did. Baker would have known that if Lincoln were assassinated, ascension to the presidency could eventually fall to Stanton— the man who opposed Lincoln's candidacy in 1860. The United States has had a succession plan in place since 1792, with the vice president replacing the fallen president, as when Zachary Taylor died in office and was succeeded by Millard Fillmore. If a more elaborate assassination plot were hatched, one that killed Vice President Andrew Johnson and Secretary of State William Seward along with President Lincoln, a skilled constitutional scholar like Edwin Stanton could attempt to manipulate the process in his favor—and perhaps even become president. This connection between Baker, Booth, and Stanton continues to intrigue and befuddle scholars. Why was Baker, a spy, paid an exorbitant amount for his services? And why did John Wilkes Booth secure a healthy payment from the same company?

Clues such as this point to Stanton's involvement, but no concrete connection has ever been proven. Circumstantially, he was involved. Secretary Stanton employed Baker, who was in regular contact with Surratt and Booth. Some historians believe that Stanton fired Baker as a cover and that the two remained in close contact.

Or so the elaborate theory goes.

Whether or not that is true, Stanton will be the sole reason that Baker's role in the dramatic events of April 1865 is hardly over.

∽

Booth is satisfied that his plan is simple enough that the synchronized slayings will not tax the mental capacities of his underlings. Now all he needs to do is find Lincoln.

The odds of the Lincolns' remaining in the White House on such an auspicious night of celebration are almost nonexistent. The president and Mrs. Lincoln are known to be fond of the theater and prone to making their public appearances in such a venue. They will be either there or at one of the many parties being held to celebrate the city's Grand Illumination.

If it is to be an Illumination party, Booth will canvass the city's notable residences for signs of a celebration. Once the president is located, the next step will be waiting for a moment when he is unguarded, whereupon Booth can use his celebrity to gain entrance and then shoot him.

If it is to be the theater, the obvious choices are either the Grover or Ford's, both of which are staging lavish productions. Booth must reacquaint himself with their floor plans so that when the moment comes he can act without thinking.

Booth turns the corner onto Pennsylvania Avenue. First stop: Grover's Theater. The assassination will be tomorrow.

# CHAPTER TWENTY-THREE

Inside the White House, just a few blocks from where John Wilkes Booth is walking the streets, a beaming Mary Lincoln holds a slim leather-bound copy of *Julius Caesar*. She is in a good mood for a change, and the new book is certainly helping her disposition. The president will be thrilled by her purchase. This is most important to Mary Lincoln. Even in her lowest moods, she craves the attention and affection of her husband.

Lincoln's fondness for all things Shakespeare is well known. While he enjoys lowbrow entertainment, like the comedian Barney Williams, who performs in blackface, he never misses the chance to attend a Shakespearean tragedy. During one two-month span in the winter of 1864, he saw *Richard III*, *The Merchant of Venice*, *Hamlet*, and, of course, *Julius Caesar*.

The actor playing all the lead roles was Edwin Booth, John's older brother. In addition to his acting, he did the Lincolns an inadvertent favor by saving the life of their eldest son. When twenty-year-old Union officer Robert Todd Lincoln was shoved from a crowded railway platform into the path of an oncoming train, it was Edwin Booth who snatched him by the coat collar and pulled him back to safety.

Robert never mentioned the incident to his father, but his command-ing officer, Ulysses S. Grant, personally wrote a letter of thanks to the actor. Edwin's brother's reaction to this incident has never been determined—if he knew at all. This is the second remarkable coinci-dence linking Robert Todd Lincoln to John Wilkes Booth, the first being his infatuation with Lucy Hale, Booth's fiancée.

Robert is due back in Washington any day, as is Grant. Lincoln's spirits will soar at the sight of both men, but in the meantime Mary cannot wait to see his face light up when she presents him with *Julius Caesar*.

Lincoln is fond of two books more than any other: the Bible and Shakespeare's collected works. Like his dog-eared Bible, Lincoln's volume of Shakespeare has become frayed and worn over the years. This brand-new copy of *Julius Caesar* will certainly keep the presi-dent's mood upbeat, which, in turn, will do wonders for Mary's morale. Their euphorias and depressions are so closely intertwined that it's hard to say which one's emotional peaks and valleys influence the other more.

∽

Lincoln is not at the White House right now. He's taken a walk over to the War Department, where he sits on a comfortable sofa, hard at work on the business of healing the nation. His first test is immediate. The Virginia legislature is about to convene in Richmond. These are the same elected representatives who once voted to leave the Union. Now this "rebel legislature" will meet in the giant columned building designed by Thomas Jefferson, determined to rebuild the shattered state and return it to its former glory.

On the surface, this is a good thing. Lincoln himself urged the leg-islature to convene during a visit to Richmond the previous week, say-ing that "the prominent and influential men of their respective counties should come together and undo their own work."

Secretary of War Edwin Stanton, the brilliant Ohio lawyer who is for whatever reason not on Booth's list of targets, and in whose office Lincoln now sits, is strongly opposed. He tells Lincoln that to "place such powers in the Virginia legislature would be giving away the scepter of the conqueror, that it would transfer the result of the

*Secretary of War Edwin M. Stanton*

victory of our arms to the very legislature which four years before said, 'give us war.'"

Lincoln disagrees. He is reluctant to see the United States Army turned into an occupying force, policing the actions of legislatures throughout the South. But he also realizes that by allowing Virginia's lawmakers to meet without close Federal observation, he is setting a dangerous precedent. There would be nothing to stop other southern states from passing laws that conspire against the Federal government—in effect, keeping the Confederacy's ideals alive.

Stanton and Lincoln were once sworn rivals, two opinionated and charismatic midwesterners who came to Washington with their own personal visions of what the country needed. They are physical opposites—Stanton's stump to Lincoln's beanpole. Stanton didn't vote for Lincoln in 1860, but that didn't stop the president from crossing party lines to name him secretary of war. Lincoln's low wartime popularity was matched only by that of Stanton, who was relentless in his prosecution of any Union officer concealing Confederate sympathies.

"He is the rock on the beach of our national ocean against which the breakers dash and roar, dash and roar without ceasing," Lincoln once said of Stanton. "I do not see how he survives, why he is not crushed and torn to pieces. Without him I should be destroyed."

As General Sam Grant glibly described Stanton: "He was an able constitutional lawyer and jurist, but the Constitution was not an impediment to him while the war lasted."

Stanton, with a graying beard extending halfway down his chest, has the sort of strong-willed personality that terrifies timid souls. The Civil War may be over, but Lincoln has made it clear that the secretary of war will be instrumental in helping the country rebuild. He trusts Stanton's counsel and uses him as a sounding board when tough decisions like this must be made. In many ways, Stanton does not behave as if he is subordinate to Lincoln. He expresses himself without fear of edit or censure, knowing that while Lincoln has strong opinions of his own, he is a good listener who can be swayed by a solid argument.

Now Stanton paces before the couch where Lincoln reclines, compiling his detailed argument against allowing the Virginia legislature to meet. He warns of the laws that might be passed, limiting the freedom of former slaves. He notes that the legislature has proven itself to be untrustworthy. And he reminds Lincoln that during his recent visit to Richmond the president made it clear that the Virginia lawmakers were being given only conditional authority—but that these same untrustworthy men are surely capable of ignoring those limits once they convene.

At last, Stanton explains his idea for temporary military governments in the southern states until order can be restored.

Lincoln doesn't speak until Stanton finishes. Almost every single one of Stanton's opinions runs contrary to Lincoln's. Nonetheless, Lincoln hears Stanton out, then lets his thoughts percolate.

As Stanton looks on, Lincoln slowly rises off the couch and draws himself up to his full, towering height. He walks to the great oak desk near the window, where he silently composes a telegram withdrawing permission for the Virginia legislature to meet. For those representatives who have already traveled to Richmond for the session, he guarantees safe passage home.

Lincoln hands the telegram to Stanton, whose thick beard cannot hide his look of satisfaction after he finishes reading. Calling the wording "exactly right," he hands the telegram to his clerk.

∽

During the course of the Civil War, Lincoln's use of telegrams—his "t-mail"—made him the first leader in world history to communicate immediately with his generals on the battlefield. He has sent, literally, thousands of these messages through the Department of War. This is his last.

On the walk back to the White House, Lincoln composes another sort of note in his head. It is to Mary, a simple invitation to go for a carriage ride on Friday afternoon. His words are playful and romantic, a reminder of the way things were before the war, and before the death of Willie. Their eldest son, Robert, is due home from the war any day. Surely, the cloud of melancholy that has hovered over the Lincolns is about to lift.

# CHAPTER TWENTY-FOUR

Thursday, April 13, 1865
Washington, D.C.
Morning

The ides. As Booth takes the train to Baltimore, hoping to reenlist a former conspirator for that night's expected executions, General Ulysses S. Grant and his wife, Julia, arrive in Washington at dawn. They have taken an overnight boat from City Point, Virginia. Grant is in no mood to be there. He is eager to push on to New Jersey to see their four children, but Secretary of War Stanton has specifically requested that the general visit the capital and handle a number of war-related issues. Grant's plan is to get in and get out within twenty-four hours, with as little fuss as possible. With him are his aide Colonel Horace Porter and two sergeants to manage the Grants' luggage.

Little does Grant know that an adoring Washington, D.C., is waiting to wrap its arms around him. "As we reached our destination that bright morning in our boat," Julia later exclaimed, "every gun in and near Washington burst forth—and such a salvo!—all the bells rang out merry greetings, and the city was literally swathed in flags and bunting."

If anything, Grant is even more beloved than the president right now. Strangers cheer the Grants' open-air carriage on its way to the Willard Hotel, on the corner of Pennsylvania Avenue and Fourteenth Street. As

*Julia Grant*

they pull up to the entrance, workers are on the roof, installing the gas jets that will spell out UNION for that evening's Grand Illumination—a mass lighting of every candle, gas lamp, and firework in the city. Thousands upon thousands of people are now streaming into Washington to witness what will be an attempt to turn night into day as yet another celebration of war's end.

Grant, who has seen more than his share of fiery explosions, could not care less about the Illumination. Their journey has been an odyssey, and the Grants are exhausted. Since leaving Lee at Appomattox, Grant has endured two days of train derailments, another day waiting for a steamer in City Point, and then the dawn-to-dusk journey up the Potomac. But standing beside his beloved Julia revives Grant.

They have been a couple for more than twenty years and have endured many a long separation, thanks to the military life. It was

Julia's letters that sustained him during the Mexican War, when he was a homesick young lieutenant. And it was Julia who stood by her husband's side during the 1850s, when he was discharged from the army and failed in a succession of businesses. They are happiest in each other's company. Both are still young—he is not quite forty-three; she is thirty-nine. They have their whole lives in front of them. The sooner they can flee Washington, D.C., and get back to normal life, the better. And right now that means getting to their room, washing up, and letting the general race over to the War Department as quickly as possible.

There's just one problem: the Grants don't have a reservation at the Willard.

∽

Grant has slept so many nights in impromptu battlefield lodgings procured on the fly by his staff that it never crossed his mind to send a telegram asking for a room. What he wants, he tells the flustered desk clerk, is a simple bedroom with an adjacent sitting room. It's understood that Colonel Porter will need a room, too. The sergeants will bunk elsewhere.

The Willard Hotel is overbooked. Yet to allow the famous Ulysses S. Grant to take a room elsewhere would be an unthinkable loss of prestige.

Some way, somehow, rooms are instantly made available. Within minutes, Julia is unpacking their suitcases. Word about their location is already flying around Washington, and bundles of congratulatory telegrams and flowers soon flood the desk and bedroom. Julia will spend the afternoon reading each one, basking in the awareness that the man whose potential she had seen so long before, when he was just a quiet young lieutenant, has ascended from anonymity and disgrace to the level of great historical figure.

Not that General Grant cares. He just wants to get on with his business and get home. Within minutes, he and Porter meet in the lobby before the short walk to the War Department. It's three blocks, just on the other side of the White House.

The two men step out onto Pennsylvania Avenue. At first the trek is easy, just two regular guys in uniform joining the sea of pedestrians, soldiers, and all those tourists pouring into the city for the Illumination. But Grant is hard to miss. Pictures of his bearded, expressionless face have been on the front pages of newspapers for more than a year. Soon the autograph seekers and the well-wishers, startled but elated by his presence, surround him. Porter tries to push them back, protecting his general in peacetime as he did in warfare. But he is just one man against many, and the diminutive Grant is swallowed by the mob. Porter pushes and elbows, grabbing Grant with one arm while shoving people back with the other. It's a benevolent crowd, cheering for Grant even as they strain to touch him. But Porter knows a simple truth: this is a perfect opportunity for a disgruntled southerner to take a shot at Grant, then disappear in an instant.

Just when the situation begins to border on pandemonium, the Metropolitan Police come to their rescue. Grant and Porter are soon on their way again, this time inside a carriage, with a cavalry escort.

An introvert, Grant is pained by the attention and stares. Once inside the War Department, he hurries to formally conclude the logistics of war. Pen in hand and cigar clenched in his teeth, he tells the quartermaster general to stop ordering supplies and suspends the draft and further recruitment. With these orders, he saves the nation $4 million per day.

Though Grant hates public appearances, the city of Washington has planned the Grand Illumination celebration for this very night, specifically so he can be there. The Capitol dome will be lit, the Willard Hotel will illuminate the word UNION, and the governmental buildings are having a competition to see which can be the most brilliantly decorated. Stanton is fussing over the War Department's display, which includes guns and flags as well as lights, while over at the Patent Office some five thousand candles will glow from every window. There will also be a massive fireworks display. And, of course, the bonfires that have blazed all week will still be burning bright. As intensely as Washington celebrated on Monday, Thursday night's Grand Illumination will be even more monumental.

That afternoon, Grant meets with Lincoln at the White House. The last time they met was the day after Petersburg fell, on that veranda in the midst of that shattered city. There, Grant promised Lincoln that he would catch Lee and end the war. Now that Grant has fulfilled that promise, a grateful Lincoln offers his congratulations. He calls for a carriage. The two men ride around the crowded streets of Washington with the top down, shocking the flood of arriving visitors, who can't believe that they are actually laying eyes on President Lincoln and General Grant. The ride is Lincoln's way of giving Grant his moment in the sun after so many months of being second-guessed and labeled a butcher and of deflecting the glory showered upon him onto the man whose genius made it all possible.

It works. The two men are loudly cheered on every street corner.

When it is done, they make plans to meet again that night for the Illumination. They will be the center of attention, these two men who won the Civil War, watched by one and all.

Meanwhile, John Wilkes Booth and his band of assassins tend to their work of sharpening knives and cleaning their pistols, eager for their night of reckoning.

# CHAPTER TWENTY-FIVE

Thursday, April 13, 1865
Washington, D.C.
Night

The four conspirators squeeze into room 6 at the Herndon House hotel, a few blocks from the White House. Booth, David Herold, Lewis Powell, and George Atzerodt lounge on the chairs and perch on the edge of the bed as Booth talks them through the plan. His recruiting trip to Baltimore was unsuccessful. He is too agitated to sit, so he paces as he thinks out loud. The wooden floor becomes a stage, and his oration a performance that takes him from stage left to stage right, then back to stage left again as he breaks down the plan. The parties outside are neither a distraction nor an offense, but a reminder of why they have gathered. Logically, each man knows that there must be plenty of Confederate sympathizers in Washington, huddled in their homes with jaws clenched as they endure the revelry. But right now the would-be assassins feel that they are the only ones who can right the grievous wrong.

Lewis Powell is the youngest and most experienced of the conspirators. He is a tall, powerfully built, and otherwise very handsome man—save for his face being deformed on one side, thanks to a mule's kick. Unlike the others, Powell has actually killed a man, and may have enjoyed it very much. During the war the Floridian fought in several major battles, was wounded at Gettysburg, successfully escaped from a prisoner-of-war camp, and worked for the Confederate Secret Service. He is a solid horseman and quick with a knife. Thanks to his military training, Powell knows the value of reconnaissance. He prepped for his attack that morning by walking past Secretary of State Seward's home on Madison Place, scoping out the best possible ways in and out of the building. He boldly struck up a conversation with Seward's male nurse, just to make sure the secretary was indeed at home.

The reconnaissance is good news for Booth. He thus knows the location of two of the intended victims. Now it is his job to find Lincoln. An afternoon talking to stage managers had led to the inescapable conclusion that Lincoln is not going to the theater tonight. Booth, it seems, will not have his grand theatrical moment. Much to his dismay, it appears as if shooting Lincoln will be as mundane as putting a bullet into his brain on a crowded street during the Grand Illumination and then running like hell.

∞

It finally dawns on one very drunk George Atzerodt that the plan has shifted from kidnapping to murder. The only reason he joined the conspiracy was that, in addition to running a small carriage-repair business in Port Tobacco, Maryland, he moonlights as a smuggler, ferrying mail, contraband, and people across the broad Potomac into Virginia. It is a hardscrabble and often dangerous existence. Atzerodt's role in the kidnapping was to be an act of commerce, not rebellion. He was to be paid handsomely to smuggle the bound-and-gagged Lincoln into the hands of the Confederates.

But there is no longer a Confederacy, no longer a kidnapping plot, no longer a need for a boat, and certainly no longer a need for a smuggler— at least in Atzerodt's mind. The thirty-year-old German immigrant slurs that he wants out.

Booth calmly springs his blackmail.

Booth cannot do without Atzerodt. His boat and his knowledge of the Potomac's currents are vital to their escape. A massive manhunt will surely begin the instant Lincoln is killed. Federal officials will seal off Washington, D.C., and canvass the Maryland and Virginia countryside, but with Atzerodt's guidance Booth and his men will rush through rural Maryland ahead of the search parties, cross the Potomac, and then follow smugglers' routes south to Mexico.

Booth has rehearsed for this moment. He knows his lines and recites them with great drama.

"Then *we* will do it," Booth says, nodding at Herold and Powell, never taking his eyes off the drunk German. "But what will come of you?"

And then, as if pulling the solution out of thin air: "You had better come along and get your horse."

At the word "horse," Atzerodt's heart skips a beat. He's trapped. Booth long ago suggested that the two men share horses from time to time. The horse a man rides is part of his identity. By sharing Booth's favorite horse—which seemed like such a simple and thoughtful gesture on the actor's part all those weeks ago—Atzerodt is now visibly connected to the assassination plot. Atzerodt has ridden Booth's horse all over Washington and has even helped him sell a few animals; so there will be no shortage of witnesses.

Atzerodt sighs and nods his head. Murder it is. There is no way out for him.

The time has come. The four men stand, aware that they are about to commit the greatest crime in the history of the United States.

∞

Before opening the door, Booth reminds them that their post-assassination rendezvous point is the road to Nanjemoy, on the Maryland side of the Potomac. Normally the sight of a lone horseman galloping out of Washington, D.C., long after dark would make the sentries guarding the bridges suspicious. But tonight is not a normal night. All those folks who've come into Washington for the Illumination will be making their way back home when it's all done. Booth and his men will easily blend in with the same drunken bleating masses who are now making that wretched noise on the streets outside room 6.

If for some reason they can't do the job tonight, they will remain in Washington and try again tomorrow.

Booth shakes hands with each man. They leave one at a time and go their separate ways.

# CHAPTER TWENTY-SIX

THURSDAY, APRIL 13, 1865
WASHINGTON, D.C.
NIGHT

There once was a fifth conspirator, the one Booth traveled to Baltimore to corral the day before. Mike O'Laughlen, a former Confederate soldier who grew up across the street from Booth, was one of the first men recruited by him last August. Just a month earlier the two men had lain in wait together for a certain carriage making its way down the lonely country road to the Soldiers' Home, only to find that its occupant was a Supreme Court justice instead of the president.

Hiding in the tall grass along the side of the road, O'Laughlen had weighed the repercussions of actually kidnapping the president of the United States and realized that he would hang by the neck until dead if caught. He was actually relieved that the carriage belonged to Salmon P. Chase instead of Lincoln.

The twenty-four-year-old engraver returned to Baltimore and put the kidnapping plot behind him. He wanted a normal life. When Booth came calling a week later with an even more far-fetched plot to kidnap the president by handcuffing him at the theater and then lowering his body to the stage, O'Laughlen shook his head and told Booth to go away.

But Booth is nothing if not relentless. In Baltimore, he tried to convince O'Laughlen to rejoin the conspiracy. O'Laughlen told the actor he didn't want any part of the killing. Yet the same day he apparently changed his mind, and he traveled to Washington a short time later. O'Laughlen started drinking the minute he arrived, bellying up to the bar at a place called Rullman's until his behavior became erratic. Like Booth, who now prowls Washington in the desperate hope of finding Lincoln, O'Laughlen prowls the bustling thoroughfares, unsure of what to do next.

Meanwhile, General Sam Grant, whose idea of a stellar evening is chain-smoking cigars and sipping whiskey, would be very happy staying in for the evening. But as Julia points out, General and Mrs. Grant have not attended a party together for quite some time. Sitting in their room on this very special night, no matter how luxurious the accommodations, would be a waste. Julia shows her husband invitation after invitation to party after party. She is thrilled to be in the city but also eager to leave as soon as possible to rejoin their four children. Knowing that they have perhaps just this one night in Washington, Grant agrees that they should venture out.

Reluctantly, Grant leaves the hotel. They engage a carriage to take them to the home of Secretary of War Stanton, who is holding a gala celebration for War Department employees. Four brass bands serenade the partygoers from nearby Franklin Square, and a fireworks demonstration will cap the night.

Grant has been a target ever since he took command of Lincoln's army. But even with all the people in the streets he is unafraid. The war is over.

The Grants arrive at Stanton's home. A bodyguard stands at the top of the steps, one of the few the general has encountered in Washington. The Grants are greeted with a loud round of applause as they join the partygoers, but they are soon lost in the sea of other prominent faces. Grant gets a drink and settles in to endure the politicking and glad-handing soon to head his way.

But the Grants have been followed. Mike O'Laughlen, wearing a dark suit, marches up the front steps of Stanton's house and tries to crash the party. The sergeant providing security brushes him off, telling the unwanted guest, "If you wish to see him, step out on the pavement, or the stone where the carriage stops."

O'Laughlen disappears into the night, only to return later asking to see Secretary Stanton. Coincidentally, Stanton and Grant are both standing just a few feet away, watching the fireworks. There is still something of the conspirator in O'Laughlen, a willingness to take risks where others might not. He takes a bold gamble, blends in with the crowd, and slips undetected into the party, despite the security detail. He then goes one better by walking over and standing directly behind Stanton.

But Mike O'Laughlen does nothing to harm the secretary of war. Nor does he bother Grant. The fact is, he doesn't know what Stanton looks like, and as a former Confederate soldier with a deep respect for rank, he is too nervous to speak with Grant.

Observers will later remember the drunk in the dark coat and suggest that his intentions were to kill the general and the secretary. Nothing could be further from the truth: the surprising fact is that O'Laughlen is actually here to warn them about Booth. But even after all those drinks, Mike O'Laughlen still can't summon the courage. He thinks of the repercussions and how if he informs on Booth, his childhood friend will most surely reveal the story about the kidnapping attempt four weeks earlier. That admission would mean the same jail sentence—or even execution—for O'Laughlen as for Booth.

No. Nothing good can come of telling Stanton or Grant a single detail of the plot. Mike O'Laughlen disappears into the night and drinks himself blind.

Meanwhile, a crowd gathers in front of Stanton's home. For all his attempts at avoiding the limelight, word of Grant's location has spread throughout the city. Cries of "Speech!" rock the night air, his admirers thoroughly unaware that Grant is terrified of public speaking.

Stanton comes to the rescue. Never afraid of expressing himself, the secretary throws out a few bon mots to pacify his audience. Grant says nothing, but the combination of a small wave to the crowd and Stanton's spontaneous words are enough to satiate Grant's fans. Soon the sidewalks are bare.

On the other side of town, John Wilkes Booth steps back into the National Hotel, frustrated and tired from hours of walking bar to bar, party to party, searching for Lincoln. The Deringer rests all too heavily in his coat pocket, in its barrel the single unfired round that could have changed the course of history. There has been no news of any other assassinations, so he can only assume that his conspirators have also failed—and he is right. Herold, Atzerodt, and Powell were all unable to conquer their fears long enough to cross the line from fanatic to assassin.

Perhaps tomorrow.

One mile away, in his White House bedroom, Abraham Lincoln slumbers peacefully. A migraine has kept him in for the night.

Hopefully that will not be the case tomorrow evening, for the Lincolns have plans to attend the theater.

# Part Three

※

# THE LONG
# GOOD FRIDAY

*The last known photograph of Lincoln,
February 1865*

# CHAPTER TWENTY-SEVEN

FRIDAY, APRIL 14, 1865
WASHINGTON, D.C.
7:00 A.M.

It is Good Friday morning, the day on which Jesus Christ was crucified, died an agonizing death, and was quickly buried. All of this after he had been betrayed by Judas and scorned by a public that had lionized him just days before.

Abraham Lincoln is a religious man but not a churchgoer. He was born into a Christian home in the wilderness, where established churches were rare. His father and mother were staunch "hard-shell" Baptists, and at a young age he attended the Pigeon Creek Baptist Church. Lincoln's church attendance became sporadic in his adult life. Nevertheless, he took comfort in reading the Bible on a daily basis and often used the words of God to make important points in his public pronouncements. Indeed, his faith has grown because of the war. But because Lincoln never attached himself to an organized religion as an adult, his ability to combine the secular and the religious in the way he goes about his life will later have everyone from atheists to humanists to Calvinists claiming that he is one of theirs. The truth is, Abraham Lincoln does believe in God and has relied on Scripture in overcoming all the challenges he has confronted.

Lincoln rises at seven A.M. Outside the White House, the Washington weather is a splendid, sunny fifty degrees. Dogwoods are blooming along the Potomac and the scent of spring lilacs carries on the morning breeze as the president throws his size 14 feet over the edge of the bed, slides them into a pair of battered slippers, pulls on an equally weathered robe, pushes open the rosewood bedroom door, says good morning to his night watchman, and walks down a second-floor hallway to the White House library. The quiet night at home has been good for his soul. Lincoln's sleep was restful. All symptoms of his migraine have disappeared.

Petitioners sleeping in the White House hallway leap to their feet upon the sight of Lincoln. They have come seeking presidential favors—a pardon, a job, an appointment. The president is courteous but evasive at their shouted requests, eager to be alone in the quiet of the library. That strangers actually sleep on the White House floor is commonplace at the time. "The multitude, washed or unwashed, always has free egress and ingress" into the White House, an astonished visitor wrote earlier in Lincoln's presidency.

The White House's open-door policy ends today.

∽

The president's favorite chair is in the exact center of the room. He sits down and opens his Bible, not because it is Good Friday but because starting the day with Scripture is a lifelong custom. Glasses balanced on the end of his prominent nose, he reads a verse, then another, before setting the Good Book on a side table. He leans back in the chair to meditate, enjoying the only quiet and solitary moments he will know this day.

Lincoln traipses down the hall to his office. His desk is mahogany, with cubbies and shelves. Behind him is the willow-lined Potomac, seen clearly outside the window.

Secretaries John Nicolay and John Hay have laid the mail on the desk, having already removed the love letters Lincoln sometimes receives from young ladies, and the assassination letters more often sent by older men. Typically, the president gets almost three hundred letters a day, of which he reads only a half dozen, at most.

Lincoln skims the mail, then jots down a few notes. Each is signed "A. Lincoln" if it is of a more official nature, or just "Yours truly," as in the case of his note to William Seward. The secretary of state continues to recover from his horrible accident, his jaw and shattered skull mending slowly. Now he lies in bed at home, a convenient stone's throw across the street from the White House.

Breakfast is scheduled for eight o'clock. Lincoln finishes his brief business and enters a small room, where he grooms himself. Daily baths and showers are rare, even in the White House. Lincoln is eager to be downstairs, for his son Robert is just back from the war and will be joining him, twelve-year-old Tad, and Mary for breakfast. More importantly, Robert was in the room when Lee surrendered at Appomattox. Though Lincoln heard the story from Grant yesterday, he is keen to hear more about this landmark event. The war's end is one topic he never gets tired of talking about.

Just twenty-one, with a thin mustache and a captain's rank, Robert is still boyish, despite his time at the front. As Lincoln sips coffee and eats the single boiled egg that constitutes his daily breakfast, Robert describes "the stately elegant Lee" and Grant, "the small stooping shabby shy man in the muddy blue uniform, with no sword and no spurs."

When Lincoln asks what it was like to be there, his son is breathless. "Oh, it was great!" the normally articulate Robert exclaims, unable to find a more expressive way to describe being present at one of the seminal moments in American history.

Robert hands Lincoln a portrait of Lee. The president lays it on the table, where it stares up at him. Lincoln tells his son that he truly believes the time of peace has come. He is unfazed by the small but bitter Confederate resistance that remains. His thoughts are far away from the likes of John Wilkes Booth.

∽

Pressing business awaits Lincoln in his office, but he allows breakfast to stretch on for almost an hour. He can permit himself this luxury, with the war finally over. At last he stands, his body stooped, now just an inch or two less than the towering height of his youth. He is relaxed and happy, even though his severe weight loss makes him look like "a skeleton with clothes," in the words of one friend.

Lincoln reminds Mary that they have a date for a carriage ride this afternoon. To Robert, he suggests that the time has come to remove the uniform, return to Harvard, and spend the next three years working on his law degree. "At the end of that time I hope we will be able to tell if you will make a good lawyer or not," he concludes, sounding more serious than he feels. The words are a sign that he is mentally transitioning from the easy part of his day into those long office hours when, even with the war concluded, the weight of the world presses down on his shoulders.

By nine A.M., President Lincoln is sitting at his desk.

Every aspect of Lincoln's early morning has the feel of a man putting his affairs in order: reading the Bible, jotting a few notes, arranging for a last carefree whirl around Washington with his loyal wife, and setting his son on a path that will ensure him a successful future. All of this is done unconsciously, of course, but it is notable.

Even if it is not mentioned on this day in the White House, the potential assassination of the president is a topic of discussion in and around Washington. The chattering class doesn't know when it might occur, but many believe an attempt will come very soon.

"To those familiar with the city of Washington," a member of his cavalry detail will later write, "it was not surprising that Lincoln was assassinated. The surprising thing to them was that it was so long delayed. It is probable that the only man in Washington who, if he thought upon the subject of all, did not think that Mr. Lincoln was in constant and imminent danger, was Mr. Lincoln himself."

But today it is as if Lincoln subconsciously knows what is about to happen.

A mile down Pennsylvania Avenue, the man who *does* know what is about to happen is also setting his affairs in order.

# CHAPTER TWENTY-EIGHT

FRIDAY, APRIL 14, 1865
WASHINGTON, D.C.
9:00 A.M.

John Wilkes Booth walks slowly down the hotel corridor, momentarily at a loss for words. He has come to say good-bye to his beloved Lucy. He struggles to think of a way to break off their secret engagement and intimate that he might never see her again. Even though their relationship has been all but dead since Newport, of all the terrible things he must do today, what he is about to do next breaks his heart like no other.

The Hales are living in the National Hotel, on the corner of Pennsylvania and Sixth. Booth lives in the same hotel, room 228. Lucy does charity work for the Sanitation Committee and even rode to the front lines of nearby battlefields to visit the troops. It's well known that her father wishes her to marry someone powerful and well connected. For Lucy to not only slink off to the room of an actor but also agree to marry him would enrage Senator Hale. So while the relationship has slowly become more public, she and Booth have kept their pending nuptials a secret.

It's nine A.M. when Booth knocks on her door. He wears a ring she gave him as a keepsake. Booth has the eccentric habit of kissing the ring absentmindedly when out drinking with friends, and he does so now, as he nervously waits for her to answer. This will be the last time he'll see her for quite a while—perhaps forever. Lucy's father has been appointed ambassador to Spain, and the entire family will accompany him abroad. Booth plans to escape to Mexico after shooting Lincoln and then perhaps sail to Spain for a clandestine visit with Lucy if all goes well.

But how to say good-bye? How to make the next few moments as touching and romantic as any farewell should be, while also not letting her know he's leaving and why?

∞

Their relationship began in 1862. Booth became enchanted after glimpsing her in a crowd and sent Lucy an anonymous Valentine's Day love letter. This was followed shortly afterward by another missive, revealing his identity. If its intended effect was to make twenty-one-year-old Lucy swoon, it worked. Booth was at the height of his fame and good looks, delighting women across the country with his performance as the male lead in a traveling production of *Romeo and Juliet*. One actress even tried to kill herself after he rebuffed her advances.

But Lucy Lambert Hale was not in the habit of throwing herself at men. So while Booth might have had the upper hand at the start, she made him work hard for her affection. The relationship simmered for two years, starting with flirtation and then blossoming into something more. The pair became intimate. When he was on the road, Booth was as faithful as a traveling thespian could be, which is to say that he made love to other women but considered them second to Lucy in his heart.

Booth is not the sort of man to mean it when he says, "I love you." For the most part, women are the objects of his own gratification. But Lucy has long treated men the same way, holding them at arm's length emotionally, basking in their charms, and then discarding them when someone newer and better comes along. In each other, Booth and Lucy met their match.

But they are also opposites in many ways. She comes from a more elite level of society, one that does not consider acting a gentlemanly career. She is an abolitionist, and he is most certainly not. He professes a heartfelt belief in the southern cause, while she is the daughter of a ferociously partisan northern senator. The engagement is doomed.

Booth has not seen Lucy since their ill-fated getaway to Newport. They haven't so much as exchanged letters or passed each other in the hallway, even though they live in the same hotel. He has no idea how she will react to his visit.

A servant answers the door and ushers him inside the suite. Lucy appears a moment later, the unfinished business of their argument hanging between them. They both know that it's over. Nothing more needs to be said, much to Booth's relief. They make small talk, skirting the obvious issue. And then it is time to say good-bye. Before leaving, Booth asks Lucy for a photograph so that he might have something to remember her by.

She steps out of the room and returns with a small portrait of her face in profile. Her hair is pulled back off her forehead and her lips are creased in a Mona Lisa smile. Booth thanks Lucy and gives her a long last look. He then turns and walks out of the Hales' suite, explaining

*Lucy Hale in the photograph she gave John Wilkes Booth*

breezily that he is off to get a shave, wondering if he will ever make it to Spain to see Lucy again.

As he walks back down the hallway, the sound of the closing door still echoing in the corridor, he admires the picture and slips it into his breast pocket, next to the pictures of four other women who have enjoyed his charms. The life of a narcissist is often cluttered.

The pictures will remain in Booth's pocket for the rest of his short life.

# CHAPTER TWENTY-NINE

FRIDAY, APRIL 14, 1865
WASHINGTON, D.C.
10:00 A.M.

Mary Lincoln has tickets for a play—and what a spectacular performance it will be. Grover's Theatre is not only staging a lavish production of *Aladdin, or The Wonderful Lamp* but is adding a grand finale for this night only, during which the cast and audience will rise as one to sing patriotic songs written especially for the occasion. Everyone in Washington is talking about it.

But Mary is torn. Word has come from James Ford, the manager of Ford's Theatre, that he is staging the wildly popular farce *Our American Cousin*. Tonight the legendary actress Laura Keene is celebrating her one thousandth performance in her signature role as Florence Trenchard. This milestone, Ford has politely suggested to Mary, is something not to be missed.

Keene, thirty-eight, is not only one of America's most famous actresses but also very successful as a theater manager. In fact, she is the first woman in America to manage her own high-profile career and purchase a theater. That theater will later be renamed the Winter Garden, and it is still in existence today at a different location in New York City. Offstage, Laura Keene's life is not so tidy—she pretends to be married to her business manager, but in truth she is secretly married to a convicted felon who has run off to Australia. During an

*Laura Keene*

extended tour of that faraway continent, Keene quarreled mightily with her costar, the equally vain Edwin Booth.

But onstage Laura Keene is a force. The gimlet-eyed actress owes much of that success to *Our American Cousin*. At first she thought very little of the script, which places a country bumpkin in the upper class of British society. But then Keene changed her mind and bought worldwide rights. Debuting seven years earlier at Laura Keene's Theatre on Broadway, it soon became the first blockbuster play in American history. It was performed in Chicago on the same night in May 1860 that Lincoln was confirmed as the Republican nominee for the presidency. Many of the play's screwball terms, like "sockdologizing" and "Dundrearyisms" (named for the befuddled character Lord Dundreary), have become part of the cultural lexicon, and several spinoff plays featuring characters from the show have been written and performed.

Despite all that, ticket sales for this run of the play have been so

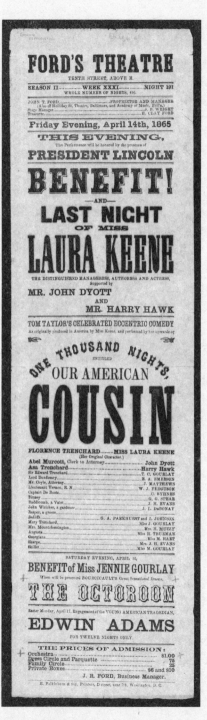

*The playbill for* Our American Cousin *from the night the Lincolns were in attendance, April 14, 1865*

sluggish that Ford's will be nearly empty. But Mary Lincoln doesn't mind. What matters most to her is that on this most patriotic of evenings, she and the president will celebrate their first visit to the theater since the war's end by enjoying the quintessential American comedy, on a night that features one of America's—if not the world's—most famous actresses.

*Aladdin* can wait.

*✑*

With this sudden and impulsive decision to attend one show and not the other, an eerie coincidence will unravel: thanks to the performance that took place in Chicago in 1860, *Our American Cousin* will bracket both the beginning and the end of the Lincoln administration.

Over breakfast a few hours earlier, Mary told the president that she wanted to go to Ford's. Lincoln absentmindedly said he would take care of it.

Now, between appointments, Lincoln summons a messenger. He wants a message delivered to Ford's Theatre, saying that he will be in attendance this evening if the state box is available. General Grant and his wife will be with him, as will Mary.

Abraham Lincoln is the undisputed leader of the world's most ascendant nation, a country spanning three thousand miles and touching two oceans. During the war, he could send men off to die with a single command to his generals. He has freed the slaves. This is a man who has the power to do almost anything he wants. And tonight, if truth be told, he would prefer to see *Aladdin*.

Yet Lincoln would never dream of contradicting Mary's wishes. His life is much easier when she is appeased. A volatile and opinionated woman whose intellect does not match her considerable capacity for rage, Mary Lincoln is short and round, wears her hair parted straight down the middle, and prefers to be called "Madame President," which some believe is pretentious, to say the least. Mary's rants about some person or situation that has angered her can sidetrack Lincoln's day and drain him of precious energy, so he does all he can to make sure nothing upsets her unstable psyche.

But to be fair, Mary Lincoln has also suffered the deaths of two

*Mary Todd Lincoln*

young sons during her twenty-two-year marriage. Lincoln dotes on her. A compassionate man, he tries more to ease the lingering pain than to merely keep the peace. Mary Lincoln is almost ten years younger than her husband, and they had an on-again, off-again courtship and even broke off their first engagement when Lincoln had cold feet about marrying her. Mary is from an affluent home, which afforded her an education that few American women enjoyed at the time. Lithe in her early twenties, Mary has put on considerable weight. And though she had many suitors as a young woman, few would now consider her to be good-looking. Nevertheless, Lincoln is enamored. The president considers Mary the love of his life. Some historians believe that because Lincoln lost his mother at the age of nine, he was drawn to women with maternal, protective instincts. Mary Lincoln certainly fits that description.

∽

Lincoln is overdue at the War Department. He also has a cabinet meeting scheduled in just over an hour. He hurriedly steps out of the White House and walks over to see Stanton. Mary demands that he wear a shawl, and so he does, not caring in the slightest that the gray garment draped over his shoulders gives him a decidedly nonpresidential appearance.

Lincoln strolls into Stanton's office unannounced, plops down on the couch, and casually mentions that he's going to the theater that night. The words are designed to provoke a reaction—and they do.

Stanton frowns. His network of spies have told him of assassination rumors. Last night, during the Illumination party at his home, Stanton adamantly warned Grant away from going to the theater with the Lincolns. Stanton is no less stern with Lincoln. He thinks the president is a fool for ignoring the assassination rumors and argues that Lincoln is risking his life.

"At least bring a guard with you," Stanton pleads, once it becomes obvious that Lincoln will not be dissuaded. That statement is the best evidence we have that Secretary of War Stanton did not wish Lincoln ill. If, as some conspiracy theorists believe, Stanton wished Lincoln dead, why would he want to provide him with protection?

The president is in a playful mood. "Stanton," Lincoln says, "did you know that Eckert can break a poker over his arm?"

Major Thomas T. Eckert is the general superintendent of the Military Telegraph Corps. He once demonstrated the shoddy nature of the War Department's fireplace irons by breaking the defective metal rods over his left forearm.

"Why do you ask such a question?" Stanton replies, mystified.

"Stanton, I have seen Eckert break five pokers, one after the other, over his arm, and I am thinking that he would be the kind of man who would go with me this evening. May I take him?"

"Major Eckert has a great deal of work to do. He can't be spared."

"Well, I will ask the major himself," Lincoln responds.

But Eckert knows better than to cross Stanton. Despite a barrage of good-natured pleading by the president, Eckert says he cannot attend the theater that evening.

His business with Stanton concluded, Lincoln wraps his shawl tightly around his shoulders and marches back to the White House for his cabinet meeting.

# CHAPTER THIRTY

Friday, April 14, 1865
Washington, D.C.
10:30 A.M.

Lincoln's messenger reaches Ford's at 10:30 A.M. "The president of the United States would like to formally request the state box for this evening—if it is available," the note reads.

The state box is available, James Ford immediately responds, barely containing his excitement. He races into the manager's office to share the good news with his brother Harry and then barks the order for the stage carpenter to come see him right this instant.

Ford's may be the city's preeminent stage, but business has been extremely slow this week. The postwar jubilation means that Washington's theatergoers are making merry on the streets, not penned together inside watching a show. In fact, Ford had been anticipating yet another dismal night. *Our American Cousin* is no match for the Grover's *Aladdin*, which has been made all the more spectacular by the postshow victory rally, thus allowing audience members to watch a play *and* make merry. Ford can almost hear the actors' words echoing off empty seats, and the punch lines that will receive a yawn instead of the guffaw a packed and energized theater so often guarantees. But now, with word that the president will be in the audience, the night should be a sellout.

Ford's was originally known as the First Baptist Church of Washington. When the Baptists moved out, in 1861, James's brother John

*Ford's Theatre, 1865*

purchased the building and turned it into a playhouse. When Ford's Athenaeum was destroyed by fire in 1862, some said it was God's will, because many churchgoers considered the theater to be the devil's playground. But John Ford was undeterred. He not only rebuilt the great brick building; he reshaped it into the nation's most modern theater.

Ford's reopened to rave reviews in August 1863. The building is flanked on either side by taverns—the Greenback Saloon to the left and Taltavul's Star Saloon to the right—so that theatergoers can pop next door for a drink at intermission. The outside of the theater itself features five decorative archways. Patrons enter through the center arch, leading directly into the ticket booth and lobby. The steps leading up from the street are granite. The unpaved streets are often muddy this time of year, so Ford has built a wooden ramp from the street into the lobby. This ensures that ladies won't soil their evening wear when stepping out of their carriages.

Inside, three seating levels face the stage. Gas lamps light the auditorium until the curtain falls, when they are dimmed by a single backstage valve. The chairs are a simple straight-backed cane but, inside his special presidential box, Lincoln prefers to sit in the red horsehair-upholstered rocking chair that Ford's reserves for his personal use.

Boxes on either side of the stage allow the more privileged patrons to look straight down onto the actors. The state box, where the Lincolns and Grants will sit this evening, is almost on the stage itself—so close that if Lincoln were to impulsively rise from his rocking chair and leap down into the actors' midst, the distance traveled would be a mere nine feet.

The state box is actually two side-by-side boxes. When not being used by the president or some other national dignitary, they are available for sale to the general public and simply referred to as boxes 7 and 8. A pine partition divides them.

On nights when the Lincolns are in attendance, the partition is removed. Red, white, and blue bunting is draped over the railing and a portrait of George Washington faces out at the audience, designating that the president of the United States is in the house. Out of respect for the office, none of the other boxes are for sale when the Lincolns occupy the state box.

Now, with the news that this will be such a night, the first thing on James Ford's mind is decorating the state box with the biggest and most spectacular American flag he can find. He remembers that the Treasury Department has such a flag. With governmental offices due to close at noon for the Good Friday observance, there's little time to spare.

By sheer coincidence, John Wilkes Booth marches up those granite front steps at that very moment. Like many actors, he spends so much time on the road that he doesn't have a permanent address. So Ford's Opera House, as the theater is formally known, is his permanent mailing address.

As James Ford reacts to Lincoln's request, an *Our American Cousin* rehearsal is taking place. The sound of dramatic voices wafts through the air. The show has been presented eight previous times at Ford's, but Laura Keene isn't taking any chances with cues or blocking. If this is to be her thousandth and, perhaps, final performance of this warhorse, she will see to it that the cast doesn't flub a single line. This bent toward perfectionism is a Keene hallmark and a prime reason she has enjoyed such a successful career.

Booth's mail is in the manager's office. As he picks up a bundle of letters, stage carpenter James J. Gifford bounds into the room, curious as to why Ford wants to see him. When the theater manager shares the exciting news about the Lincolns, Clifford is ecstatic, but Booth pretends not to hear, instead staring straight down at his mail, acting as if he is studying the return addresses. He grins, though he does not mean to. He calms himself and makes small talk with Ford, then says his good-byes and wanders out into the sunlight. Booth sits on the front step, half-reading his mail and laughing aloud at his sudden good fortune.

Ford walks past, explaining that he is off to purchase bunting—and perhaps a thirty-six-star flag.

∞

Until this moment, Booth has known what he wants to do and the means with which he will do it. But the exact details of the murder have so far eluded him.

Sitting on the front step of Ford's Theatre on this Good Friday morning, he knows that he will kill Lincoln tonight and in this very theater. Booth has performed here often and is more familiar with its hidden backstage tunnels and doors than he is with the streets of Washington. The twofold challenge he now faces is the traditional assassin's plight: find the most efficient path into the state box in order to shoot Abraham Lincoln and then find the perfect escape route from the theater.

The cast and crew at Ford's treat Booth like family. His eccentricities are chalked up to his being a famous actor. The theatrical world is full of a hundred guys just as unpredictable and passionate, so nobody dreams that he has a burning desire to kill the president. So it is, as Booth rises to his feet and wanders back into the theater to plan the attack, that it never crosses anyone's mind to ask what he's doing. It's just John being John.

The seats are all empty. The house lights are up. Onstage, the rehearsal is ending.

John Wilkes Booth prowls Ford's Theatre alone, analyzing, scrutinizing, estimating. His journey takes him up the back stairs to the state box, where he steps inside and looks down at the stage. A music stand provides an unlikely burst of inspiration. He hefts it in his hand, nervous but elated, knowing how he will make use of it tonight. By the time he is done, Booth has come up with an audacious—and brilliant—plan of attack.

On Booth's mind are these questions: Will he commit the perfect crime? And will he go down in history as a great man?

# CHAPTER THIRTY-ONE

—

FRIDAY, APRIL 14, 1865
WASHINGTON, D.C.
11:00 A.M.

A hazy sun shines down on Washington's empty streets. The city is so quiet it seems to be asleep. The Good Friday observance means that its citizens are temporarily done celebrating the war's end. They are now in church or at home repenting, leaving the local merchants to lament the momentary loss of the booming business they've enjoyed the past few days.

Hundreds of miles to the south, in Fort Sumter, South Carolina, a massive celebration is about to take place, commemorating the raising of the Stars and Stripes. Major General Robert Anderson stands before forty-five hundred people as the very flag that was lowered there four years earlier, marking the beginning of the war, now climbs the flagpole. A minister offers a prayer of thanksgiving. The Union is reunited.

Back in Washington, General Grant walks to the White House, feeling conflicted. He was supposed to meet with Lincoln at nine A.M., but the president rescheduled for eleven so that Grant can attend the cabinet meeting. Now he feels obligated to attend the theater tonight with the Lincolns. But Julia Grant, who thinks Mary Lincoln is unstable and a gossip, has bluntly refused. When the theater invitation arrived from Mary Lincoln earlier that morning, Julia replied with a firm no, stating that the Grants would be leaving town that afternoon and noting, "We will not, therefore, be here to accompany the President and Mrs. Lincoln to the theatre." She is, in fact, adamant that they catch the afternoon train out of Washington. Going to the theater with Mary Lincoln is out of the question.

General Grant is caught in the middle. Lincoln has become such an ally and dear friend that turning down his invitation seems rude. But displeasing his wife, who has endured many a sacrifice these past years, is equally daunting.

The two soldiers standing guard at the White House gate snap to attention as their general in chief arrives. Grant tosses them a return salute with the casual ease of a man who has done it thousands of times, never breaking stride as he continues on to the front door.

The doorman nods graciously as Grant steps inside, dressed in his soldier's uniform, moving past the police bodyguard currently on duty and a rifle-bearing soldier also in dress uniform. Then it's up the stairs to Lincoln's second-floor office, where another soldier stands guard. Soon Grant is seated in Lincoln's cabinet meeting, somewhat surprised by the loose way in which such matters are conducted. He assumed that Lincoln's entire cabinet would be in attendance, particularly since there are so many pressing matters of state to discuss. But a quick glance around the room shows no sign of Secretary of War Stanton or Secretary of the Interior John P. Usher. Secretary of State William Seward, home recovering from his carriage accident, is represented by his son Frederick. And as Lincoln leans back in his chair along the south window, the half-filled room feels more like a collegiate debating club than a serious political gathering. Lincoln guides the dialogue, which jumps from elation at the war's end to other topics and back, taking no notes as he soaks in the various opinions. His behavior is that of a first among equals rather than the ultimate decision maker.

∽

The meeting is into its second hour as Grant is shown into the room, and his entrance injects a new vitality—just as Lincoln intended. The cabinet, to a man, is effusive in praise of the general and begs to hear details of the Appomattox surrender. Grant sets the scene, describing the quaint McLean farmhouse and the way he and Lee sat together to settle the country's fate. He doesn't go into great detail, and he makes a point of praising Lee. The cabinet members are struck by his modesty but clamor for more.

Lincoln tries to draw him out. "What terms did you make for the common soldiers?" the president asks, already knowing the answer.

"To go back to their homes and families, and they would not be molested, if they did nothing more."

There is a point to Lincoln's inviting Grant to this meeting, as evidenced by this new line of inquiry. Lincoln hopes for a certain pragmatic lenience toward the southern states, rather than a draconian punishment, as his vice president, Andrew Johnson, favors. Lincoln has not seen Johnson since his second inauguration. But Lincoln's lenient plan for the South is not borne solely out of kindness nor with just the simple goal of healing the nation. The South's bustling warm-water ports and agricultural strength will be a powerful supplement to the nation's economy. With the nation mired in more than $2 billion of wartime debt, and with Union soldiers still owed back pay, extra sources of income are vitally needed.

Grant's simple reply has the desired effect. Lincoln beams as the cabinet members nod their heads in agreement.

"And what of the current military situation?"

Grant says that he expects word from Sherman any minute, saying that General Joe Johnston has finally surrendered. This, too, is met with enthusiasm around the table.

Throughout the proceedings, Grant's feeling of unease about that evening's plans lingers. He makes up his mind to tell Lincoln that he will attend the theater. Doing otherwise would be ungracious and disrespectful. Julia will be furious, but eventually she will understand. And then, first thing in the morning, they can be on the train to New Jersey.

∾

The cabinet meeting drags on. One o'clock rolls past. One-thirty.

A messenger arrives carrying a note for Grant. It's from Julia and she's not happy. Mrs. Grant wants her husband back at the Willard Hotel immediately, so that they can catch the 6:00 P.M. to Burlington, New Jersey.

General Grant's decision has now been made for him. After months and years of men obeying his every order, he bows to an even greater authority than the president of the United States: his wife.

"I am sorry, Mr. President," Grant says when the cabinet meeting ends, just after one-thirty. "It is certain that I will be on this afternoon's train to Burlington. I regret that I cannot attend the theater."

Lincoln tries to change Grant's mind, telling him that the people of Washington will be at Ford's to see him. But the situation is out of the general's hands. Lincoln senses that and says good-bye to his dear friend.

The Grants will make their train. Julia is so eager to leave town that she has chosen the local, which takes thirteen long hours to reach Burlington. The faster option would be the seven-thirty express in the morning, but that would mean a night at the theater with the daft and unbalanced Mary Lincoln. Julia Grant's mind is made up.

What Ulysses S. Grant does not know is that he will be returning to Washington by the same train within twenty-four hours.

# CHAPTER THIRTY-TWO

Two thousand years after the execution of Jesus, there are still many unanswered questions about who was directly responsible for his death and what happened in the aftermath. And so it is, on Good Friday 1865, that a series of bizarre occurrences will take place.

In the hours to come guards will inexplicably leave their posts, bridges that should be closed will miraculously be open, and telegrams alerting the army to begin a manhunt for Lincoln's killer will not be sent—all happenings that have been tied to a murky conspiracy that most likely will never be uncovered. What we do know is that in these hours, John Wilkes Booth is putting the final touches on his murderous plan.

Booth is on an emotional roller coaster, his spirits rising and falling as he ponders the assassination and its consequences, all the while running down his checklist, completing the tasks that must be done for tonight. He is dressed in dashing fashion, with tight black pants, a tailored black coat, and a black hat. With those clothes and his broad black mustache, he couldn't look more like a villain. The only thing he wears that isn't black are his boots—they're tan.

The first stop is Mary Surratt's boardinghouse on H Street. She is walking out the door for a trip into the country to collect on an old debt, but Booth catches her just in time. He hands her a spyglass wrapped in brown paper and tied with a string, telling her to make sure that it doesn't get wet or break. One of Surratt's tenants, Louis Weichmann, is a soldier and government clerk whose job deals with the care and housing of prisoners of war. Weichmann senses that there's something shady about Booth, having listened to his rants and spent enough time around the Surratts to discern the pro-Confederate leanings of the crowd. So he leans in to eavesdrop as Mary and Booth confer by the marble fireplace.

Mary catches him. She calmly orders Weichmann to leave her house at once and pick up a horse and buggy for her journey.

By the time Weichmann returns with the horse and buggy, Booth is gone, walking the five blocks to Herndon House, where Lewis Powell is lying on the bed, staring at the ceiling. He and Booth discuss the evening's plan. The trick in killing Secretary of State Seward, Booth reminds him, isn't the actual murder—Seward is still barely conscious and in great pain after his carriage accident. He is incapable of putting up any resistance.

No, the hard part will be getting in and out of Seward's home. There is at least one male military nurse to protect the secretary, along with Seward's wife and three of his children. In a worst-case scenario, Powell will have to kill them all, Booth says. Powell, mentally impaired since that long-ago mule kick to the head, says he has no problem with mass murder.

Then Booth is on the move again, headed for Pumphrey's stable to arrange for his getaway horse. He prefers a small sorrel, but it's already gone for the day. Instead, Booth rents a compact bay mare with a white star on her forehead. Pumphrey warns Booth that although the mare is just fourteen hands high, she's extremely high-spirited. She mustn't be tied to a post if he leaves her anywhere, because she'll pull away and escape. Better to have someone hold her reins at all times.

The bay tries to bite Booth as the groom cinches the English saddle under her belly and adjusts her stirrups. To demonstrate her high spirits, the groom smacks the mare on the rump. She jumps and kicks, much to Booth's delight.

∽

Booth saddles up. He likes the horse with the black mane and tail, but the stirrups don't feel right. The groom shortens them one notch and Booth is on his way, walking the mare up Sixth Street to Pennsylvania Avenue, where he jabs his spurs into her flanks so she'll run. It's a ludicrous idea. The street is jammed with pedestrians and carriages. Union soldiers, returning from the front, march in loose formation, dog-tired and in no mood for a horseman to romp through their ranks. But today Booth is above the law. He gallops the bay down Pennsylvania, ignoring the angry curses hurled in his mud-splattered wake.

Booth stops at Grover's Theatre, where the marquee announces THE GORGEOUS PLAY OF ALADDIN, OR THE WONDERFUL LAMP. He doesn't have any business there, but theaters are safe refuges no matter what city he's visiting. Booth knows not only the insides of the building but also each nearby bar and restaurant, where he's sure to see a friendly face. On a day like today, when his stomach is churning and he's battling with all his might to stay calm and focused, nothing could be more natural than making his way to a theater, just to experience a few moments of calm reassurance. For the child of actors, raised on greasepaint and footlights, it's like going home.

Against Pumphrey's explicit direction, he ties the mare to a hitching post, then wanders up to Deery's tavern and orders a bottle. Alone at the bar, nursing a brandy and water to the sounds of the clacking of billiard balls from the nearby table, he pauses to reflect on what he is about to do. Getting into the theater should be easy enough. Getting past the bodyguard at the door to the state box, however, might get bloody. And the odds of killing Lincoln and escaping are low. He accepts all that.

But what if nobody knows it's him?

What if the euphoric triumph of shooting Lincoln is followed by the devastating letdown of anonymity—that is, until he reaches some safe refuge where he can shout his accomplishment to the world and then parlay his infamy into some even greater glory. But what if no one believes him? What if John Wilkes Booth shoots the president and makes a clean getaway, only to be ignored when he tells everyone that he's the man who did it?

This cannot be. Booth craves the limelight too much. He needs to make sure he'll get immediate credit for such a bold and dramatic act.

∽

Booth tosses a dollar onto the bar and walks downstairs to the Grover's manager's office. It's empty. Sitting at the desk, Booth removes paper and an envelope from the pigeonholes. He then writes a letter to the editor of the *National Intelligencer* stating, in specific terms, what he is about to do.

He signs his name, then adds those of Powell, Atzerodt, and Herold. They are all members of the same company, in theatrical terms. They deserve some sort of billing—even if they might not want it.

After sealing the envelope, Booth steps outside. He is pleased to see that his feisty bay is still where he left her. A motley and dispirited group of Confederate prisoners is marching down the street as he saddles up. "Great God," he moans, mortified by such a sad sight. "I no longer have a country."

But seeing those downtrodden rebels is yet another reminder of why Booth has embraced violence. Thus fortified, Booth spies fellow actor John Matthews in front of the theater. Booth leans down from his horse to hand him the envelope and gives him specific instructions to mail it the next morning. However, hedging his bets in case things go bad, Booth says he wants the letter back if he finds Matthews before ten tomorrow morning.

It's a petty and spiteful trick, designed to implicate Matthews, who will be onstage in the role of Richard Coyle during *Our American Cousin*. Booth had asked him to be part of the conspiracy and was turned down. The night after his aborted kidnapping attempt on the Soldiers' Home road four weeks earlier, Booth even lounged on Matthews's bed in a small boardinghouse across from Ford's Theatre, trying to cajole the fellow actor to join him.

But Matthews continued to refuse. Now Booth is getting his revenge, implicating Matthews by association.

Matthews, completely unsuspecting, is distracted by an unusual sight. "Look," he says to Booth. "Over there."

Booth is stunned to see General and Mrs. Grant leaving town in an open carriage piled high with luggage. Julia is inside, with another female passenger, while the general sits up top, next to the coachman.

Booth trots after them, just to see for himself. He parades his horse past the carriage, turns around, and guides the bay back toward the Grants at a walk. He stares as the carriage passes, glaring at Sam Grant with such intensity that Julia will later recall quite vividly the crazed man who stared them down. It is only after the assassination that Mrs. Grant will realize who he was.

∽

"I thought he was going to Ford's tonight, with Lincoln," Booth says to a stranger.

"Somebody said he's going to Jersey," the man responds, confirming Booth's worst fears. Glumly, he realizes that one of his two primary targets will not be at Ford's this evening. He wheels the horse around and heads for that theater.

Washington, D.C., is a relatively small city. All the locations

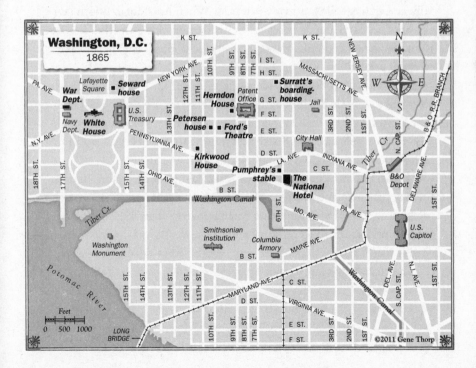

associated with Booth's activities throughout the week are situated close together. Mary Surratt's boardinghouse is just a few blocks from the National Hotel, which is just a few blocks from Kirkwood House, where Vice President Johnson is staying, which is just a few blocks from the White House, which is right across the street from Secretary Seward's home. The National, the White House, and Mary Surratt's boardinghouse constitute the three corners of a broad triangle. Within that triangle are all the other locations. And in the very center is Ford's Theatre, which is right across the alley from Herndon House, where Lewis Powell is now eating an early dinner of cold beef and potatoes before checking out.

The alley is known as Baptist Alley, due to Ford's origins as a house of worship. A maid at Ford's hears the sound of galloping hooves coming from the alley. When she looks outside, she sees a most unusual sight: the famous actor John Wilkes Booth racing a horse north up the alley from E Street, then galloping out the other end on F Street. He does this twice. The maid, Margaret Rozier, watches as Booth dismounts after the second dry run of his escape, not in a million years imagining what she has just witnessed. When he is done, Booth stops at Ford's stage door, where he invites stagehands Jim Maddox and Ned Spangler to join him for a drink next door at Jim Ferguson's Greenback Saloon.

As they come back outside after their drink, Booth mounts the bay and says hello to Jim Ferguson himself. Ferguson has heard about the Lincolns and is making plans to see *Our American Cousin* tonight. "She is a very nice horse," Booth says, noting the way Ferguson admires her. "She can gallop and can almost kick me in the back."

Booth prods her with his spurs and gallops back to the National Hotel, his errands complete. The energy whooshes out of him as the alcohol wears off and the brute realization of what he is about to do hits him hard. His face is so pale that the desk clerk inquires about his health.

Booth says he's fine, orders a cup of tea, and heads upstairs to rest.

# CHAPTER THIRTY-THREE

FRIDAY, APRIL 14, 1865
WASHINGTON, D.C.
3:30 P.M.

"Crook," Abraham Lincoln says to his bodyguard, "I believe there are men who want to take my life. And I have no doubt that they will do it."

The two men are walking down Pennsylvania Avenue, on their way back to the War Department for their second meeting of the day. Lincoln wants a short session with Stanton to discuss the fate of a Confederate ringleader who very recently made the mistake of crossing the border from Canada back into the United States. Stanton is in favor of arresting the man, while Lincoln prefers to let him slip away to England on the morning steamer. As soon as Lincoln makes his point, he aims to hurry back to the White House for the carriage ride he promised Mary.

William Crook is fond of the president and deeply unsettled by the comments.

"Why do you think so, Mr. President?"

Crook steps forward as they come upon a group of angry drunks. He puts his body between theirs and Lincoln's, thus clearing the way for the president's safe passage. Crook's actions, while brave, are unnecessary—if the drunks realize that the president of the United States is sharing the same sidewalk, they give no notice.

Lincoln waits until Crook is beside him again, then continues his train of thought. "Other men have been assassinated," Lincoln says.

"I hope you are mistaken, Mr. President."

"I have perfect confidence in those around me. In every one of you men. I know that no one could do it and escape alive," Lincoln says. The two men walk in silence before he finishes his thought: "But if it is to be done, it is impossible to prevent it."

At the War Department, Lincoln once again invites Stanton and telegraph chief Major Thomas Eckert, the man who can break fireplace pokers over his arms, to attend *Our American Cousin* that night. Both men turn him down once again. Lincoln is upset by their rejection, but he doesn't show it outwardly. The only indication comes on the walk back to the White House, when he admits to Crook, "I do not want to go." Lincoln says it like a man facing a death sentence.

∽

Inside the White House, Lincoln is pulled into an unscheduled last-minute meeting that will delay his carriage ride. Lincoln hides his exasperation and dutifully meets with New Hampshire congressman Edward H. Rollins. But as soon as Rollins leaves, yet another petitioner begs a few minutes of Lincoln's time. A weary Lincoln, all too aware that Mary will be most upset if he keeps her waiting much longer, gives former military aide Colonel William Coggeshall the benefit of a few moments.

Finally, Lincoln marches down the stairs and heads for the carriage. He notices a one-armed soldier standing off to one side of the hallway and overhears the young man tell another, "I would almost give my other hand if I could shake that of Lincoln."

Lincoln can't resist. "You shall do that and it shall cost you nothing, boy," he exclaims, smiling broadly as he walks over and grasps the young man's hand. He asks his name, that of his regiment, and in which battle he lost the arm.

Only then does Lincoln say his farewells and step outside. He finds Mary waiting at the carriage. She's in a tentative mood—they've spent so little time alone in the past few months that being together, just the two of them, feels strange. She wonders if Lincoln might be more comfortable if they brought some friends along for the open-air ride.

"I prefer to ride by ourselves today," he insists. Lincoln helps her into the barouche and then is helped up from the gravel driveway to take his seat beside her. The four-wheeled horse-drawn carriage features two facing double seats for passengers and a retractable roof. The driver sits in a box seat up front. Lincoln opts to keep the roof open, then covers their laps with a blanket, even though the temperature is a warm sixty-eight degrees.

The war has been hard on their marriage. Mary is delighted beyond words to see that Lincoln is in a lighthearted mood. She gazes into her husband's eyes and recognizes the man who once courted her.

"Dear Husband," she laughs, "you startle me by your great cheerfulness. I have not seen you so happy since before Willie's death."

"And well I may feel so, Mary. I consider this day, the war has come to a close." The president pauses. "We must both be more cheerful in the future—between the war and the loss of our darling Willie we have been very miserable."

Coachman Francis Burns guides the elegant pair of black horses down G Street. The pace is a quick trot. Behind them ride two cavalry escorts, just for safety. The citizens of Washington are startled to see the Lincolns out on the town. They hear loud laughter from Mary as the barouche passes by and see a grin spread across the president's face. When a group calls out to him as the carriage turns onto New Jersey Avenue, he doffs his trademark stovepipe hat in greeting.

∽

Throughout the war, Lincoln has stayed in the moment, never allowing himself to dream of the future. But now he pours his heart out to Mary, talking about a proposed family trip to Palestine, for he is most curious about the Holy Land. And after he leaves office he wants the family to return to their roots in Illinois, where he will once again hang out his shingle as a country lawyer. The "Lincoln & Herndon" sign has never been taken down, at Lincoln's specific request to his partner.

"Mary," Lincoln says, "we have had a hard time of it since we came to Washington, but the war is over, and with God's blessing we may hope for four years of peace and happiness, and then we will go back to Illinois and pass the rest of our lives in quiet. We have laid by some money, and during this term we will try to save up more."

The carriage makes its way to the Navy Yard, where Lincoln steps on board USS *Montauk*. His intent is just a cursory peek at the storied ironclad, with its massive round turret constituting the deck's superstructure. But soon its crew mobs Lincoln, and he is forced to politely excuse himself so that he can return to Mary. Unbeknownst to Lincoln, the *Montauk* will soon serve another purpose.

Lincoln offers a final salute to the many admirers as coachman Burns turns the carriage back toward the White House. It's getting late, and the Lincolns have to be at the theater.

John Wilkes Booth is expecting them.

# CHAPTER THIRTY-FOUR

FRIDAY, APRIL 14, 1865
WASHINGTON, D.C.
7:00 P.M.

William Crook stands guard outside Lincoln's office door. The twenty-six-year-old policeman and presidential bodyguard has had a long day, having arrived at the White House at precisely eight A.M. His replacement was supposed to relieve him three hours ago, but John Parker, as always, is showing himself to be lazy and unaccountable. Crook is deeply attached to Lincoln and frets about his safety. How this drunken slob Parker was designated as the president's bodyguard is a great mystery, but Crook knows that the president does not involve himself in such things.

After their carriage ride, the Lincolns eat dinner with their sons, and then Crook walks the president back to the War Department for a third time, to see if General Sherman has sent a telegraph stating the disposition of his troops in the South. Lincoln has become so addicted to the telegraph's instant news from the front that he still can't let go of the need for just one more bit of information, even though the prospect of another great battle is slim.

Then Crook walks back to the White House with Lincoln, his eyes constantly scanning the crowds for signs that someone means his employer harm. He remembers well the advice of Ward Hill Lamon, the walrus-mustached, self-appointed head of Lincoln's security detail, that Lincoln should not go out at night, under any circumstances. "Especially to the theater," Lamon had added.

But tonight, Lincoln is going to the theater—and it's no secret. The afternoon papers printed news about him attending *Our American Cousin* with General Grant and their wives, almost as if daring every crackpot and schemer with an anti-North agenda to buy a ticket. Indeed, ticket sales have been brisk since the announcement, and— recent outpourings of affection notwithstanding—Lincoln's status as the most hated man in America certainly means that not everyone at Ford's will be there out of admiration for the president.

Lincoln, however, doesn't see it like that. Even though Mary says the carriage ride gave her a headache that has her second-guessing the night out, the president feels obligated to go. He might feel differently if he hadn't missed the Grand Illumination last night. That, plus the fact that the Grants aren't going, makes Lincoln's obligation all the more urgent—he knows his constituents will be deeply disappointed if both of America's two most famous men fail to appear.

And then there's the minor issue of disappointing the Grants' last-minute replacements. Just when it seemed like everyone in Washington was terrified of attending the theater with the Lincolns, Mary found guests, the minor diplomat Major Henry Reed Rathbone and his fiancée (and stepsister) Clara Harris, who watched Lincoln's speech with Mary three nights before. Mary is deeply fond of Clara, the full-figured daughter of Senator Ira Harris of New York. They enjoy an almost mother-daughter relationship. Just as important, Major Rathbone is a strapping young man who saw service during the war; he has the sort of physical presence Lincoln might need in a bodyguard, should such services be required.

The president doesn't know either of them. When he received news that this unlikely couple would be their guests, he was enjoying a quiet dinner with Tad and Robert. Lincoln's response was neither joy nor disappointment but merely a silent nod of acknowledgment.

William Crook is a straightforward cop, not one to search for conspiracies or malcontents where none exist. Yet the bodyguard in him wonders about the tall, athletic Rathbone and whether or not he poses a security risk. What better way to kill the president than shooting him in his own box during the play?

Finally, Crook hears feet thudding up the stairs. Parker ambles down the hallway, patting the bulge in his jacket to show that he is armed. He is a thirty-four-year-old former machinist from Frederick County, Virginia, and the father of three children. Parker served in the Union army for the first three months of the war, then mustered out to rejoin his family and took a job as a policeman in September 1861, becoming one of the first 150 men hired when Washington, D.C., formed its brand-new Metropolitan Police Department.

Throughout his employment, Parker's one distinguishing trait has been an ability to manufacture controversy. He has been disciplined for, among other things, swearing at a grocer, swearing at a supervising officer, insulting a woman who had requested police protection, and being drunk and disorderly in a house of prostitution. At his trial, the madam testified that not only was Parker drunk and disorderly but that he had been living in the whorehouse for five weeks before the incident. Apparently, the authorities chose to ignore that testimony. The trial took place before a police board, rather than in the criminal courts. The board found no wrongdoing by Parker and quickly acquitted him.

⁂

And so Parker continued his questionable behavior. He appeared before the police board just two weeks later for sleeping on duty. Ninety days after that, another police board: this time for using profane language to a private citizen. Both charges were dismissed.

His innocence proven again and again, Parker had no qualms about putting his name into the pool when, late in 1864, the Metropolitan Police Department began providing White House bodyguards. It was prestigious duty and kept him from being drafted back into the army. Mary Lincoln herself wrote the letter exempting him from service. So far, the only blemish on Parker's record while serving the president is a penchant for tardiness, as Crook knows all too well. So when Parker finally appears several hours late for his shift, Crook is upset but not surprised.

Crook briefs Parker on the day's events, then explains that the presidential carriage will be stopping at Fourteenth and H to pick up Major Rathbone and Miss Harris. The presence of two additional passengers means that there will be no room for Parker. "You should leave fifteen minutes ahead of the president," says Crook, pointing out that Parker will have to walk to Ford's Theatre—and that he should arrive before the presidential party in order to provide security the instant they arrive.

As Crook finishes, Lincoln comes to his office door. A handful of last-minute appointments have come up, and he is eager to get them out of the way so he can enjoy the weekend.

"Good night, Mr. President," Crook says.

He and the president have repeated this scene a hundred times, with Lincoln responding in kind.

Only this time it's different.

"Good-*bye*, Crook," Lincoln replies.

All the way home, that subtle difference nags at William Crook.

## CHAPTER THIRTY-FIVE

FRIDAY, APRIL 14, 1865
WASHINGTON, D.C.
8:00 P.M.

As Lincoln is bidding farewell to William Crook, Booth is gobbling down a quick dinner in the National Hotel's dining room. Food, sleep, and adrenaline have him feeling sober once more. *Our American Cousin* starts at eight, and his plan will go into action shortly after ten P.M. If all goes well, any residual effects of the afternoon's alcohol will have worn off by then. In fact, Booth is feeling so good that he starts drinking again. What he is about to do is very grave, indeed. Liquid courage will make sure he doesn't get stage fright and miss his cue.

That cue is simple: there is a moment in the third act when the actor Harry Hawk, playing the part of Asa Trenchard, is the only person on stage. He utters a line that never fails to make the audience convulse with laughter. "Don't know the manners of good society, eh?" he says to the character of the busybody, Mrs. Mountchessington, who has insulted him before exiting the stage. "Well, I guess I know enough to turn you inside out, old gal—you sockdologizing old man-trap."

The instant that the punch line hits home and the Ford's audience explodes, Booth will kill Lincoln. If everything goes according to plan, he will already be concealed inside the state box. All he needs to do is pull out his Deringer and fire. Booth will toss the pistol aside after shooting Lincoln, then use his Bowie knife to battle his way out, if cornered.

His plan is to keep moving forward at all times—forward from the back wall of the box, forward to Lincoln's rocking chair, forward up and over the railing and then down onto the stage, forward to the backstage door, forward to Maryland, and then forward all the way to Mexico, exile, and safety.

But Booth will stop for an instant in the midst of all that rapid movement. The actor in him cannot resist the chance to utter one last bold line from center stage. After leaping from the balcony Booth will stand tall and, in his best elocution, announce, *"Sic semper tyrannis"*: Thus always to tyrants.

The Latin phrase is meant to sound smart, the sort of profound parting words that will echo down the corridors of history. He has stolen it, truth be told, from the state of Virginia. It is the commonwealth's motto.

No matter. The words are perfect.

∽

Booth plans to have another last-minute rendezvous with his co-conspirators at eight P.M. He returns to his room and polishes his Deringer, then slips a single ball into the barrel. The gun goes into his pocket. Into his waistband goes the Bowie knife in its sheath. Outside he can hear Washington coming to life once again, with still more of the endless postwar parties, bonfires, and street corner sing-alongs that annoy him no end.

Booth packs a small bag with a makeup pencil, false beard, false mustache, wig, and a plaid muffler. As he is about to leave the hotel on his deadly errand, he realizes that his accomplices might be in need of firearms. So he slips a pair of revolvers into the bag. Their firepower far exceeds the Deringer's.

And yet what Booth leaves behind is just as powerful: among the personal effects that authorities will later find are a broken comb, tobacco, embroidered slippers, and one very telling scrap of paper. On it are written the keys to top-secret coded Confederate messages that link him with Jefferson Davis's office in Richmond and with the million-dollar gold fund in Montreal. Finally, Booth leaves behind a valise filled with damning evidence that implicates John Surratt and, by extension, his mother, Mary.

Booth could have destroyed these items, but such is his malevolence that if he is ever apprehended or killed, he wants everyone else to go down as well. He also wants to show the world that he, Booth, was the mastermind behind killing Abraham Lincoln.

He walks downstairs and slides his key across the front desk. "Are you going to Ford's tonight?" he asks George W. Bunker, the clerk on duty.

"No," comes the reply.

"You ought to go," Booth says with a wink on his way out the door. "There is going to be some splendid acting."

∽

Booth laughs at his own joke as he steps into the night air. Washington is covered in a fine mist, giving the streetlights and the Capitol dome a ghostly appearance. Booth feels like he is viewing the city through frosted glass.

He trots his horse over to Ford's. Once again he examines his escape route, then slides down from the saddle and ties the mare to a hitching post. He steps into a nearby tavern, where he runs into Ford's orchestra director, William Withers Jr., who's having a last quick drink before the eight P.M. curtain. They talk shop, the conversation veering toward mutual friends in the theater. Withers mentions Booth's late father. When Booth suggests that he is the better actor of the two, Withers laughingly shoots back that Booth will never be as talented as his father.

Booth's face hardens, but he manages a thin smile. Focusing his gaze on Withers, he utters the truest sentence he will ever speak: "When I leave the stage I will be the most talked about man in America."

# CHAPTER THIRTY-SIX

Friday, April 14, 1865
Washington, D.C.
8:05 p.m.

"Would you have us be late?" Mary Lincoln chides her husband, standing in his office doorway. Speaker of the House Schuyler Colfax dropped by a half hour ago and was immediately granted a few minutes of Lincoln's time. But those few minutes have stretched into half an hour and, across town, the curtain has already risen on *Our American Cousin*. Making matters worse, the Lincolns still have to stop and pick up their theater guests. They'll be lucky to arrive at Ford's in time for the second act.

It is five minutes after eight. Mary wears a gray dress that shows her ample bosom and a matching bonnet. She is eager to get to the theater but tentative in her approach because Mr. Lincoln's moods have been so unpredictable lately.

Once again, he has lost all track of time. Speaker Colfax stopped in to discuss the possibility of a special session of Congress. Colfax has plans to leave in the morning on a long trip to California but says he will cancel it if Lincoln calls the special session. Lincoln won't hear of it. He tells Colfax to enjoy himself and to enlist the support of the western states in reuniting America.

As he makes to leave, Colfax pauses at the door. He is a true admirer of Lincoln's. Colfax has heard rumors of violence against Lincoln and mentions how afraid he was when Lincoln visited Richmond a week earlier. "Why, if anyone else had been president and gone to Richmond, I would have been alarmed, too," Lincoln chuckles. "But I was not scared about myself a bit."

Lincoln asks Colfax if he has plans for the evening, and, if not, would he be interested in attending *Our American Cousin*? Colfax replies that although he is deeply honored by the invitation, he cannot go.

This marks a half dozen rejections for Lincoln today. First the Grants, then Stanton and Thomas Eckert, then his son Robert just a half hour earlier, and now the Speaker of the House.

Former Massachusetts congressman George Ashmun waits to see Lincoln as Colfax exits. But Mary's pleas finally have an effect. It is time to leave for the theater. Lincoln hastily pulls a card from his jacket pocket and jots a small note inviting Ashmun to return at nine in the morning.

Finally, Lincoln walks downstairs and out onto the front porch, where the presidential carriage awaits.

∽

The roof is now closed, which is a comfort on this misty night. Footman Charles Forbes helps Mary up the steps and into her seat as Lincoln says a few final words to Ashmun and Colfax, who have followed him outside. Suddenly, yet another caller steps out of the night, seeking a few moments of Lincoln's time. The president hears the footsteps on the gravel and the familiar voice of former Illinois congressman Isaac Arnold yelling his name.

Lincoln is about to climb into the carriage, but he waits until Arnold is close enough that they can shake hands. Arnold was a staunch backer of Lincoln's during the war's darkest hours, and the resulting dip in the president's popularity cost him his seat in the House. The least Lincoln can do is acknowledge him. He bends his head to listen as Arnold whispers a quiet petition in his ear.

Lincoln nods but refuses to give an immediate answer. "Excuse me now," he begs. "I am going to the theater. Come see me in the morning."

The Harris residence, at H and Fifteenth Streets, is almost right across the street from the White House, so the Lincolns have little time alone before picking up their guests. But in that short interval Lincoln turns lighthearted and happy, chatting excitedly about the night. Mary is delighted at her husband's sudden jocularity and his ability to seemingly leave the burdens of the White House behind the instant they leave the grounds.

As the carriage threads the seven blocks to the theater, Rathbone, with his muttonchops and broad mustache, sits facing Lincoln, talking about his experiences in the war. Along the way, another impromptu victory parade on Pennsylvania Avenue slows their progress and makes them even later for the show. Once they finally approach Ford's, they can smell and see the tar torches casting their ghostly yellow light on the front of the theater. The carriages of theatergoers line Tenth Street. A crowd of soldiers gathers, there to see Lincoln and Grant. A barker calls out, "This way to Ford's!"

Driver Francis Burns steps down and walks the horses the final few feet to the theater, fearful that the commotion might cause them to bolt. The two cavalry escorts trailing the carriage wheel their horses back to their barracks, knowing that they will return and finish their guard duty once the show ends.

It is eight twenty-five when Lincoln steps through the front door of the theater. A young boy, in a moment he will remember for the rest of his life, shyly offers him a program. The president accepts it with a smile. Now rejoined by bodyguard John Parker, the Lincolns and their guests climb the stairs leading to their box. Onstage, the actors are more than aware that the audience is in a foul mood. Having bought tickets in hopes of seeing Lincoln and Grant, the theatergoers had monitored the state box, only to find that neither was in house.

So when Lincoln finally arrives, there is relief onstage. Laura Keene ad-libs a line that refers to Lincoln, making the audience turn toward the back of the theater in order to witness his appearance. William Withers, the orchestra director who had a drink with John Wilkes Booth less than an hour ago, immediately stops the show's music and instructs the band to perform "Hail to the Chief."

The audience members rise to their feet and cheer, making a noise that Withers can only describe as "breathtaking." Lincoln does not seek out such adulation. Indeed, he has "an almost morbid dread" of causing a scene. But he works the crowd for full effect, allowing Rathbone and Harris to enter the state box first, followed by Mary. Then Lincoln strides forth so the crowd can see him. As patriotic cheering fills the house, he honors his constituents by standing at the edge of the box and bowing twice.

Only when the applause dies down does Lincoln ease into the rocking chair on the left side of the box. A curtain partially shields him from the audience, giving him privacy should he decide to nod off and take a nap. The crowd can see him only if he leans forward and pokes his head over the ledge; otherwise he is entirely invisible to everyone in the theater, except for those in the state box and the actors onstage.

Lincoln takes advantage of the privacy, reaching out for Mary's hand and holding it lovingly. She blushes at such scandalous behavior. "What will Miss Harris make of my hanging on to you so?" she giggles to her husband.

"She will think nothing about it," he replies, squeezing her hand but not letting go.

∽

Behind Lincoln, a single door leads into the state box. On the other side of the door is a narrow unlit hallway. At the end of the hallway is yet another door. This is the only route to and from the state box, and it is John Parker's job to pull up a chair and sit in front of this door, making sure that no one goes in or out.

But on the night of April 14, 1865, as Abraham Lincoln relaxes in his rocking chair and laughs out loud for the first time in months, John Parker gets thirsty. He is bored, and he can't see the play. Taltavul's saloon calls to him. Pushing his chair against the wall, he leaves the door to the state box unguarded and wanders outside. Footman Charles Forbes is taking a nap in the driver's seat of Lincoln's carriage, oblivious to the fog and drizzle.

"How about a little ale?" Parker asks, knowing that Forbes will be an eager drinking buddy. The two walk into Taltavul's and make themselves comfortable. The show won't be over for two more hours—plenty of time to have a couple beers and appear perfectly sober when the Lincolns need them again.

President Abraham Lincoln's only bodyguard, a man with a career-long history of inappropriate and negligent behavior, has left his post for the last time. Incredibly, he will never be punished for this gross dereliction of duty.

## CHAPTER THIRTY-SEVEN

---

FRIDAY, APRIL 14, 1865
WASHINGTON, D.C.
8:45 P.M.

Less than two hours to go.

John Wilkes Booth summarizes the final details with his co-conspirators as the Lincolns settle into their seats. Though Lewis Powell checked out of his hotel room hours earlier, the four men meet outside the Herndon House because of its close proximity to Ford's. With the exception of Atzerodt, each man is on horseback. Though he has been drinking steadily on and off all day, Booth is thinking and acting clearly. None of the co-conspirators has any cause to doubt him.

First, and most important, Booth tells them, the precise time of the president's assassination will be ten-fifteen P.M. Unlike the night before, when the assassination plans had a haphazard quality, tonight's events are timed to the minute. Shows at Ford's usually start promptly. If that's the case, then Harry Hawk will be alone onstage, delivering his punch line, at precisely ten-fifteen.

Second, Booth tells them, the murders of Seward and Johnson must also take place at ten-fifteen. The precision is vital. There can be no advance warning or alarm to the intended targets. The attacks must be a complete surprise. Booth hopes to create the illusion that Washington, D.C., is a hotbed of assassins, resulting in the sort of mass chaos that will make it easier for him and his men to escape. With officials looking everywhere for the killers, on streets filled with bonfires and spontaneous parades and hordes of drunken revelers, blending in to the bedlam should be as simple as staying calm.

Next comes the list of assignments. The job of murdering of Secretary of State Seward will be a two-man affair, with Lewis Powell and David Herold now working together. Powell will be the man who actually walks up to the door, finds a way to enter the house, and commits the crime. The ruse that will get him in the door is a fake bottle of medication, which Powell will claim was sent by Seward's physician.

Herold's role is to assist in the getaway. He knows Washington's back alleys and shortcuts and will guide Powell, who knows little about the city, to safety. During the murder, Herold must wait outside and hold their horses. Once Powell exits the house, the two men will gallop across town by a roundabout method in order to confuse anyone trying to give chase. Then they will leave town via the Navy Yard Bridge and rendezvous in the Maryland countryside.

As for George Atzerodt, he will act alone. Killing Vice President Andrew Johnson does not look to be a difficult task. Though Johnson is a vigorous man, he is known to be unguarded and alone most of the time. Atzerodt is to knock on the door of his hotel room and shoot him when he answers. Atzerodt will also escape Washington via the Navy Yard Bridge, then gallop into Maryland to meet up with the others. From there, Atzerodt's familiarity with smugglers' trails will allow him to guide the men into the Deep South.

Once the plans are finalized, Booth will head for Ford's. There he will bide his time, making sure the theater's entries and exits are unguarded, that the secret backstage passageways are clear, and that his horse is ready and waiting.

❧

Booth clears his throat just before they ride off in their different directions. He tells them about the letter he wrote to the *National Intelligencer*, implicating all of them in this grand triple assassination. The message is clear: there is no going back. If the men object to Booth outing them, there is no historical record to show it.

Booth looks over his gang. These four unlikely men are about to change the course of history, just as surely as Grant or Lincoln or Lee or any of the hundreds of thousands of men who died during the Civil War. They are now ninety minutes away from becoming the most wanted men in all of the world.

He wishes them good luck, then spurs his horse and trots off to Ford's.

# CHAPTER THIRTY-EIGHT

FRIDAY, APRIL 14, 1865
WASHINGTON, D.C.
9:30 P.M.

Booth guides his mare into the alley behind Ford's. The night is quiet, save for the peals of laughter coming from inside the theater. He dismounts and shouts for Ned Spangler to come hold his horse. The sceneshifter appears at the back door, visibly distressed about the possibility of missing an all-important stage cue. Booth doesn't care. He demands that Spangler come outside and secure the animal. The last thing Booth needs is for his escape to be thwarted by a runaway mare.

Spangler, completely unaware of the assassination plot, insists that he can't do the job. Booth, ever persuasive, insists. The unshaven, heavy-lidded stagehand weakens but does not capitulate. His employment is contingent on moving the right scenes at the right time. He is willing to do anything for a great actor such as Booth—anything but lose his job. Leaving Booth in the alley, Spangler dashes back into the theater and returns with Joseph Burroughs, a young boy who does odd jobs at Ford's and goes by the nickname "Peanut John." Booth hands Peanut John the reins and demands that he remain at the back door, holding the horse, until he returns. The boy must not leave that spot for any reason.

Peanut John, hoping that Booth will give him a little something for the effort, agrees. He sits on the stone step and shivers in the damp night air, his fist clutched tightly around those reins.

Booth slides into the theater. The sound of the onstage actors speaking their lines fills the darkened backstage area. He speaks in a hush as he removes his riding gloves, making a show of saying hello to the cast and crew, most of whom he knows well. His eyes scrutinize the layout, memorizing the location of every stagehand and prop, not wanting anything to get in the way of his exit.

There is a tunnel beneath the stage, crossing from one side to the other. Booth checks to make sure that nothing clutters the passage. Nobody guesses for an instant that he is checking out escape routes. When he reaches the far side, Booth exits Ford's through yet another backstage door. This one leads to an alley, which funnels down onto Tenth Street.

There's no one there.

In one short dash through Ford's Theatre, Booth has learned that his escape route is not blocked, that nobody is loitering in the alley who could potentially tackle him or otherwise stop him from getting away, and that the cast and crew think it's the most normal thing in the world for him to stroll into and out of the theater.

And, indeed, no one questions why he's there nor finds it even remotely suspicious.

∽

Feeling very pleased with himself, Booth pops in Taltavul's for a whiskey. He orders a whole bottle, then sits down at the bar. Incredibly, Lincoln's bodyguard is sipping a large tankard of ale just a few feet away.

Booth smiles as he pours water into his whiskey, then raises the glass in a toast to himself.

*What am I about to do? Can I really go through with this?*

He pushes the doubts from his head. *We are at war. This is not murder. You will become immortal.*

At ten P.M. Booth double-checks to make sure John Parker is still drinking at the other end of the bar. Then, leaving the nearly full whiskey bottle on the bar, he softly lowers his glass and walks back to Ford's.

# CHAPTER THIRTY-NINE

———

Friday, April 14, 1865
Washington, D.C.
10:00 p.m.

The third act is under way. Soon the play will be over, and Lincoln can get back to the White House. Meanwhile, the unheated state box has gotten chilly. Abraham Lincoln drops Mary's hand as he rises to put on his overcoat, tailored in a black wool specially for his oversized frame by Brooks Brothers. The silk lining is decorated with an eagle clutching a banner in its beak. The words on the streamer are Lincoln's unspoken manifesto, and every time he slips on the coat he is reminded of his mission. "One country, one destiny," it reads, quite simply.

Sitting back down in the horsehair rocker, Lincoln shifts his gaze from the performers directly below him. He pushes back the privacy curtain, then leans forward over the railing to look down and to the left, at the audience.

Lincoln lets go of the curtain and returns his attention to *Our American Cousin*.

It is seven minutes after ten. At the exact same moment, John Wilkes Booth strolls through the front door of Ford's—heart racing, whiskey on his breath, skin clammy to the touch. He is desperately trying to appear calm and cool. Always a man of manners, Booth takes off his hat and holds it with one hand. When ticket taker John

Buckingham makes a joke of letting him in for free, "courtesy of the house," Booth notices the bulge in Buckingham's lip and asks if he has any extra tobacco. Like so many other minor theater employees, Buckingham is in awe of Booth's celebrity. Not only does he hand over a small plug of tobacco, he also summons the courage to ask if he might introduce Booth to some close friends who happen to be at the show. "Later," Booth promises with a wink.

Buckingham notes the deathly pallor on Booth's face and how incredibly nervous the normally nonchalant actor seems to be. As Booth walks off, Buckingham's fellow Ford's employee Joseph Sessford points out that Booth has been in and out of the theater all day. "Wonder what he's up to?" Sessford mutters to Buckingham. They watch as Booth climbs the staircase to the dress circle, which accesses the hallway to the state box. But neither man thinks Booth's unusual behavior merits closer scrutiny. They watch him disappear up the stairs and then once again return their attention to the front door and to the patrons late in returning from intermission.

∞

At the top of the stairs, Booth enters the dress circle lobby. He is now inside the darkened theater, standing directly behind the seats of the second-level audience. He hums softly to himself to calm his nerves. In hopes of increasing the theater's capacity for this special performance, Ford's management has placed extra chairs in this corridor, and now Booth walks past two Union officers sitting in those seats. They recognize the famous actor and then turn their focus back to the play. They make no move to stop him, because they have no reason to.

Booth approaches the door leading into the state box. It is attended by a White House messenger but not a pistol-packing bodyguard. He sees the chair where John Parker should be sitting and breathes a sigh of relief that the bodyguard is still in the saloon. Handing the messenger one of his calling cards, Booth steps through the doorway without a question.

In the theater below, a young girl who came to the theater hoping to see Lincoln has spent the night staring up at the state box, waiting for him to show his face. Now she is awed by the sight of John Wilkes Booth, the famous and dashing actor, standing in the shadows above her. At the same time, her heart leaps as Lincoln moves his gaze from the stage to the audience, once again poking his head out over the railing. Finally, with the play almost over, she has seen the president! She turns to the man next to her, Taltavul's owner, Jim Ferguson, and grins at her good fortune.

She turns to get another glimpse of Booth, but by then he has already pushed through the door and now stands in the darkened hallway leading into the state box. He is completely alone. If he wants, he can go back out the door and get on with his life as if nothing has happened. The letter boasting of his deed has not yet been sent. Other than the other members of the conspiracy, no one will be the wiser. But if he walks forward down the hallway, then through the rear door of Lincoln's box, his life will change forever.

Booth has a head full of whiskey and a heart full of hate. He thinks of the Confederate cause and Lincoln's promise to give slaves the vote. And then Booth remembers that no one can put a stop to it but him. He is the one man who can, and will, make a difference. There will be no going back.

Earlier that day Booth spied a wooden music stand in the state box. He now jams it into the side of the door leading to the corridor. The music stand has become a dead bolt, and Booth double-checks to make sure it is lodged firmly against the wooden door frame. This seals the door shut from the inside. When he is done, the door might as well be locked, so perfect is his blockade. It's impossible to push open from the other side. No one in the theater can get in to stop him.

Booth then creeps down the hallway. Booth's second act of preparation that afternoon was using a pen knife to carve a very small peephole in the door of the state box. Now he looks through that hole to get a better view of the president.

∽

As Booth already knows, the state box is shaped like a parallelogram. The walls to the left and right of Lincoln slant inward. Booth sees that Clara Harris and Major Rathbone sit along the wall to his far right, at an angle to the stage, and the Lincolns sit along the railing. The Lincolns look out directly onto the stage, while Clara and her beau must turn their heads slightly to the right to see the show—if they look directly forward they will be gazing at Mary and Abraham Lincoln in profile.

But it is not their view of Lincoln that matters. What matters is that Booth, through the peephole, is staring right at the back of Lincoln's head. He can hear the players down below, knowing that in a few short lines Harry Hawk's character Asa Trenchard will be alone, delivering his "sockdologizing old man-trap" line.

That line is Booth's cue—and just ten seconds away.

Booth presses his black hat back down onto his head, then removes the loaded Deringer from his coat pocket and grasps it in his right fist. With his left hand, he slides the long, razor-sharp Bowie knife from its sheath.

Booth takes a deep breath and softly pushes the door open with his knife hand. The box is dimly lit from the footlights down below. He can see only faces. No one knows he's there. He presses his body against the wall, careful to stay in the shadows while awaiting his cue. Abraham Lincoln's head pokes over the top of his rocking chair, just four short feet in front of Booth; then once again he looks down and to the left, at the audience.

"You sockdologizing old man-trap" booms out through the theater.

The audience explodes in laughter.

# CHAPTER FORTY

FRIDAY, APRIL 14, 1865
WASHINGTON, D.C.
10:15 P.M.

A few blocks away, someone knocks hard on the front door of the "Old Clubhouse," the home of Secretary of State William Seward. The three-story brick house facing Lafayette Park, across the street from the White House, took that name from its day as the headquarters of the elite Washington Club. Tragedy paid a visit to the building in 1859, when a congressman shot his mistress's husband on a nearby lawn. The husband, Philip Barton Key, was a United States attorney and the son of Francis Scott Key, who wrote "The Star-Spangled Banner." Key's body was carried inside the club, where he passed away in a first-floor parlor.

That tragedy, however, will pale in comparison with what will happen in the next ten minutes.

There is another sharp knock, even though it's been only a few seconds since the first one. This time the pounding is more insistent. Secretary Seward does not hear it, for he is sleeping upstairs, his medication causing him to drift between consciousness and unconsciousness. William Bell, a young black servant in a pressed white coat, hurries to the entryway.

"Yes, sir?" he asks, opening the door and seeing an unfamiliar face.

A handsome young man with long, thick hair stares back from the porch. He wears an expensive slouch hat and stands a couple inches over six feet. His jaw is awry on the left, as if it was badly broken and then healed improperly. "I have medicine from Dr. Verdi," he says in an Alabama drawl, holding up a small vial.

"Yes, sir. I'll take it to him," Bell says, reaching for the bottle.

"It has to be delivered personally."

Bell looks at him curiously. Secretary Seward's physician had visited just an hour ago. Before leaving, he'd administered a sedative and insisted that there be no more visitors tonight. "Sir, I can't let you go upstairs. I have strict orders—"

"You're talking to a white man, boy. This medicine is for your master and, by God, you're going to give it to him."

When Bell protests further, Lewis Powell pushes past him, saying, "Out of my way, nigger. I'm going up."

Bell simply doesn't know how to stop the intruder.

∽

Powell starts climbing the steps from the foyer to the living area. Bell is a step behind at all times, pleading forgiveness and politely asking that Powell tread more softly. The sound of the southerner's heavy work boots on the wooden steps echoes through the house. "I'm sorry I talked rough to you," Bell says sheepishly.

"That's all right," Powell sighs, pleased that the hardest part of the plot is behind him. He feared he wouldn't gain access to the Seward home and would botch his part of the plan. The next step is locating Seward's bedroom.

Out front, in the shadow of a tree across the street, David Herold holds their horses, prepared for the escape.

∽

But now the secretary's son Frederick stands at the top of the stairs in a dressing gown, blocking Powell's path. He was in bed with his wife, but the sound of Powell's boots woke him. Young Seward, fresh off a heady day that saw him represent his father at Lincoln's cabinet meeting, demands to know Powell's business.

Politely and deferentially, Powell holds up the medicine vial and swears that Dr. Verdi told him to deliver it to William Seward and William Seward only.

Seward takes one look at Powell and misjudges him as a simpleton. Rather than argue, he walks into his father's bedroom to see if he is awake.

This is the break the assassin is looking for. Now he knows exactly which room belongs to the secretary of state. He grows excited, eager to get the job done as quickly as possible. He can feel the revolver stuffed inside his waistband.

Frederick Seward returns. "He's sleeping. Give it to me."

"I was ordered to give it to the secretary."

"You cannot see Mr. Seward. I am his son and the assistant secretary of state. Go back and tell the doctor that I refused to let you go into the sickroom, because Mr. Seward was sleeping."

"Very well, sir," says Powell, handing Frederick the vial. "I will go."

As Frederick Seward accepts the vial, Powell turns and takes three steps down the stairs. Suddenly he turns. He sprints back up to the landing, drawing a navy revolver. He levels the gun, curses, and pulls the trigger.

But the gun jams. Frederick Seward will later tell police he thought he was a dead man. Frederick cries out in fear and pain, throwing up his arms to defend himself. He has the advantage of standing one step higher than Powell but only for a second. The two men grapple as Powell leaps up onto the landing and then uses the butt of his gun to pistol-whip Frederick. Finally, Frederick Seward is knocked unconscious. His body makes a horrible thud as he collapses to the floor, his skull shattered in two places, gray brain matter trickling out through the gashes, blood streaming down his face.

"Murder, murder, murder!" cries William Bell from the ground floor. He sprints out the front door and into the night, screaming at the top of his lungs.

∽

Across the street, David Herold holds the two getaway horses. Bell's cries are sure to bring soldiers and police to the house within minutes. Suddenly, the long list of reasons why Herold wants to be part of the

Lincoln conspiracy are forgotten. He panics. He ties Powell's horse to a tree, spurs his own mount, and gallops down Fifteenth Street.

Back inside the Seward home, Lewis Powell isn't done. He pounds on Frederick's head without mercy, blood spattering the walls and his own hands and face. The beating is so savage that Powell's pistol literally falls to pieces in his hands. Only then does he stand up straight and begin walking toward the secretary of state's bedroom.

# CHAPTER FORTY-ONE

---

Friday, April 14, 1865
Washington, D.C.
10:15 p.m.

The commotion in the hallway and the sound of a body dropping heavily to the hardwood floor have alerted twenty-year-old Fanny Seward to the intrusion. The daughter of the secretary of state is clad only in a nightdress and has been sitting at the foot of her father's bed, trying to coax him to sleep. Also inside the room is Sergeant George Robinson, sent by the army to watch over Seward. Now Private Robinson pushes his full weight against the door, even as the assassin tries to fight his way in. Soon Lewis Powell forces open the door and slashes at Robinson with his Bowie knife, cutting the soldier's forehead to the bone and almost putting out an eye. As Robinson crumples to the ground, Fanny Seward places herself between Powell and her father. "Please don't kill him," she begs, terrified. "Please, please don't kill him."

Secretary Seward then awakens on the bed. Something about the word "kill" jars him from his slumber.

Powell punches Fanny Seward hard in the face, instantly knocking her unconscious. A split second later he is on the bed, plunging his knife downward into Seward's neck and shoulders.

The room is pitch-black, save for the sliver of light from the open door. Powell's first thrust misses, making a hollow thud as it slams into the headboard. Seward desperately tries to roll away from his attacker and squeeze down into the gap between the mattress and the wall.

He doesn't succeed. Powell kneels over him, stabbing Seward again and again and again. The secretary wears a splint on his broken jaw, which, luckily, deflects the knife away from the jugular vein, but it does little to protect the rest of his skull. The right side of his face is sliced away from the bone and now hangs like a flap. Blood jets from three deep punctures in his neck, drenching his now-useless bandages, his nightdress, and the white bedsheets and spattering all over Powell's torso.

The assassin is almost finished. Powell brings up his knife for one final killer blow. But at that exact moment, Seward's son Augustus enters the room. He is thirty-nine, a decorated graduate of West Point and a career army officer. He has fought in the Mexican War, battled the Apache, and seen action in the Civil War. Never once has he been injured. But now, that changes. Powell leaps at August Seward, stabbing him seven times. In the midst of the attack, Private Robinson staggers to his feet and rejoins the fight. For his trouble, Robinson is stabbed four more times.

∽

Powell is finally exhausted. Lying in front of him are four human beings, all of them still alive. But Powell doesn't know that. He steps over Fanny's limp body and races from the room, still clutching his knife. At that very moment, State Department messenger Emerick Hansell arrives at the Seward home on official business. He sees Powell, covered with blood, running down the steps and turns to flee for his life. But Powell catches him, stabbing the courier just above the fourth vertebrae. Powell is in such a hurry, fortunately, that he pulls the knife back out before it can go any deeper, thus sparing Hansell's life.

"I'm mad! I'm mad!" Powell screams as he runs into the night, hoping to scare off anyone who might try to stop him.

He is, however, anything but mad. Powell is as lucid as he is powerful. He now turns all his focus to the getaway. With adrenaline coursing through his veins, his senses heightened, and his broad shoulders aching from fists rained down upon him in the fight, he hurls the blood-covered knife into the gutter. He then looks right and left into the darkness for David Herold and their getaway horses. Seeing nothing, he listens for a telltale clip-clop of approaching horseshoes.

"Murder! Murder!" William Bell cries from the porch, risking his life by chasing after Powell. Soldiers come running from a nearby sentry box. Powell sees his horse now, tied to the tree where Herold left it. Realizing he has been betrayed, Powell feels his heart sink. He knows that without Herold he will be lost on the streets of Washington. Still, he can't very well just stand around. He needs to get moving. Powell unties the horse and mounts up. He has the good sense to wipe the blood and sweat from his face with a handkerchief. Then, instead of galloping away, he kicks his heels gently into the horse's flanks and trots casually down Fifteenth Street, trailed all the while by William Bell and his shouts of "Murder!" But instead of stopping him, the unsuspecting soldiers ignore the black man and run right past Powell.

After a block and a half, Bell falls behind. He eventually returns to the Seward home, where four gravely injured men and one woman lie. Incredibly, they will all recover. But this horrific night will haunt them for the rest of their lives.

Lewis Powell trots his horse toward the darkness on the edge of town. There he hides in a field and wonders if he will ever find a way out of Washington. Powell's thoughts then turn to President Lincoln and Vice President Johnson. They should be dead by now.

# CHAPTER FORTY-TWO

FRIDAY, APRIL 14, 1865
WASHINGTON, D.C.
10:15 P.M.

As John Wilkes Booth tiptoes into the state box and Lewis Powell knocks on William Seward's front door, George Atzerodt, the would-be assassin of Vice President Andrew Johnson, is drinking hard, late for his date with destiny.

If any man in Washington has incurred the wrath of the Confederacy, it is Johnson, the former governor of Tennessee, whom many southerners consider a rank traitor. Johnson's bitter words are seldom compatible with Lincoln's. So it is no surprise that his views on punishing the South stand in stark contrast to Lincoln's lenience. "And what shall be done with the leaders of the rebel host? I know what I would do if I were president. I would arrest them as traitors, I would try them as traitors, and, by the Eternal, I would hang them as traitors," Johnson shouted from the steps of the War Department as recently as Monday night.

Like Johnson, Atzerodt the carriage painter is staying at Kirkwood House, on the corner of Pennsylvania Avenue and Twelfth Street, four blocks from the White House and just one block from Ford's Theatre. He has passed the time aimlessly since his meeting with Booth and the other conspirators, drawing attention to himself through the simple act of trying not to draw attention to himself.

At nine-thirty he visits Naylor's stable on E Street to pick up his horse. The owner knows George Atzerodt and his friend David Herold and does not care for either of them. Nevertheless, when a nervous, sweating Atzerodt asks if he'd like to get a drink, Naylor answers with a quick "Don't mind if I do." He is concerned about Herold, who rented a horse from him earlier that day and is long overdue. Naylor hopes that Atzerodt will disclose his friend's location after a drink or two.

They leave Atzerodt's mare and walk to the bar of the Union Hotel. Atzerodt, whom Naylor suspects has been drinking for some time, orders a stiff whiskey; Naylor chugs a tankard of ale. Atzerodt pays. They return to the stable after just one round, with Naylor none the wiser about Herold's location.

"Your friend is staying out very late with his horse," Naylor finally prods. Atzerodt has just handed him a five-dollar tip for boarding his horse.

"He'll be back after a while," Atzerodt glibly replies as he mounts the mare.

But Atzerodt is too wasted on alcohol to ride a straight line. He almost falls out of the saddle when the mare takes a sudden turn. On a hunch, Naylor decides to follow Atzerodt on foot. The trail, however, is only a block long. Atzerodt dismounts and ties the horse at a hitching post in front of Kirkwood House. Naylor waits across the street, just out of sight. When Atzerodt walks back out a few minutes later and trots the mare over toward Ford's Theatre, Naylor gives up the surveillance and returns to his stable.

∽

Andrew Johnson, meanwhile, is behaving very much like a man waiting to be summoned. He eats an early dinner alone. He turns down a last-minute invitation to attend *Our American Cousin*. His assistant is out for the night, and Johnson has no one to talk with. So he goes up to his room and lies down on his bed, fully clothed, as if some great incident is about to occur and he needs to be ready to spring into action on a moment's notice. Johnson is a boorish man. Largely uneducated, he learned to read and write late in his life. A tailor by trade, he entered politics in his twenties and worked his way up to the Senate. He owes a lot to President Lincoln, who first appointed him the military governor of Tennessee and then chose him to run on the vice presidential ticket after Lincoln asked Hannibal Hamlin of Maine to step down. Hamlin was a hard-core northerner and Lincoln needed a southern presence on the ticket.

Up until this point, Johnson has had no power at all. He is simply a figurehead.

∽

At ten-fifteen George Atzerodt is back inside Kirkwood House, getting thoroughly smashed in the bar. Truth be told, even more than when he tried to bow out a few days earlier, the German-born carriage painter wants no part of murder. A few floors above him, Johnson lies alone in his room. In his lifetime he will suffer the ignominy of impeachment and endure the moniker of "worst president in history." Andrew Johnson will not, however, suffer the far worse fate of death at the hand of an assassin. For that, Johnson can thank the effects of alcohol, as a now very drunk George Atzerodt continues to raise his glass.

# CHAPTER FORTY-THREE

FRIDAY, APRIL 14, 1865
WASHINGTON, D.C.
10:15 P.M.

John Wilkes Booth takes a bold step out of the shadows, Deringer clutched in his right fist and knife in his left. He extends his arm and aims for the back of Abraham Lincoln's head. No one sees him. No one knows he is there.

Booth squeezes the trigger. Unlike the crazed Richard Lawrence, whose pistols misfired when he attempted to assassinate Andrew Jackson, Booth feels his gun kick. The ball launches down the barrel as the audience guffaws at the play. Abraham Lincoln has chosen this precise moment to lean forward and turn his head to the left for another long look down into the audience. A half second later, he would have been leaning so far forward that the ball would have missed his skull completely. But the president is not so lucky. The man who has worried and fretted and bullied America back from the brink of disaster, holding fast to his faith in the Union at a time when lesser men argued that it should be dissolved, feels a split second snap of pain—and then nothing at all.

"The ball entered through the occipital bone about one inch to the left of the median line and just above the left lateral sinus, which it opened," the autopsy will read. "It then penetrated the dura matter, passed through the left posterior lobe of the cerebrum, entered the left lateral ventricle and lodged in the white matter of the cerebrum just above the anterior portion of the left corpus striatum."

The president's calvarium—or skullcap—will be removed with a saw. A surgeon will probe the exposed brain before slicing into it with a scalpel, using the path of coagulated blood to trace the trajectory of the ball. This will show that the ball entered behind the left ear and traveled diagonally across the brain, coming to rest above the right eye.

Yet the autopsy will be inconclusive. Four different doctors will examine the body. Each will have a different conclusion about what happened once the sphere of Britannia metal poked a neat round hole in Lincoln's skull and then pushed fragments of that bone deep into Lincoln's brain as it traveled precisely seven and a half inches before plowing to a stop in the dense gray matter.

∽

At ten-fifteen on the night of April 14, 1865, President Abraham Lincoln slumps forward in his rocking chair. Mary Lincoln, lost in the play until this very instant, stops laughing. Major Henry Reed Rathbone snaps his head around at the sound of gunfire—a sound he knows all too well from the battlefield. He's had his back to the door, but in an instant he's on his feet, striking a defensive pose.

John Wilkes Booth drops the Deringer and switches the knife to his right hand. Just in time, for Major Rathbone sets aside his own safety and vaults across the small space. Booth raises the knife to shoulder level and brings it down in a hacking motion. Rathbone throws his left arm up in a defensive reflex and instantly feels the knife cut straight down through skin and biceps to the bone.

Booth moves quickly. He steps to the front of the box, ignoring a stricken Mary Lincoln. "Freedom!" he bellows down to the audience, though in all the laughter and the growing confusion as to why the cast has added the sound of gunfire to the scene, his words are barely heard. Harry Hawk stands alone on stage, staring up at the state box with growing concern.

Booth hurls his body over the railing. Up until this point, he has performed every single aspect of the assassination perfectly. But now he misjudges the thickness of the massive United States flag decorating the front of the box. He means to hold on to the railing with one

hand as he vaults, throwing his feet up and over the edge, then landing on the stage like a conquering hero.

This sort of leap is actually his specialty. Booth is famous among
the theatrical community for his unrehearsed gymnastics, sometimes
inserting jumps and drops into Shakespeare plays on a whim. During
one memorable performance of *Macbeth*, his fall to the stage was several feet longer than the fall from the state box.

But Booth's right spur gets tangled in the flag's folds. Instead of a
gallant two-footed landing on the stage, Booth topples heavily from
the state box. He drops to the boards awkwardly, left foot and two
hands braced in a bumbling attempt to catch his fall.

The fibula of Booth's lower left leg, a small bone that bears little
weight, snaps two inches above the ankle. The fracture is complete,
dividing the bone into two neat pieces. If not for the tightness of
Booth's boot, which forms an immediate splint, the bone would poke
through the skin.

Now Booth lies on the stage in front of a nearly packed house. His
leg is broken. He holds a blood-smeared dagger in his right hand. The
sound of gunfire has just ricocheted around Ford's. Major Rathbone is
bleeding profusely from a severe stab wound. And just above him,
slumped forward as if very drunk or very asleep, the president of the
United States is unconscious.

∽

Yet still nobody knows what happened. James Ford steps out of the
box office and thinks Booth is pulling some crazy stunt to get attention. Observers in the audience have heard the pop and are amazed
by the sudden appearance of a famous matinee idol making a cameo
on the stage right before their very eyes—perhaps adding some comi-
cal whimsy to this very special evening. Harry Hawk still holds center
stage, his head turned toward Booth, wondering why in the world he
would intrude on the performance.

Time stops for a second—but only one.

Then the assassin takes charge. "Booth dragged himself up on one
knee," Hawk will later remember, "and was slashing that long knife
around him like one who was crazy. It was then, I am sure, I heard him
say, 'The South shall be free!' I recognized Booth as he regained his

feet and came toward me, waving his knife. I did not know what he had done or what his purpose might be. I did simply what any man would have done—I ran."

Booth scurries to his feet and limps off the stage, "with a motion," observes one spectator, "like the hopping of a bull frog."

"Stop that man!" Major Rathbone screams from above.

"Won't somebody please stop that man!" Clara Harris echoes.

"What is the matter?" cries a voice from the audience.

"The president has been shot!" she shouts back.

The reverie is shattered, and with it all the joy of Washington's postwar celebration. The theater explodes in confusion. In an instant, the audience is on its feet. It is a scene of utter chaos, "a hell of all hells." Men climb up and over the seats, some fleeing toward the exits while others race to the stage, hoping to climb up into the box and be part of the action. Women faint. Children are trapped in the panic. "Water!" some yell, tending to the collapsed.

A former congressman yells something far more pointed: "Hang the scoundrel!"

Meanwhile, Booth passes within inches of leading lady Laura Keene as he limps off the stage. William Withers, the orchestra leader with whom he had a drink just hours earlier, stands between Booth and the stage door. Withers is paralyzed with fear, but Booth assumes he is intentionally blocking the way and slashes at him, "the sharp blade ripping through the collar of my coat, penetrating my vest and under garments, and inflicting a flesh wound in my neck," Withers will later testify.

Only one man is bold enough to give chase. Set carpenter Jake Ritterspaugh and Booth reach the stage door at the very same time. Booth thrusts the knife blade at him. Ritterspaugh leaps back. And in that instant, Booth is gone, squeezing through the door and hauling himself up into the saddle.

Rather than give Peanut John the shiny nickel the boy had hoped for, Booth kicks him hard and bludgeons him with the butt of his knife.

"He kicked me! He kicked me!" the boy moans, falling to the ground.

At the same instant, yet another spontaneous torchlight parade blocks Booth's getaway on Tenth Street. He swerves into the alley, spurs his horse down the cobblestones dividing two large brick buildings, and then turns onto F Street, completely avoiding the procession.

In an instant, John Wilkes Booth disappears into the night.

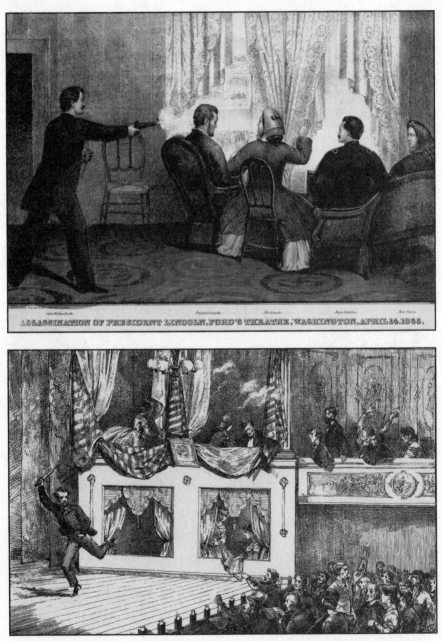

ASSASSINATION OF PRESIDENT LINCOLN, FORD'S THEATRE, WASHINGTON, APRIL 14.1865.

*Editorial illustrations depicting the assassination of President Lincoln*

# CHAPTER FORTY-FOUR

Friday, April 14, 1865
Washington, D.C.
10:20 P.M.

Booth slows the mare to a walk. Word is already spreading through Washington that the president has been shot. The news is shouted, breathlessly exclaimed, passed from citizen to citizen, bonfire to bonfire. People aren't racing away from Ford's, they're racing *to* Ford's, to see for themselves if these wild rumors are true. Victory marches turn into mobs of the curious and scared, determined to fight their way to the theater.

When a drunk shouts into the night, "I'm glad it happened!" a furious mob beats and kicks him unconscious, tearing off his clothes, and hauls his limp body to a lamppost for a lynching. Ironically, he will be rescued by the Union cavalry.

Now another troop of cavalry is summoned to Ford's and plunges recklessly through the throngs assembling outside. Inside, the crowd surges toward the stage, trapping small children in its midst, chanting all the while that Booth must be lynched. Laura Keene has the presence of mind to march to center stage and cry out for calm and sanity, but her words go unheeded. The crush against the stage is made worse as the news explodes into the street in front of Ford's Theatre. Passersby rush inside to see for themselves, some of them hoping that

Booth is still trapped inside but most just wanting a glimpse of the injured president.

Across town at Grover's Theatre, the patriotic celebration is in full swing. A young boy is reciting a poem when a man bursts into the theater and shouts that the president has been shot. As the crowd reacts in horror, a young soldier stands and yells for everyone to sit still. "It's a ruse of the pickpockets," he says, explaining that thieves spread such disinformation to fleece the crowd as people rush for the exit.

The six hundred theatergoers take their seats once again. The boy onstage exits, his poetry reading complete. But he is back just seconds later, struggling to control his voice as he shares the horrific news that President Lincoln has, indeed, been shot. Tad Lincoln, the president's twelve-year-old son, is in the audience with a White House staffer. Stunned, he returns to the White House, where he collapses into the arms of the doorkeeper, shouting, "They've killed Papa dead! They've killed Papa dead."

∽

Soon more bad news begins to spread: Secretary Seward has been assaulted in his bed.

At Rullman's Hotel, on Pennsylvania Avenue, the bartender shouts out the mournful news that Lincoln has been shot. Mike O'Laughlen, the would-be conspirator who stalked the Grants last night, drinks in the corner. He is drunk again but still coherent enough to know in an instant that Booth is the killer—and that he must get out of town before someone implicates him, too.

In front of the Willard Hotel, the stable foreman John Fletcher is still seething that David Herold hasn't return the roan he rented earlier. At that very moment, Herold trots past. "You get off that horse now!" Fletcher cries, springing out into the street and grabbing for the bridle. But Herold spurs the horse and gallops away. Acting quickly, Fletcher sprints back to his stable, saddles a horse, and races after him.

In the midst of all this, a lone rider galloping away from the chaos at Ford's would most certainly attract attention. So Booth guides the mare slowly up and down the streets and alleys of Washington, even as his veins course with adrenaline and euphoria, and pandemonium breaks out all around him. Despite his considerable celebrity, Booth blends in and proceeds unmolested through the streets. It is Friday night, after all, a time when Washington comes to life. There are plenty of men trotting horses through town. It's only when Booth finally nears the end of his three-mile journey to the Navy Yard Bridge that his fears about being caught force him to spur the horse and ride hard to freedom.

It is ten forty-five when Booth pulls back on the reins once again and canters up to the wooden drawbridge by the Navy Yard—almost thirty long minutes since the Deringer did its deadly job. Booth approaches like a man confident that his path will go unblocked. "Where are you going, sir?" cries the military sentry. His name is Silas T. Cobb, and his long and boring shift will be over at midnight. He notices the lather on the horse's flanks, a sign that it's been ridden hard.

"Home. Down in Charles," Booth replies.

"Didn't you know, my friend, that it is against the laws to pass here after nine o'clock?" Cobb is required to challenge anyone entering or exiting Washington, but the truth of the matter is that the war has ended and with it the formal restrictions on crossing the bridge after curfew. He wants no trouble, just to finish his shift in peace and get a good night's sleep.

"No," lies Booth. He explains that he's been waiting for the full moon to rise, so that he might navigate the darkened roads by night. And, indeed, a waning moon is rising at that very moment.

"I will pass you," Cobb sighs. "But I don't know I ought to."

"Hell, I guess there'll be no trouble about that," Booth shoots back. Ignoring the rule that horses be walked across the bridge, he trots the mare into the night.

Booth is barely across the Potomac when David Herold approaches Silas T. Cobb. He gives his name as just "Smith." Once again, after a brief discussion, Cobb lets him pass.

One more rider approaches Cobb that night. He is John Fletcher, the stable foreman who is following David Herold. Fletcher can clearly see Herold on the other side of the bridge, now disappearing into the Maryland night.

"You can cross," Cobb tells him, "but my orders say I can't let anyone back across the bridge until morning."

The Maryland countryside, with its smugglers and spies and illicit operatives, is the last place John Fletcher wants to spend the night. He turns his horse's reins back toward his stable, settling on the hope that Herold and the missing horse will one day make the mistake of riding back into Washington.

In fact, Fletcher will never see the horse again, for it will soon be shot dead, its body left to rot in the backwoods of Maryland—yet another victim of the most spectacular assassination conspiracy in the history of man.

# CHAPTER FORTY-FIVE

FRIDAY, APRIL 14, 1865
WASHINGTON, D.C.
10:20 P.M.

Lincoln's life is slipping away. Mary Lincoln lays her head to the president's breast as Major Rathbone uses his one good arm to yank the music stand from its notch in the doorway. Booth's knife missed a major artery by just one-third of an inch. Otherwise Rathbone would now be dead.

The major swings open the outer door of the state box. Dozens of unruly theatergoers fill the dress circle and try to fight their way into the state box. "Doctors only!" Rathbone shouts as blood drips down his arm and pools on the floor. The truth is that the major needs medical attention, but all eyes are on Lincoln.

"I'm bleeding to death!" Rathbone shouts as a twenty-three-year-old doctor, Charles Leale, fights his way forward. Dr. Leale came to the theater solely because he wanted to see Lincoln in person. Now he is the first physician to come upon the crime scene. Leale reaches out a hand and lifts Rathbone's chin so that he might look into his eyes and gauge his physical condition. Noting in an instant that Rathbone is quite obviously not bleeding to death, Dr. Leale turns his attention to Lincoln.

"Oh, Doctor," sobs Mary Lincoln as Leale slowly removes her from her husband's body. "Can he recover? Will you take charge of him?"

"I will do what I can," Dr. Leale says calmly. With a nod to the crowd of men who have followed him into the box, the young doctor makes it clear that Mary must be removed. She is ushered to a couch on the other side of the box, next to Clara Harris, who begins stroking her hand.

Leale asks for a lamp and orders that no one else be admitted to the state box except for physicians. Then he stands in front of the rocking chair, facing Lincoln's slumped head. He pushes the body upright, the head lolling back against the rocker. He can feel the slightest breath from Lincoln's nose and mouth, but Leale is reluctant to touch the body without making a preliminary observation. One thing, however, is quite clear: Lincoln is not dead.

Dr. Leale can't find any sign of injury. Onlookers light matches so that he can see better, and the call goes out for a lamp. The front of Lincoln's body shows no sign of physical violence, and the forward slumping indicates that the attack must have come from behind. Yet there's no visible entry wound or exit wound. If Dr. Leale didn't know better, he would swear that Lincoln simply dozed off and will awaken any minute.

"Put him on the floor," the doctor orders. Gently, ever so gently, Lincoln's long torso is lifted by men standing on both sides of the rocking chair and then lowered to the carpet.

⁂

Based on Major Rathbone's wounds, and the fact that he didn't hear any gunshot during the performance, Leale deduces that Lincoln was stabbed. He rolls the president on one side and carefully searches for a puncture wound, his fingers slipping along the skin, probing for a telltale oozing of blood. But he feels nothing, and when he pulls his hands away, they're completely clean.

He strips Lincoln to the waist and continues the search, cutting off the president's white shirt with a pocketknife. But his skin is milky white and smooth, with no sign of any harm. Leale lifts Lincoln's eyelids and examines the pupils. Finding clear evidence that the right eye's optic nerve has somehow been cut, he decides to reexamine. Perhaps Lincoln was stabbed in the back of the skull. Head wounds are notorious bleeders, so such a wound is unlikely, but there has to be some explanation.

Dr. Leale, more befuddled by the mystery with each passing moment, runs his hands through Lincoln's hair. This time they come back blood-red.

Alarmed, Leale examines the president's head a second time. Beneath the thick hair, just above and behind the left ear, hides a small blood clot. It's no bigger than the doctor's pinkie, but when he pulls his finger away, the sensation is like a cork being removed from a bottle. Blood flows freely from the wound, and Lincoln's chest suddenly rises and falls as pressure is taken from his brain.

Dr. Leale has been a practicing physician for all of two months, having just graduated from Bellevue Hospital Medical College. He wears an army uniform, as befitting a doctor who currently works in the Wounded Commissioned Officers' Ward at the U.S. Army's General Hospital in nearby Armory Square. The bulk of his medical education took place during the Civil War, so despite his short time as a practicing physician, he has seen more gunshot wounds than most doctors see in a lifetime. Yet he encountered those wounds in hospitals far removed from the battlefield, when the patients were in advanced stages of recovery. He has never performed the sort of critical life-saving procedures that take place immediately after an injury.

But now Dr. Leale somehow knows just what to do—and he does it well.

∽

Working quickly, Leale straddles Lincoln's chest and begins resuscitating the president, hoping to improve the flow of oxygen to the brain. He shoves two fingers down Lincoln's throat and presses down on the back of the tongue, just in case food or drink is clogged in the esophagus. As he does so, two other doctors who were in the audience arrive on the scene. Though far more experienced, army surgeon Dr. Charles Sabin Taft and Dr. Albert King defer to Dr. Leale. When he asks them to stimulate the blood flow by manipulating Lincoln's arms in an up-and-down, back-and-forth manner, they instantly kneel down and each

take an arm. Leale, meanwhile, presses hard on Lincoln's torso, trying to stimulate his heart.

Then, as Leale will one day tell an audience celebrating the one
hundredth anniversary of Lincoln's birth, he performs an act of great
and urgent intimacy: "I leaned forcibly forward directly over his body,
thorax to thorax, face to face, and several times drew in a long breath,
then forcibly breathed directly into his mouth and nostrils, which
expanded the lungs and improved his respirations."

Dr. Leale lies atop Lincoln, his lips locked with Lincoln's, offering
what looks to be a lover's kiss. The theater below is a madhouse. Men
in the box around him look on, recognizing that Leale is performing
a medical procedure, but struck by the awkward pose nonetheless.

Dr. Leale doesn't care. Every bit of his energy is poured into accom-
plishing the impossible task of saving Lincoln. Finally, he knows in his
heart that the procedure has worked. He will later recall, "After waiting a moment, I placed my ear over his thorax and found the action of
the heart improving. I arose to the erect kneeling posture, then watched
for a short time and saw that the president could continue independent
breathing and that instant death would not occur. I then announced
my diagnosis and prognosis."

But Dr. Leale does not utter the hopeful words the onlookers wish
to hear. They have seen the president breathe on his own. They know
that his heart is functioning. Clearly, they think the president might
survive.

Only Dr. Leale has seen the dull look in Lincoln's pupils, a sure
sign that his brain is no longer functioning. "His wound is mortal,"
Leale announces softly. "It is impossible for him to recover."

∽

A soldier vomits. Men remove their caps. Mary Lincoln sits just a few
feet away but is in too much shock to comprehend what's been said.
Someone hands Dr. Leale a dram of brandy and water, which he slowly
dribbles into Lincoln's mouth. The president's prominent Adam's apple
bobs as he swallows.

The pandemonium in the theater, meanwhile, has not diminished.
The frenzy and shouting are deafening. No one in the state box speaks
as Dr. Leale works on Lincoln, but its list of occupants has grown

larger and more absurd. With John Parker, Lincoln's bodyguard, still strangely missing, no one is blocking access to the little room. To one side, on the couch, the distraught Mary Lincoln is being comforted by Clara Harris. Major Rathbone drips blood on the carpet, trying to stanch the flow by holding tight to the injured arm. There are three doctors, a half dozen soldiers, and a small army of theater patrons who have battled their way into the box. And then, almost absurdly, the actress Laura Keene forces her way into their midst and kneels at Lincoln's side. She begs to be allowed to cradle Lincoln. Dr. Leale, somewhat stunned but knowing it can do no harm, agrees.

Keene lifts the president's head into her lap and calmly strokes his face. Before becoming an actress she worked for a time as a restorer of old paintings, so she is more than familiar with the world of art and sculpture. She knows that this moment is Michelangelo's *Pietà* come to life, with her as Mary and Lincoln as Christ. Surrounded on all sides by what can only be described as anarchy, Laura Keene nurtures the dying man. The war years have been hard on her—drink has made her face puffy, and the constant wartime barnstorming has done little to stop her slowly declining popularity. The chestnut-eyed actress with the long auburn hair knows that this moment will put her name in papers around the world, so there is more than a touch of self-indulgence in her actions. But Laura Keene is not maudlin or the slightest bit dramatic as Abraham Lincoln's blood and brains soak into the lap of her dress. Like everyone else in the state box, she is stunned. Just a few minutes before, the president of the United States had been a vibrant and larger-than-life presence. Now everything has changed.

# CHAPTER FORTY-SIX

The president of the United States cannot die on a dirty floor. No one knows how much longer he will live, but he must be moved. Dr. King suggests they move him to the White House, where he can pass the final moments of life in the comfort of his own bed. But Dr. Leale knows better than to attempt a bumpy carriage ride through Washington, D.C., particularly through panicked crowds that will necessitate the driver stopping and starting and turning quite suddenly. "He will be dead before we get there," Leale says firmly.

The young doctor agrees, however, that Lincoln should be resting in a bed, not on the floor. Dr. Taft sends a soldier to scour nearby boarding-houses for an empty room. Four other young soldiers are ordered to lift Lincoln back into the rocking chair and carry the president out of the theater.

But Dr. Leale overrules Taft. The logistics of carrying a rocking chair containing a man with very long legs borders on the absurd. Just getting down to the lobby involves navigating sharp angles, a narrow corridor, two small doorways, and a flight of stairs. A stretcher would be ideal, but none is available. Leale orders the four soldiers to stop gawking and get to work. They will lock their hands beneath the president and form a sling. Two will lift the torso, while two will carry the legs. They will transport Lincoln headfirst. Leale will walk backward, cradling Lincoln's head in his hands.

Laura Keene steps aside. She can't help but marvel at Lincoln's upper body, still possessing the lean musculature of the young wrestler renowned for feats of strength. The youthful power and appearance of his chest is in marked contrast to that famously weathered face. The only clue that this great body is actually dying is that his skin is pale and growing more so by the moment.

The four soldiers—John Corry, Jabes Griffiths, Bill Sample, and Jacob Soles of the Pennsylvania Light Artillery—now slip their hands under that torso and raise Lincoln to a sitting position. Dr. Leale, with help from the other two physicians, dresses the president in his frock coat and buttons it.

"Guards," barks Leale. "Clear the passage."

As if leading a processional, Laura Keene waits for the body to be lifted. She then marches out of the box, followed by the backward-walking Leale, the four soldiers, and Dr. King, who supports a shoulder, if only so he can remain a part of the action. Through the hallway, out into the dress circle, and down the stairs they travel. Mary Lincoln follows in their wake, stunned and shaky as she walks.

∽

Their progress is slow, for two reasons. The first is that theatergoers block the way, desperate for a peek—desperate to be able to say they saw Lincoln's corpse. The faithful make the sign of the cross and mumble a quiet prayer as Lincoln passes before their very eyes.

"Clear the way," Leale barks. Soldiers in the crowd respond, jumping forth to push back the mob. It becomes a wrestling match. Chairs are destroyed. Punches are thrown. Noses are bloodied. A Union officer finally draws his sword and threatens to cut down any man standing in Lincoln's path. This manages to quiet the crowd but only for an instant.

The second reason for the dawdling pace is that the bullet hole in Lincoln's head is clotting at an amazing rate. When this happens, Lincoln appears to be in obvious discomfort from increased pressure against his brain. So despite the anarchy all around him, Dr. Leale orders the processional halted every few feet. Then he slips his fore-finger into Lincoln's skull to clear the hole, bringing forth even more blood but taking pressure off the president's brain.

They finally reach the lobby but don't know where to go next. By now, soldiers have found the partition usually used to divide the state box. At seven feet long and three inches thick, it makes a perfect stretcher for Abraham Lincoln. His body is shifted onto the board.

Dr. Leale and the other two surgeons decide they will carry Lincoln into Taltavul's, right next door. A soldier is sent to clear the tavern. But he soon comes back with word that Lincoln will not be allowed inside—and for very good reason. Peter Taltavul is a patriot, a man who spent twenty-five years in the Marine Corps band. Of all the people in the crowd on this frenzied night, he is one of the few who has the foresight to understand the significance of the presidency and how the night's events will one day be viewed. "Don't bring him in here," Taltavul tells the soldier. "It shouldn't be said that the president of the United States died in a saloon."

But where should they bring him?

Leale orders that Lincoln be lifted and carried to the row houses across the street. There is an enormous crowd in front of Ford's. It will be almost impossible to clear a path through their midst, but it's vital that Leale get Lincoln someplace warm and clean, immediately. The pine stretcher is lifted and Lincoln's body is carried out into the cold, wet night, the procession lit by that murky yellow light from the tar torches. Lincoln's carriage, with its magnificent team of black chargers, is parked a few feet away.

Then his bodyguards arrive. Not John Parker, for the instant he heard that Lincoln was shot he vanished into the night, continuing his villainy. No, it is the Union Light Guard, otherwise known as the Seventh Independent Company of Ohio Volunteer Cavalry, that gallops to the rescue. These are the men who have served as Lincoln's bodyguards during his rides around the city and out to the Soldiers' Home. They raced over from their stables next to the White House when they heard about the shooting. Rather than dismount, they work with other soldiers on the scene to make a double-wide corridor from one side of Tenth Street to the other. Leale and the men carrying Lincoln make their way down Ford's granite front steps and onto the muddy road, still not knowing where they will finally be able to bring him but glad to be away from the chaos and frenzy of Ford's.

∽

Only more chaos awaits them in the street. The violent mob has swelled from dozens to hundreds in mere minutes, as people from all around Washington have sprinted to Ford's Theatre. Many are drunk. All are confused. And no one is in charge.

"Bring him in here," a voice shouts above the madness.

Henry S. Safford is a twenty-five-year-old War Department employee. He has toasted the Union victory every night since Monday, and tonight he was so worn out that he stayed in to rest. He was alone in his parlor, reading, when the streets below him exploded in confusion. When Safford stuck his head out the window to see what was happening, someone shouted the news that Lincoln had been shot. Safford raced downstairs and out into the crowd, but "finding it impossible to go further, as everyone acted crazy or mad," he retreated back to the steps of the Federal-style brick row house in which he rents a room from a German tailor named William Petersen. Safford stood on the porch and watched in amazement as Lincoln's failing body was conveyed out of Ford's. He saw the confusion on Dr. Leale's face as the contingent inched across Tenth Street, and witnessed the way Dr. Leale stopped every few feet and poked his finger into Lincoln's skull to keep the blood flowing. He saw Leale lifting his own head and scanning the street front, searching for someplace to bring Lincoln.

Now Safford wants to help.

"Put him in here," he shouts again.

Dr. Leale was actually aiming for the house next door, but a soldier had tried and found it locked. So they turn toward Safford. "This was done as quickly as the soldiers could make a pathway through the crowd," a sketch artist will remember later. Just moments earlier he had been so enthralled with the happy crowd in front of Ford's that he had impulsively grabbed a pad and begun drawing—"women with wide skirts and wearing large poke bonnets were as numerous as the men. . . . The scene was so unusual and inspiring."

But now he is sketching a melee and the sad scene of "the prostrate form of an injured man."

He will later say, "I recognized the lengthy form of the president by the flickering light of the torches, and one large gas lamp. The tarrying at the curb and the slow, careful manner in which he was carried across the street gave me ample time to make an accurate sketch. It was the most tragic and impressive scene I have ever witnessed."

∽

Leale and his stretcher bearers carry Lincoln up nine short, curved steps to the front door of the Petersen house. "Take us to your best room," he orders Safford. And though he is hardly the man to be making that decision, Safford immediately realizes that his own second-floor room will not do. He guides the group down to the spacious room of George and Huldah Francis, but it is locked. Safford leads them deeper into the house, to a room that is clearly not Petersen's finest—but that will have to do. He pushes open the door, which features a large glass window covered by a curtain, and sees that it is empty.

The room is that of William Clark, a twenty-three-year-old army clerk who is gone for the night. Clark is fastidious in his cleanliness, so at just under ten feet wide and eighteen feet long, furnished with four-poster bed, table, bureau, and chairs, the bedroom is a cramped though very neat space.

But Lincoln is much too big for the bed. Dr. Leale orders that the headboard be broken off, but it won't break. Instead, the president is laid down diagonally on the red, white, and blue bedspread. The lumpy mattress is filled with corn husks. His head points toward the door and his feet toward the wall. Ironically, John Wilkes Booth often rented this very room during the previous summer. In fact, as recently as three weeks ago, Booth lolled on the very bed in which Lincoln is now dying.

∽

Everyone leaves but the doctors and Mary Lincoln. She stares down at her husband, still wearing his boots, pants, and frock coat; there are two pillows under his head, and that bearded chin rests on his chest. Now and then he sighs involuntarily, giving her hope.

"Mrs. Lincoln, I must ask you to leave," Dr. Leale says softly.

Mary is like a child, so forlorn that she lacks the will to protest as others make her decisions for her. The first lady steps out of William Clark's rented room, into the long, dark hallway.

"Live," she pleads to her husband before she leaves. "You must live."

# CHAPTER FORTY-SEVEN

SATURDAY, APRIL 15, 1865
WASHINGTON, D.C.
MIDNIGHT TO DAWN

D r. Leale strips Lincoln's body. He, too, marvels at the definition of the muscles on the president's chest, shoulders, and legs. This is clearly the body of a man who has led a vigorous life. Dr. Leale searches the body for signs of another wound but finds none. The area around Lincoln's eyes and forehead is becoming swollen and black and blue, like a boxer's face after a tough fight.

Moving down the long and slender frame, Leale is disturbed to feel that Lincoln's feet are now icy to the touch, which he immediately treats by applying a mustard plaster to every inch of the front of Lincoln's body, from shoulders down to ankles. "No drug or medicine in any form was administered to the president," he will later note. "But the artificial heat and mustard plaster that I had applied warmed his cold body and stimulated his nerves."

He then covers the president with a blanket as Dr. Taft begins the process of removing the ball from Lincoln's head. Taft inserts his index finger into the wound and pronounces that the bullet has penetrated beyond the fingertip.

Meanwhile, Lincoln's pockets are emptied and his belongings carefully cataloged: an Irish linen handkerchief with the embroidered letter *A*; money, both Confederate and U.S.; newspaper clippings; an ivory pocketknife; and a pair of gold-rimmed glasses whose broken frame the president had mended with string.

More brandy and water is poured between Lincoln's lips. The Adam's apple once again bobs during the first spoonful but not at all for the second. With great difficulty, the doctors gently turn Lincoln on his side so that the excess fluid will run from his mouth and not choke him.

Lincoln is battling to stay alive. This is quite clear to each doctor. A normal man would be dead by now.

∽

The surgeon general of the army, Dr. Joseph Barnes, arrives and takes control of the scene. Barnes is closely followed by future surgeon general Charles H. Crane. Dr. Leale has been bold and aggressive these past few hours since the shooting. He now explains his course of action in great detail to two of the most powerful and well-regarded physicians in America. Both men agree with Leale's assessment and treatment, much to the young physician's relief.

The human brain is the most complex structure in all the world's biology, a humming and whirring center of thought, speech, motor movement, memory, and thousands of other minute functions. It is protected on the outside by the skull and then by a layer of connective-tissue membranes that form a barrier between the hard bone of the cranium and the gelatinous, soft tissue of the brain itself. Lincoln's brain, in which a Nélaton's probe (a long, porcelain, pencil-like instrument) is now being inserted in hopes of finding the bullet, contains vivid memories of a youth spent on the wild American frontier. This brain dazzled with clarity and brilliance during great political debates. It struggled with war and the politics of being president, then devised and executed solutions to the epic problems of the times. It imagined stirring speeches that knit the country together, then made sure that the words, when spoken, were uttered with exactly the right cadence, enunciation, and pitch. It guided those long slender fingers as they signed the Emancipation Proclamation, giving four million slaves their freedom. Inside his brain, Lincoln imagined the notion of "One country, one destiny." And this brain is also the reservoir of Lincoln's nightmares—particularly the one in which, just two weeks earlier, he envisioned his own assassination.

Now, thanks to a single round metal ball no bigger than a marble, Lincoln's brain is finished. He is brain-dead.

∞

Dr. Leale realizes that he is no longer needed in that cramped bedroom. But he does not leave. Emotion supersedes professional decorum. Leale, like the others, can barely hold back his tears. He has noticed that Lincoln is visibly more comfortable when the wound is unclogged. So he sits next to Lincoln's head and continues his solitary vigil, poking his finger into the blood clot every few minutes, making sure there's not too much pressure on Lincoln's brain.

A light rain is falling outside, but the crowd is eager for news and will not leave. In the room next door, Secretary of War Stanton has arrived and now takes charge, acting as interim president of the United States. Word of the assassination has brought a crowd of government officials to the Petersen house. The police investigation is beginning to take shape. It is clear that Booth shot Lincoln, and many believe that the actor also attacked Seward in his bed. Vice President Andrew Johnson, whose luck held when his assassin backed out, now stands in the next room, summoned after learning of Lincoln's plight.

All the while, Dr. Leale maintains his vigil by the dim candlelight. The occupants of the bedroom change constantly, with clergymen and officials and family members stepping in for a moment to pay their respects. More than sixty-five persons will be allowed inside before the night is through. The most frequent presence is Mary Lincoln, who weeps and even falls to her knees by the bedside whenever she is allowed a few moments with her husband. Leale takes care to spread a clean white handkerchief over the bloody pillow whenever she is about to walk in, but the bleeding in Lincoln's head never ceases, and before Mary Lincoln departs the handkerchief is often covered in blood and brain matter.

At three A.M., the scene is so grisly that Mary is no longer admitted.

The various doctors take turns recording Lincoln's condition. His respiration is shallow and fast, coming twenty-four to twenty-seven times a minute. His pulse rises to sixty-four at five-forty A.M., and hovers at sixty just a few moments later. But by then Leale can barely feel it.

Another doctor makes notes on Lincoln's condition:

"6:30—still failing and labored breathing."

"6:40—expirations prolonged and groaning. A deep, softly sonorous cooing sound at the end of each expiration, audible to bystanders."

"6:45—respiration uneasy, choking and grunting. Lower jaw relaxed. Mouth open. A minute without a breath. Face getting dark."

"6:59—breathes again a little more at intervals."

"7:00—still breathing at long pauses; symptoms of immediate dissolution."

With the president's death imminent, Mary Lincoln is once again admitted. Dr. Leale stands to make room. She sits in the chair next to Lincoln and then presses her face against her husband's. "Love," she says softly. "Speak to me."

A "loud, unnatural noise," in Dr. Leale's description, barks up from Lincoln's lungs. The sound is so grotesque that Mary collapses. As she is carried from the room she steals one last glimpse of her husband. She has known him since he was just a gangly country lawyer and has shared almost half her life with him. This will be the last time she sees him alive.

"I have given my husband to die," she laments, wishing that it could have been her instead.

Dr. Leale can't find a pulse. Lincoln's breathing becomes guttural, then ceases altogether before starting again. The room fills with a small army of elected officials, all of whom wish to witness the historic moment of Lincoln's death. Outside, it is dawn, and the crowds have grown even larger, with everyone waiting for a sliver of news.

In the bedroom, Robert Lincoln sobs loudly, unable to control his grief. He stands at the head of the bed and looks down at his father. Dr. Barnes sits in the chair, his finger on Lincoln's carotid artery, seeking a pulse. Dr. Leale has moved to the other side of the bed and wedged himself against the wall. He once again holds Lincoln's hand, simultaneously using his index finger to feel for a pulse on Lincoln's wrist.

There is no death rattle. Lincoln draws his last breath at seven twenty-one. His heart beats for another fifteen seconds, then stops altogether at ten seconds past seven twenty-two A.M.

More than twenty men are packed into the bedroom. Nobody says a word for five long minutes. Dr. Barnes reaches into his vest

pocket for a pair of silver coins, which he places over Lincoln's eyes—
one of which is now completely black and blue. Dr. Leale, meanwhile,
folds the president's arms across his chest and carefully smooths his
hair.

He barely hears Secretary Stanton rumble, "Now he belongs to the
ages."

*Sketch created at the deathbed of President Lincoln*

# Part Four

❧

# THE CHASE

*John Wilkes Booth in portrait*

## CHAPTER FORTY-EIGHT

SATURDAY, APRIL 15, 1865
MARYLAND COUNTRYSIDE
EARLY MORNING

John Wilkes Booth and David Herold, the most wanted men in the United States of America, have successfully fled into the Maryland countryside. They met up at the rendezvous spot in the dead of night. With no sign that Atzerodt or Powell managed to escape Washington, Booth and Herold pushed on with their flight, galloping their horses south, toward Virgina. However, Booth's leg injury is so severe, and their horses so tired, that they were forced to find a place to rest. They are now hiding in the house of the eminent physician and Confederate sympathizer Dr. Samuel Mudd.

Somewhere in Washington, George Atzerodt and Lewis Powell are still on the loose.

The authorities don't know any of that yet—no numbers, no identities, and no motives. But even before Lincoln breathed his last, they began the intricate process of unraveling the mystery of his death.

Investigators stumble upon Atzerodt's trail first. After failing to carry out the assassination of Vice President Johnson, the carriage painter spent the night wandering aimlessly about Washington, getting thoroughly drunk in a number of bars and making sure to dispose of the knife he was supposed to use to kill the vice president. Other than plotting against the president of the United States, he has committed no crime. Atzerodt has a reputation for being dim, but he is canny enough to know that once he threw his knife into a gutter, the only obvious piece of evidence connecting him with the conspiracy was being seen publicly on Booth's horse. It might take days for authorities to make that connection. If he maintains a low profile and keeps his wits about him, there is every chance that he can get out of Washington and get on with a normal life.

Atzerodt is all too aware that returning to his room at Kirkwood House would be a very stupid idea. So just before three A.M. he checks into the Pennsylvania House hotel, where he is assigned a double room. His roommate, at a time when Atzerodt needs to be as far away from the long arm of the law as possible, is a police lieutenant named W. R. Keim. The two men know each other from Atzerodt's previous stays at the Pennsylvania House. They lie on their backs in the darkness and have a short conversation before falling asleep. Keim is stunned by the slaying of Lincoln. As drunk as he is, Atzerodt does an artful job of feigning sadness, saying that the whole Lincoln assassination is a terrible tragedy.

Lieutenant Keim never suspects a thing.

∽

But events are already conspiring against Atzerodt. Even as he sleeps off his long, hard night of drinking and walking, detectives sent to protect Andrew Johnson are combing through Atzerodt's belongings at Kirkwood House. A desk clerk remembers seeing a "villainous-looking" individual registered in room 126. Atzerodt took the only room key with him when he fled, so detectives have to break down the door to investigate. Quickly canvassing the empty room, they come up with the first solid leads about Lincoln's murder. In the breast pocket of a dark coat hanging on a wall peg, they discover a ledger book from the Ontario Bank in Montreal. The name written inside the cover is that of John Wilkes Booth, whom scores of eyewitnesses have already identified as Lincoln's killer. The book confirms the connection between Atzerodt and Booth.

A quick rifling of the bed produces a loaded revolver under the pillow and a Bowie knife hidden beneath the covers. And that is just the beginning. Room 126 soon becomes a treasure trove of evidence:

a map of southern states, pistol rounds, a handkerchief embroidered with the name of Booth's mother, and much more.

Investigators now have two suspects: Booth and Atzerodt. Warrants are issued for their arrests.

∽

At the same time, an anonymous tip leads investigators to raid Mary Surratt's boardinghouse on H Street in the dead of night. Nothing is found, but Surratt's behavior is suspicious enough that detectives decide to keep an eye on her and the house. A similar anonymous tip leads police to room 228 at the National Hotel—Booth's room—which is quickly ripped apart. Booth has left behind an abundance of clues—among them a business card bearing the name "J. Harrison Surratt" and a letter from former conspirator Samuel Arnold that implicates Michael O'Laughlen. More and more, it is becoming obvious that John Wilkes Booth did not act alone.

∽

A few blocks away, detectives question Secretary of State Seward's household staff, which adds two more nameless individuals to the list: the man who attacked Seward and his accomplice, who was seen waiting outside. This brings the number of conspirators to six: Booth, Atzerodt, O'Laughlen, Arnold, and Seward's two unknown attackers. John Surratt becomes a suspect because police are watching his mother.

The detectives, thrilled at their brisk progress, are sure they will arrest each and every member of the conspiracy within a matter of days.

Meanwhile, Washington is in a state of shock. Flags are flown at half-mast. Vice President Andrew Johnson is sworn in as the seventeenth president of the United States. Secretary of State Seward is not dead, as is widely rumored. But he is very badly injured.

He will be in a coma through Saturday but will awaken on Easter Sunday. Gazing out the window, he will see the War Department's flags at half-mast and immediately know what has happened. "The president is dead," Seward will sigh.

When his nurse insists that this is not the case, Seward will hold his ground. "If he had been alive he would be the first to call on me," he will say, "but he has not been here, nor has he sent to know how I am, and there's the flag at half-mast." Then he will turn his head from the window, tears streaming down his cheeks, their salt mingling with the blood of his still-fresh wounds.

∽

But now it is still Saturday morning. Black crepe replaces the red, white, and blue bunting on government buildings. Liquor outlets are shut down so that angry Washingtonians don't find yet another excuse to begin drinking and perhaps, in their drunken anger, start looting. Multiracial crowds gather in front of the Petersen house, grateful to merely be in the presence of the hallowed ground where Lincoln died. Just across the street, Ford's Theatre has instantly gone from a Washington cultural hub to a pariah; the good fortune of having Lincoln attend *Our American Cousin* will soon put the theater out of business. The government will decree that the building may never again be used as a place of public amusement.

The cast of *Our American Cousin* is so afraid of being attacked by angry mobs that the actors and actresses lock themselves inside the theater after the shooting. One of their own, Harry Hawk, has already been taken into police custody for sharing the same stage as Booth.

Throughout the nation, as the news spreads, Abraham Lincoln's worst fears are being realized. Outraged northerners mourn his loss and openly rant about revenge, while southerners rejoice in the death of the tyrannical man who wouldn't give them the freedom to form their own nation. The Civil War, so close to being finally over, now seems on the verge of erupting once again.

∽

Believing that catching Lincoln's killer will help quell the unrest, Secretary of War Stanton spends Saturday expanding the search, making the hunt for Lincoln's killers the biggest criminal dragnet in American history. Soldiers, cavalry, and every imaginable form of law enforcement throughout the northern states are called off every other task and ordered to devote all their energies to finding John Wilkes Booth and his band of killers. In the same manner that Grant attempted to besiege Petersburg by throwing a noose around the city, Stanton hopes to throw a giant rope around the Northeast, then slowly cinch the knot tighter until he squeezes out the killers. He also sends a telegram to New York City, recalling Lafayette Baker, his former spymaster and chief of security. The strange connection between Stanton and Baker now becomes even stronger.

Why does Stanton call for Baker, of all people?

✑

As all this is going on, George Atzerodt wakes up at dawn on Saturday morning, still drunk after just two hours of sleep. He is somehow oblivious to the fact that people might be looking for him. Nor does he have any idea that the man who assaulted Secretary Seward, Lewis Powell, is also still stuck in Washington, hiding out in a cemetery after being thrown from his horse. Atzerodt knows he must get out of Washington, but first he needs money to fund his escape. He has no plan, and he is under no delusion that he will find a way to meet up with John Wilkes Booth; nor does he want to.

Atzerodt leaves the Pennsylvania House and walks across the city to nearby Georgetown, where he makes the unusual gesture of calling on an old girlfriend. He tells her he is going away for a while, as if she might somehow want to come along. And then as mysteriously as he appeared, Atzerodt leaves the home of Lucinda Metz and pawns his revolver for ten dollars at a nearby store. He uses the money to buy a stagecoach ticket into Maryland, taking public transportation at a time when all common sense cries out for a more inconspicuous means of escape.

But now fate is smiling upon George Atzerodt. Nobody stops the stagecoach as it rolls out of Washington and into Maryland. Even when the stage is halted and searched by Union soldiers miles outside the capital, nobody suspects that the simple-witted Atzerodt is capable of being resourceful enough to take part in the conspiracy. In fact, Atzerodt is so unassuming that the sergeant in charge of the soldiers actually shares a few glasses of cider with the conspirator.

In this way, George Atzerodt stumbles deeper and deeper into the countryside, on his way, he believes, to safety and freedom.

# CHAPTER FORTY-NINE

---

John Wilkes Booth is miserable. Flat on his back on a bed in the country home of Confederate sympathizer Samuel Mudd, Booth screams in pain as the thirty-one-year-old doctor cuts off his boot and gently presses his fingers into the grossly swollen ankle. As if shattering his fibula while leaping to the stage wasn't bad enough, Booth's horse threw him during his thirty-mile midnight ride through Maryland, hurling his body into a rock. Booth is sore, hungover, exhausted, and experiencing a new and nagging anxiety: that of the hunted.

After the assassination, Booth and David Herold rode hard all night, stopping only at a small tavern owned by Mary Surratt to pick up some Spencer rifles she'd hidden for them. Herold was glib, boasting to the Confederate proprietor that they'd killed the president. But he also had his wits about him, buying a bottle of whiskey so Booth could enjoy a nip or two to dull the pain. Then they rode on, ten more hard miles on tree-lined country roads, for Booth every mile more painful than the last. It was the actor's leg that made them detour to Mudd's house. Otherwise they would have reached the Potomac River by sunrise. With any luck, they might have stolen a boat and made the crossing into Virginia immediately.

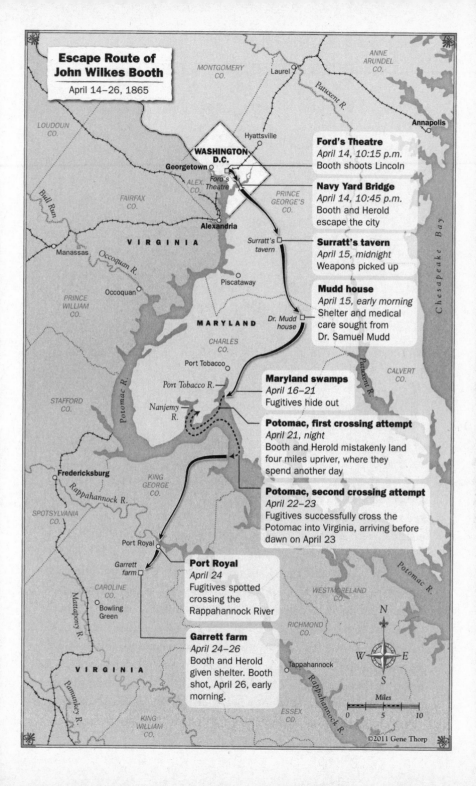

**Escape Route of John Wilkes Booth**
April 14–26, 1865

**Ford's Theatre**
*April 14, 10:15 p.m.*
Booth shoots Lincoln

**Navy Yard Bridge**
*April 14, 10:45 p.m.*
Booth and Herold
escape the city

**Surratt's tavern**
*April 15, midnight*
Weapons picked up

**Mudd house**
*April 15, early morning*
Shelter and medical
care sought from
Dr. Samuel Mudd

**Maryland swamps**
*April 16–21*
Fugitives hide out

**Potomac, first crossing attempt**
*April 21, night*
Booth and Herold mistakenly land
four miles upriver, where they
spend another day

**Potomac, second crossing attempt**
*April 22–23*
Fugitives successfully cross the
Potomac into Virginia, arriving before
dawn on April 23

**Port Royal**
*April 24*
Fugitives spotted
crossing the
Rappahannock River

**Garrett farm**
*April 24–26*
Booth and Herold
given shelter. Booth
shot, April 26, early
morning.

ANNE ARUNDEL CO.

MONTGOMERY CO.

Laurel

Annapolis

Hyattsville

WASHINGTON D.C.

Georgetown

Ford's Theatre

LOUDOUN CO.

FAIRFAX CO.

ALEX. CO.

PRINCE GEORGE'S CO.

Bull Run

Alexandria

Manassas

VIRGINIA

Surratt's tavern

Occoquan R.

PRINCE WILLIAM CO.

Occoquan

Piscataway

MARYLAND

Dr. Mudd house

Chesapeake Bay

Patuxent R.

CHARLES CO.

Port Tobacco

Port Tobacco R.

Nanjemy R.

Patuxent R.

CALVERT CO.

STAFFORD CO.

Potomac R.

Fredericksburg

Rappahannock R.

KING GEORGE CO.

SPOTSYLVANIA CO.

Port Royal

Garrett farm

CAROLINE CO.

Bowling Green

Mattapony R.

VIRGINIA

KING WILLIAM CO.

Pamunkey R.

WESTMORELAND CO.

RICHMOND CO.

Tappahannock

Potomac R.

Rappahannock R.

ESSEX CO.

N
W E
S

Miles
0    5    10

©2011 Gene Thorp

*Dr. Samuel Mudd*

Still, they're close. Very close. By choosing to take shelter at Mudd's rather than stay on the main road south to the Potomac, they have veered off the fastest possible route. But Mudd's two-hundred-eighteen-acre estate is just north of Bryantown, south and east of Washington, and fully two-thirds of the way to the Potomac River.

Booth's pants and jacket are now spattered with mud. His handsome face, so beloved by women everywhere, is unshaven and sallow. But more than anything else, John Wilkes Booth is helpless. Almost overnight he has become a shell of himself, as if assassinating Lincoln has robbed him of the fire in his belly, and the pain of his shattered leg has transformed him from daredevil to coward. He is now completely dependent upon David Herold to lead their escape into the South. At a time when Booth needs all his wiles and resources to complete the second half of the perfect assassination, he is too distraught and in too much agony to think straight.

Dr. Mudd says he's going to splint the leg. Booth lies back and lets him, despite the knowledge that this means he will no longer be able to slip his foot into a stirrup. Now he must ride one-legged, half on and half off his horse—if he can ride at all.

∽

Mudd finishes splinting the leg, then leaves Booth alone to get some rest. The actor is in an upstairs room, so if anyone comes looking, he won't be found right away. He wraps a shawl around his neck and face to conceal his identity, and he has plans to shave his mustache. But otherwise, he does absolutely nothing to facilitate his escape. The pain is too great. It will take a miracle for Booth to travel even one mile farther.

He rolls over and closes his eyes, then falls into a deep sleep, sure that he is being hunted but completely unaware that more than a thousand men on horseback are within a few miles of his location—and that Lafayette Baker is now on the case.

# CHAPTER FIFTY

Lafayette Baker is in his room at New York's Astor House hotel when he hears that Lincoln has been shot. The disgraced spy, who was sent away from Washington for tapping Secretary Stanton's telegraph lines, is not surprised. His first thought, as always, is of finding a way to spin this tragedy for his own personal gain. Baker loves glory and money. He understands in an instant that the man who finds Lincoln's killer will know unparalleled wealth and fame. Baker longs to be that man.

It's noon on Saturday when a telegram arrives from Stanton, summoning him to "come here immediately and find the murderer of our president."

If Baker were an ordinary man and not prone to weaving elaborate myths about himself, that telegram would be a very straightforward call to battle. But Baker is so fond of half-truths and deception that it's impossible to know if he is traveling to Washington as a sort of super-sleuth, handpicked by Stanton to find Lincoln's killers, or if he is traveling to Washington to find and kill Booth before the actor can detail Secretary Stanton's role in the conspiracy. Whatever the case, at a time when Baker could have been anywhere in the world, Stanton knew exactly where to find the fired spy so that he could be summoned to the capital.

Lafayette Baker takes the overnight train to Washington, arriving at dawn. The city is in chaos, and he will later describe the looks on people's faces as "inexpressible, bewildering horror and grief." Baker travels immediately to the War Department, where he meets with Stanton. "They have killed the president. You must go to work. My whole dependence is upon you," the secretary tells him. The entire detective forces of New York, Baltimore, Philadelphia, and Boston have traveled to Washington and are devoting their considerable professional talents to finding the killers. But Stanton has just given Baker carte blanche to move in and take over the entire investigation.

One of Baker's specialties is playing the part of the double agent. Even though there is evidence that Baker and Booth are somehow connected to each other through the 178½ Water Street, New York, address, Baker claims that he knows nothing about the case or about the suspects. His first act is to post a reward for $30,000 leading to the arrest and conviction of Lincoln's killers. He also has photographs of John Surratt, David Herold, and John Wilkes Booth plastered all around town.

One of several reward posters for
the capture of John Wilkes Booth

# CHAPTER FIFTY-ONE

SATURDAY–SUNDAY, APRIL 15–16, 1865
MARYLAND COUNTRYSIDE

David Herold needs a buggy. It's the most obvious solution to John Wilkes Booth's plight. With a buggy they can travel quickly and in relative comfort. He asks Dr. Mudd to loan them his, but the doctor is reluctant; secretly harboring fugitives is one thing, but allowing the two most wanted men in America to ride through southern Maryland in his personal carriage would surely implicate Mudd and his wife in the conspiracy. Their hanging—for that is surely the fate awaiting any Lincoln conspirator—would leave their four young children orphans.

Instead, Mudd suggests that they ride into Bryantown to pick up some supplies and check on the latest news. With Booth still passed out upstairs, Herold agrees to the journey. But as they draw closer and closer to the small town, something in Herold's gut tells him not to take the risk. A stranger like him will be too easily remembered by such a tight-knit community. He is riding Booth's bay now, because it's too spirited for the actor to control with his broken leg. Herold lets Mudd go on without him, then wheels the mare back to the doctor's home.

Good thing. The United States cavalry now has Bryantown surrounded. They're not only questioning all its citizens, they're not letting anyone leave, either.

This is the sort of savvy, intuitive thinking that separates David Herold from the other members of Booth's conspiracy. Atzerodt is dim. Powell is a thug. And Booth is emotional. But the twenty-two-year-old Herold, recruited to the conspiracy for his knowledge of Washington's backstreets, is intelligent and resourceful. He was educated at Georgetown College, the finest such institution in the city. He is also an avid hunter, which gives him a full complement of the outdoor skills that Booth now requires to escape, the additional ability to improvise in dangerous situations, and an instinctive sixth sense about tracking—or, in this case, being tracked.

But now Herold is just as exhausted as Booth. He didn't endure the same extreme adrenaline spike last night, if only because he didn't kill anyone. But he experienced a definite and sustained rush as he galloped over the Navy Yard Bridge, then along the dangerous darkened roads of Maryland. He's had time to think and to plan, and he knows that constant forward movement is the key to their survival. Otherwise, Herold has no doubt that the cavalry will be on their trail in no time.

❧

Clearly, they cannot stay at Dr. Mudd's any longer. Just before dusk, Herold rouses Booth and helps him down the stairs and up into the saddle. Herold guides them south through the countryside, aiming for the Zekiah Swamp, with its quicksand bogs and dense stands of old-growth hardwoods. The few trails that exist are almost impossible to see in the dark, and the pair are soon lost and frustrated. They turn back toward Mudd's farm but remain out of sight, plotting their next move.

The next twelve hours bring an enduring awareness that they are neither safe nor welcome anywhere.

Easter Sunday dawns hard and bleak. Herold and Booth are camped in a stand of pines a quarter mile off the main road. A cold front is racing across Maryland, and they shiver in the damp swampy air, just a few short miles from the final obstacle to their escape into Virginia, the Potomac River. Booth isn't wearing a boot on his injured leg, and his foot and ankle are in pain and quite cold from walking on swampy ground in the thin shoes he took from Mudd. Yet Herold doesn't dare make a fire. Beside him, Booth is curled up in the fetal position, head resting on one hand. Each man clutches his revolver as a stiff wind bends the towering pines. The last sympathizer they visited, the wealthy owner of forty slaves in this still-lawless region, promised to send a man to ferry them across to safety. The rescue signal will be a soft whistle, a pause, and then another soft whistle.

So now they wait. Hour after brutally cold hour, they wonder who will deliver them from this hell. Booth says little, except to cry out in pain or mutter something about not being taken alive. He still has some fight in him. Now and then they hear the jangle of bridles from the nearby road. And all the while, a gnawing little voice in Herold's gut tells him that they have been betrayed—that the whistle, when it comes, will be their only warning before United States cavalry confirm their position and ride in with guns blazing.

Late Sunday afternoon they hear the first whistle. Then a second. Confederate sympathizer Thomas Jones calls out to them in a low voice, announcing that he is walking into their camp.

# CHAPTER FIFTY-TWO

There is nothing dashing or heroic about the man who has come to save the lives of Booth and Herold. Thomas Jones is a broken man, a forty-four-year-old smuggler who has done time in prison, outlived his wife, and lost his home. He now earns his living by transporting everyone from secret agents to diplomats across the Potomac River to the South. On average, he makes the crossing three times a night. He is so skilled that northern newspapers secretly enlisted his help to get their product into the South during the war. A favorite technique employed by the silver-haired and low-key Jones is to begin his first crossing just before dusk, when the angle of the sun makes it impossible for sentries on the opposite shore to see small craft on the water. It is a brazen and brilliant tactic. Clearly, if any man can get Booth and Herold to safety, it's Thomas Jones.

On his first visit to the campsite he merely wanted to get a look at the men he would be helping, to see if they were mentally and physically capable of enduring what might be a very long wait until it is safe to cross.

His second visit comes one day later. It's also the second day in the pine forest for Booth and Herold. They once again hear the whistle from the trees. Booth is even worse today, the pain in his leg so severe that he doesn't do much more than whimper. Herold stands, carbine pointed toward the sound of approaching footsteps, until Jones finally appears in their thicket, his pockets overflowing with ham, butter, bread, and a flask of coffee. In his hands he holds the one thing Booth wants to see more than any other: newspapers.

Cavalry are combing the countryside, he cautions the killers, and he reminds them to be patient. It might take several days before things die down. No matter how cold it gets, no matter how extreme the conditions, they must be prepared to hunker down in the woods until the coast is clear. As soon as it is, he'll let them know.

Booth argues that their lives are in danger and that they can't stay here any longer. But the thunder of hoofbeats from the nearby road stops him short—it's Union cavalry and far too close for comfort.

"You see, my friend," Jones whispers. "You must wait." He tells them to kill the horses, lest their whinnying give the killers away.

Prior to the assassination, Booth would have continued to argue and then done as he pleased. But now he quietly gives in. "I leave it all with you," he says to Jones.

Jones departs quickly. His visits are uplifting to Booth and Herold, a welcome break from the monotony of sitting still for hours and hours out in the open. They don't even dare build a shelter, for fear the noise will attract unwelcome attention. Jones doesn't just bring food and newspapers; he also offers hope, his cool confidence suggesting that all will be well, just so long as they are patient.

∽

With a sigh, Booth turns his attention to the newspapers. He reads about the extent of the search. But his melancholy soon turns to rage as he learns that his monumental actions are not being applauded. Far from it. He is being labeled a scoundrel and a coward for shooting Lincoln in the back. Washington newspapers assail him as the war's ultimate villain and note that any "kindly feeling" toward the South or its sympathizers has disappeared, thanks to his actions. Booth's achievement is described in the Richmond papers as "the most deplorable calamity, which has ever befallen the people of the United States." And finally, the nation's most staunchly anti-Lincoln paper, the *National Intelligencer*, is now crying out that Lincoln was a true American hero. The very newspaper that the actor had once hoped would print the letter explaining his actions is instead portraying him as an abomination.

Booth, overcome with despair, sets the papers aside. As is his new habit, he regales Herold with a monologue on the killings—regrets, desires, and misunderstandings. Then he takes out his diary and begins keeping a journal of their time in the wilderness. In it, he writes his reflections on killing Lincoln, just to make sure that his point of view is properly recorded for posterity. "I struck boldly and not as the papers say. I walked with a firm step through a thousand of his friends, was stopped, but pushed on," Booth writes. "I can never repent it, though we hated to kill. Our country owed all her troubles to him, and God simply made men the instrument of his punishment."

Booth writes and rants and writes some more. Then he sleeps. Then he awakens and writes some more. There's nothing else to do with his time. So it is with the world's two most wanted men, bored to tears in a Maryland swamp.

# CHAPTER FIFTY-THREE

MONDAY, APRIL 17, 1865
MARY SURRATT'S BOARDINGHOUSE
NIGHT

Mary Surratt has been a suspect since the night Lincoln was shot. An anonymous tipster alerted Washington police that the boardinghouse on H Street was the hub of the conspiracy. Detectives questioned her at two o'clock that morning, even as Lincoln lay dying. The widow was forthcoming about the fact that John Wilkes Booth had paid her a visit just twelve hours earlier and that her son John had last been in Washington two weeks earlier. When a thorough search of the house turned up nothing, the police left. No arrest was made.

Now they are back. One of her boarders, Louis Weichmann, has volunteered volumes of information to the authorities about the comings and goings of Booth and the conspirators at Mary Surratt's boardinghouse. This eyewitness information has confirmed not only that Booth is at the heart of the plan but that Mary Surratt is complicit.

It is well past midnight when police surround the house. She answers a knock at the door, thinking it is a friend. "Is this Mrs. Surratt's house?" asks a detective.

"Yes."

"Are you Mrs. Surratt?"

"I am the widow of John H. Surratt."

"And the mother of John H. Surratt Jr.?"

"Yes."

"Madam, I have come to arrest you."

Three policemen step inside. Mary's twenty-two-year-old daughter, Anna, is also taken into custody. Just before they are led outside, Mary asks permission to kneel in prayer. She is a devout Catholic and prays "the blessing of God upon me, as I do in all my actions."

The house is quiet. Her words echo through the half-lighted rooms as the detectives awkwardly wait for Mary to finish praying and rise to her feet.

Then there's another knock on the door.

When the detectives open it, they are shocked by the sight of a six-foot-two man with a pickax slung over his shoulder, wearing a shirt-sleeve on his head like a stocking cap. His boots are coated with mud and he is unshaven. As he steps inside, they see that there appears to be blood on his sleeves. The detectives quickly close the door behind him.

Lewis Powell, starved and famished after three days of sleeping in the woods, instantly realizes he has made a grave error. "I guess I am mistaken," he quickly tells the detectives, turning to leave.

The police send Mary and Anna Surratt out the door, where carriages wait to take them to jail. Then they focus their attention on the tall stranger with the pickax.

Powell gives his name as Lewis Payne and fabricates an elaborate story, saying that he has come to Mary Surratt's at her behest, in order to dig a ditch for her in the morning. The police press him, asking about Powell's address and place of employment. When he can't answer in a satisfactory manner, they arrest him. At the police station he is strip-searched, and an unlikely collection of items, including cash, a compass, a pocketknife, and a newspaper clipping of Lincoln's second inaugural address, are found in his pockets.

So far, all evidence points to "Payne's" involvement in the assassination. His height and rugged build clearly match the description of Secretary Seward's attacker. The police summon the young black servant who had given the description to the station. William Bell has been interrogated a number of times since the attacks, so as he is called back to the station once again his attitude is weary. The late hour does not help.

However, when a lineup of potential suspects is paraded into the room before him, Bell becomes instantly euphoric. He marches right up to Powell and presses his finger against the lips of the man who mocked him, insulted him with a racial slur, and very nearly killed his employer and several members of the family and staff. "He is the man," Bell proclaims.

This is the last moment in Lewis Powell's life when he is able to move his arms freely and walk without hearing the clank of chains. Manacles are placed on his wrists. A ball and chain will be attached to each ankle in the days to come, the unyielding iron cutting deeply into his flesh every time he takes a step. A canvas hood will soon be placed over his head, with only a small hole through which he can draw breath and eat.

And yet there is much worse to come for Lewis Powell.

# CHAPTER FIFTY-FOUR

Tuesday, April 18, 1865
Maryland Swamps
Day and night

The military sweep through southern Maryland is ongoing and intense. Searches of towns and homes have turned up nothing, and it is clear that the time has come to scour more daunting terrain for Booth and Herold. A combined force of seven hundred Illinois cavalry, six hundred members of the Twenty-second Colored Troops, and one hundred men from the Sixteenth New York Cavalry Regiment now enter the wilderness of Maryland's vast swamps.

"No human being inhabits this malarious extent" is how one journalist describes this region. "Even a hunted murderer would shrink from hiding there. Serpents and slimy lizards are the only living denizens. . . . Here the soldiers prepared to seek for the President's assassins, and no search of the kind has ever been so thorough and patient."

The method of searching the swamps is simple yet arduous. First, the troops assemble on the edge of bogs with names like Allen's Creek, Scrub Swamp, and Atchall's Swamp, standing at loose attention in the shade of a thick forest of beech, dogwood, and gum trees. Then they form two lines and march straight forward, from one side to the other. As absurd as it seems to the soldiers, marching headlong into cold mucky water, there is no other way of locating Booth and

Herold. Incredibly, eighty-seven of these brave men will drown in their painstaking weeklong search for the killers.

"The soldiers were only a few paces apart," the journalist reports, "and in steady order they took to the ground as it came, now plunging to their armpits in foul sluices of gangrened water, now hopelessly submerged in slime, now attacked by legions of wood ticks, now attempting some unfaithful log or greenishly solid morass, and plunging to the tip of the skull in poisonous stagnation. The tree boughs rent their uniforms. They came out upon dry land, many of them without a rag of garment, scratched and gnashed, and spent, repugnant to themselves, and disgusting to those who saw them."

The soldiers detain anyone with anti-Union leanings. For many of the arrested, their only crime is either looking or behaving suspiciously. Taking them into custody is the best possible way to ensure that no suspect is overlooked.

Hundreds of these suspects soon fill Washington's jails.

But not a single trace of Booth or Herold can be found anywhere.

∽

Back in Washington, Lafayette Baker follows their progress. Since arriving in the capital two days earlier, Baker has distanced himself from the other investigators, "taking the usual detective measures, till then neglected," of offering the reward, circulating photos of the suspects, and sending out a small army of handpicked detectives to scour the countryside. But he is hampered by the lack of railroads and telegraph lines through the rough and lawless countryside. There is, however, a telegraph line at Point Lookout, a former Union prisoner of war camp at the mouth of the Potomac River. To keep himself informed of all activities in the area, he dispatches a telegraph operator by steamship to that location and orders him to tap into the existing line.

Now, safe in the knowledge that he has established the broadest possible dragnet, Baker waits for that telegraph line to sing.

# CHAPTER FIFTY-FIVE

TUESDAY, APRIL 18, 1865
MARYLAND COUNTRYSIDE
AFTERNOON

The moment Dr. Samuel Mudd has been dreading for two days comes while he is in the fields, working his crops. The cavalry unit galloping up his driveway is not there by accident. There are at least two dozen riders, not including his cousin George. It was George to whom Mudd confided that two strangers had spent the night of Lincoln's assassination in his home. They spoke after Easter services, even as Booth and Herold were still very much in the vicinity. Mudd took pains to state that his life was in danger, should these two men ever come back. The story was a cover, intended to make it look as if he had no knowledge of the strangers' identities. It was Mudd's hope that George would act as an intermediary, alerting the police to the fact that his Good Samaritan cousin might just have "accidentally" aided the men who killed Lincoln.

George, however, is a devoted Union sympathizer. Instead of the police, George has brought the cavalry, with their rifles, sabers, and no-nonsense military bearing. The riders dismount. Lieutenant Alexander Lovett is in charge and quickly begins a line of questioning to determine exactly who and what Samuel Mudd saw that night.

Mudd is not a brave man and is quickly rattled. His lips turn blue, even as his face turns chalk white. The story he fabricated and rehearsed in his head so many times suddenly eludes him. Rather than present himself as eager for the "entire strangers" to be captured, Mudd is vague and contrary. He mentions that one stranger had a broken leg and that he had done the neighborly thing by splinting it before sending the men on their way. When Lovett asks him to repeat parts of the story, Mudd frequently contradicts his own version of events.

Lieutenant Lovett is positive that Samuel Mudd is lying. But he does not arrest him—not now, at least. He is determined to find evidence that will link Mudd to the two strangers. He bawls the order to mount up, and the cavalry trots back out to the main road.

Mudd, his heart beating in relief, can only wonder when they will return.

# CHAPTER FIFTY-SIX

George Atzerodt has chosen to escape via a northeast route, rather than push south like Booth and Herold. This takes him into a much more pro-Union territory, where the Lincoln assassination has people demanding vengeance on the perpetrators. On the surface, Atzerodt's plan is an act of genius, allowing one of the most wanted men in America to literally hide in plain sight.

But the increasingly unbalanced George Atzerodt is not a genius. His escape is not a premeditated act of egress but a random wandering from home to home, accepting sanctuary and comfort wherever he can find it. He dawdles when he should be making continuous progress. After four days on the run he makes a critical mistake, boldly supporting Lincoln's assassination while eating dinner with strangers. His statements quickly make their way to U.S. marshals.

Now, as Atzerodt takes refuge at a cousin's house in the small community of Germantown, Maryland, twenty miles outside of Washington, a cavalry detachment knocks at the door. Entering the house, they find Atzerodt sharing a bed with two other men. "Get up and dress yourself," a sergeant commands.

There is no fight, no attempt to pretend he shouldn't be arrested. George Atzerodt goes meekly into custody, where he is soon fitted with wrist shackles, a ball and chain on his ankle, and a hood over his head, just like Lewis Powell.

Less than three months later, George Atzerodt—the twenty-nine-year-old drifter who stumbled into the conspiracy and stumbled right back out without harming a soul—hangs by the neck until dead.

# CHAPTER FIFTY-SEVEN

FRIDAY, APRIL 21, 1865
WASHINGTON, D.C.
7:00 A.M.

One week after the assassination, even as John Wilkes Booth is still alive and hiding in a Maryland swamp, the body of Abraham Lincoln is loaded aboard a special train for his return home to Illinois. General Ulysses S. Grant supervises the occasion. The body of Lincoln's late son Willie rides along in a nearby casket. Abraham Lincoln once confided to Mary that he longed to be buried someplace quiet, and so it is that the president and his dear son are destined for Springfield's Oak Ridge Cemetery.

But even after the burial, Lincoln's body will never quite be at rest. In the next 150 years, Lincoln's casket will be opened six times and moved from one crypt to another seventeen times. His body was so thoroughly embalmed that he was effectively mummified.

The funeral, which is quite different from the actual burial, of course, was held on Wednesday, April 19. Six hundred mourners were ushered into the East Room of the White House. Its walls were decorated in black, the mirrors all covered, and the room lit by candles. General Ulysses S. Grant sat alone nearest his dear departed friend, next to a cross of lilies. He wept.

Mary Lincoln is still so distraught that she will spend the next five weeks sobbing alone in her bedroom; she was notably absent from the

*The president's funeral procession down Pennsylvania Avenue*

list of recorded attendees. The sound of hammers pounding nails all night long on Tuesday, creating the seating risers for the funeral guests, sounded like the horrible ring of gunfire to her. Out of respect for her mourning and instability, President Andrew Johnson will not have the platforms torn down until after she moves out, on May 22.

Immediately after the funeral, Lincoln's body was escorted by a military guard through the streets of Washington. One hundred thousand mourners lined the route to the Capitol, where the body was once again put on view for the public to pay their last respects.

And now, two days later, there is the matter of the train. In a trip that will re-create his journey to the White House five years earlier—though in the opposite direction—Lincoln's special train will stop along the way in twelve cities and pass through 444 communities. In what will be called "the greatest funeral in the history of the United States," thirty million people will take time from their busy lives to see this very special train before its great steel wheels finally slow to a halt in his beloved Springfield.

The unfortunate mementos of his assassination remain behind in Washington: the Deringer bullet and the Nélaton's probe that pinpointed its location in his brain will soon be on display in a museum, as will the red horsehair rocker in which he was shot. He also leaves behind the messy unfinished business of healing the nation. And while Abraham Lincoln has gone home to finally get the rest he has so long deserved, that unfinished business will have to wait until his murderer is found.

# CHAPTER FIFTY-EIGHT

---

Samuel Mudd is not home when Lieutenant Lovett and the cavalry return. Lovett sends farmhand Thomas Davis to find him. Mudd is having lunch nearby and quickly returns to his farm to face Lovett.

The terror of their previous encounter returns. He knows that Lovett has spent the previous three days searching the area around his property for evidence. Mudd's face once again turns a ghostly white. His nervousness is compounded as Lovett questions him again, probing Mudd's story for discrepancies, half-truths, and outright lies.

This time Lovett does not ride away. Nor is he content to search the pastures and outer edges of the farm. No, this time he wants to go inside Mudd's home and see precisely where these strangers slept. Lovett gives the order to search the house.

Mudd frantically gestures to his wife, Sarah, who walks quickly to him. He whispers in her ear, and she races into the house. The soldiers can hear her footsteps as she climbs the stairs to the second floor, then returns within just a moment. In her hands are two items: a razor and a boot. "I found these while dusting up three days ago," she says as she hands them to Lovett.

Mudd explains that one of the strangers used the razor to shave off his mustache. The boot had come from the stranger with the broken leg.

Lovett presses Mudd on this point, asking him if he knew the man's identity.

Mudd insists that he didn't.

Lovett cradles the long riding boot in his hands. It has been slit down one side by Mudd, in order that he might pull it from Booth's swollen leg to examine the wound.

Lovett asks if this is, indeed, the boot the stranger wore.

Mudd agrees.

Lovett presses Mudd again, verifying that the doctor had no knowledge of the stranger's identity.

Mudd swears this to be truth.

And then Lovett shows Mudd the inside of the riding boot, which would have been clearly visible when Mudd was removing it from the stranger's leg.

Mudd's world collapses. His story is shattered in an instant.

For marked inside the boot, plain for all to see, is the name "J. Wilkes."

Dr. Samuel Mudd is under arrest.

And while Lieutenant Lovett has just made a key breakthrough in the race to find John Wilkes Booth and David Herold, the truth is that nobody in authority knows where they are.

∞

Lafayette Baker, however, has a pretty good idea.

Baker keeps a host of coastal survey maps in his office at the War Department. With "that quick detective intuition amounting almost to inspiration," in his own words, he knows that Booth's escape options are limited. When news of the discovery of the abandoned riding boot makes its way back to Washington, Baker concludes that Booth cannot be traveling on horseback. And though traveling by water is more preferable, once Booth is flushed from the swamps—for that is surely where he is hiding—he won't follow the Maryland coastline. There are too many deep rivers to cross, and he would be easily spotted. Lafayette Baker also deduces that Booth won't head toward Richmond if he gets across the Potomac because that would lead him straight into Union lines.

Lafayette Baker is already convinced that John Wilkes Booth must aim for the mountains of Kentucky. "Being aware that nearly every rod of ground in Lower Maryland must have been repeatedly passed over by the great number of persons engaged in the search," he will later write, "I finally decided, in my own mind, that Booth and Herold had crossed over the river into Virginia. The only possible way left open to escape was to take a southwestern course, in order to reach the mountains of Tennessee or Kentucky, where such aid could be secured as would insure their ultimate escape from the country."

It's as if he already knows Booth's plan.

To get to Kentucky, Booth must cross the great breadth of Virginia, following almost the exact same path General Lee took in his escape from Petersburg. But he has no horse, which means traveling by water or on the main roads in a buggy, and he must cross treacherous territory to get south of Richmond.

Baker studies his maps, searching for the precise spot where Booth might cross the Potomac. His eyes zoom in on Port Tobacco. "If any place in the world is utterly given over to depravity, it is Port Tobacco," he will quote a journalist as saying in his memoirs. "Five hundred people exist in Port Tobacco. Life there reminds me, in connection with the slimy river and the adjacent swamps, of the great reptile period of the world, when iguanodons and pterodactyls, and plesiosauri ate each other."

Lafayette Baker is wrong—but not by much.

# CHAPTER FIFTY-NINE

FRIDAY, APRIL 21, 1865
MARYLAND SWAMPS
NIGHT

Six days. Six long, cold miserable days. That's how long Booth and Herold have now been in the swamp, scratching at wood ticks, shivering under thin, damp wool blankets, and eating just the one meal a day provided by Thomas Jones. The silence has been almost complete, save for the times when Union warships on the Potomac fire their big guns to salute their fallen president.

The newspapers delivered daily by Jones continue to be a source of information and misery, as it becomes more and more clear that Booth's actions have condemned him. Booth would rant about that injustice if he had the energy. The fact is, he and Herold long ago tired of speaking in a whisper. And even if they hadn't, they have nothing to talk about.

The sizzle of happiness that accompanied killing Lincoln is long gone. Booth is a man accustomed to the finest things in life, and his miserable existence in the swamp has him longing for the tender flesh of Lucy Hale, a bottle of whiskey, a plate of oysters, and a warm bed.

Booth is just settling in for another night in the swamp when he hears the first whistle. Herold hears it, too, and is on his feet in an instant. Grabbing his rifle, Herold warily approaches the sound and returns with Jones. "The coast seems to be clear," Jones tells them, his voice betraying the sense of urgency. "Let us make the attempt."

Their camp is three miles from the river. Getting to the Potomac undetected means traveling down well-used public roads. Despite the darkness, they might run into a cavalry detail at any moment, but it is a chance they have to take.

Booth can't walk, so Jones loans him his horse. Herold and Jones help Booth into the saddle. The actor clings precariously to the horse's mane, desperate not to fall off.

Jones tells them to wait, then walks ahead to make sure the coast is clear. Only when he whistles that all is well do they follow. This is how they travel to the river, the ever vigilant Jones utilizing the smuggling skills he honed so well during the war to lead them to safety. Their pace is frustratingly slow to Booth, who wants to canter the horse as quickly as he can manage to the river, but Jones is taking no chances.

∽

When they approach Jones's house, Booth begs to be allowed inside for a moment of warmth. He badly wants to get to the river, but he is also addicted to creature comforts. After six days out in the cold, something as simple as standing before a roaring fireplace feels like a version of heaven. Jones won't hear of it, reminding them that his servants are home and could possibly give them away. Instead, Jones walks inside and returns with hot food, reminding the two fugitives that this might be the last meal they eat for a while.

They press on to the river. Jones has hidden a twelve-foot-long boat at the water's edge, tied to a large oak tree. The bank is steep, and Booth must be carried down the slope. But soon he sits in the stern, grasping an oar. Herold perches in the bow. The night is still dark, for the moon has not risen. A cold mist hovers on the surface of the wide and treacherous Potomac. Safety is just across the river in Virginia, where the citizens are solidly pro-Confederacy. It's so close they can see it. But getting there means navigating unseen currents and tides that can force them far downriver—or even backward. The river is two miles wide at this point and constantly patrolled by Union warships. Some are merely heading into Washington's Navy Yard after time at sea, while others are specifically hunting for two men in a small boat. It is common naval practice for ships to douse their running lights at night, all the better to thwart smugglers. Booth and

Herold might actually run headlong into a ship without even seeing it in the total darkness.

"Keep to that," Jones instructs Booth, lighting a small candle to illuminate Booth's compass and pointing to the southwesterly heading. The actor has carried the compass since the assassination, just for a moment such as this. "It will bring you into Machodoc Creek. Mrs. Quesenberry lives near the mouth of this creek. If you tell her you come from me, I think she will take care of you."

"God bless you, my dear friend," says Booth. "Good-bye."

They shove off. Jones turns his back and returns home, his work complete. No other man has risked as much, nor shown as much compassion for Booth and Herold, as Jones. He did not do it because he applauded the assassination—in fact, Jones is disgusted by Booth's action. Rather, he helped the two men out of compassion for men in trouble and a last-ditch bout of loyalty to the Confederacy. His deeds will go unpunished. When his part in the conspiracy will be revealed later on, the testimony will come from a non-white resident of southern Maryland and thus will be ignored.

Booth and Herold, meanwhile, paddle hard for the opposite shore. That is: Herold paddles hard. Booth sits in the back and dangles his oar in the water under the pretense of steering.

Herold paddles for several hours against a daunting current, but they're going the wrong way. Booth's compass may be a prized possession, but it's useless if not utilized properly.

❦

Things go from bad to worse. The fugitives almost paddle headlong into the *Juniper*, a Federal gunboat. And yet if anyone on the deck of the eighty-footer sees them they don't cry out.

Finally, they land, four miles upriver from where they departed, still in Maryland. Their escape is not going well. They are forced to hide themselves and their boat in the brush for yet another day.

And so, after one last, long twenty-four hours of hiding from the thousands of soldiers now combing the countryside looking for them, John Wilkes Booth and David Herold once again set out under cover of darkness rowing hard for Virginia. This time they make it.

Next stop: Kentucky.

# CHAPTER SIXTY

MONDAY–TUESDAY, APRIL 24–25, 1865
VIRGINIA-MARYLAND BORDER
DAY

Samuel H. Beckwith is in Port Tobacco, the "Gomorrah," in Lafayette Baker's words, of Maryland. He is the telegraph operator specially detailed by Baker to keep the detective apprised of all actions in the Booth dragnet. Now he telegraphs a coded message back to Washington, stating that investigators have questioned local smugglers and learned that Booth and Herold have gone across the Potomac River.

The evidence is, in fact, erroneous. It refers to a group of men smuggled into Virginia on Easter Sunday, not Booth and Herold. Lafayette Baker immediately reacts, however, sending twenty-five members of the Sixteenth New York Cavalry by the steamship *John S. Ide* from Washington downriver to Belle Plain, Virginia. All of the men have volunteered for the mission. The senior officers are Baker's cousin Lieutenant Luther Baker and Colonel Everton Conger, a twenty-nine-year-old, highly regarded veteran of the Civil War.

Lafayette Baker sees them off. "I want you to go to Virginia and get Booth," he says and then puts his cousin in charge, despite the lower rank.

The *Ide* pushes back at two P.M., for a four-hour voyage. It arrives at the simple wharf and warehouse along the shore just after dark. The men immediately spur their horses down the main road of Belle Plain, Virginia, and then into the countryside, knocking on farmhouse doors and questioning the occupants. They stop any and all riders and carriages they encounter, pressing hard for clues as to Booth's whereabouts.

But nobody has seen Booth or Herold—or, if they have, they're not talking. By morning the cavalry squad is in Port Conway, more than ten miles inland from the Potomac. Exhausted, their horses wrung out from the long night, the soldiers are starting to feel as if this is just another futile lead. Conger has promised them all an equal share of the more than $200,000 in reward money awaiting those who capture Booth. This spurred them to ride all night, but now the prize seems unattainable. They are growing fearful that the *Ide* will return to Washington without them, leaving them to wait days for another ship.

During their trip south, Lieutenant Luther Baker made the rather wise decision to give the command back to Conger. "You have been over the ground," he told the veteran.

Then, just as they are about to give up and go home, on the shores of the Rappahannock River, at a ferry crossing known as Port Royal, two men positively identify photographs of Booth and Herold. They passed through the previous day and were traveling with a small group of Confederate veterans.

By this time, the twenty-five cavalry soldiers are exhausted, "so haggard and wasted with travel that they had to be kicked into intelligence before they could climb to their saddles," Lieutenant Baker will later recall.

But climb into their saddles they do, for hours and hours of more searching.

∽

At two o'clock in the morning, at a handsome whitewashed farm three hundred yards off the main road, they finally come to a halt. The ground is soft clay, so their horses' hooves make no sound. The soldiers draw their carbines from their scabbards as Lieutenant Baker dismounts and opens the property's main gate. He has no certain knowledge of anything nefarious. It is just a hunch.

Fanning out, the riders make a circle around the house and barn.

In a very few minutes, Lieutenant Baker's hunch will make history.

# CHAPTER SIXTY-ONE

---

Wednesday, April 26, 1865
Garrett farm, Virginia
Dusk to dawn

Until just a few hours ago, John Wilkes Booth was happier and more content than at any time since killing Lincoln. His broken leg notwithstanding, his three days in Virginia, with its pro-Confederate citizens and custom of hospitality, have made him think that escape is a likely possibility. He even disclosed his identity to a group of former southern soldiers he met along the road. To everyone else who's asked, he's a former soldier who was injured at Petersburg and is on his way home.

He's spent the last day at the farmhouse of Richard Garrett, whose son John just returned home from the war. The Garretts do not know Booth's true identity and believe his story about being a former soldier. He's enjoyed hot meals and the chance to wash and sleep. But an hour before sunset came word that Federal cavalry were crossing the ferry over the Rappahannock River.

Booth reacted to the news with visible fear. The Garretts, seeing this, grew suspicious and insisted that both men leave. Booth and Herold refused, though not in a belligerent manner. Not knowing what to do and not wanting to create a problem with the two armed strangers, John Garrett sent them to sleep in the barn. Now Booth and Herold hide in a forty-eight-by-fifty-foot wooden structure, filled with hay and corn. Tobacco-curing equipment is stored inside, and thick cedar beams provide sturdy structural support. Worried that Booth and Herold plan to steal their horses and escape in the night, John and his brother William sleep outside the barn, armed with a pistol.

Booth doesn't realize the Garrett brothers are outside guarding the barn; nor does he know that the cavalry is surrounding the house. All he is sure of is that at two A.M. the dogs begin barking. Then a terrified John Garrett steps into the barn and orders the men to give up their weapons. The building is surrounded, he tells them.

"Get out of here," Booth cries, "or I will shoot you. You have betrayed me."

∽

Garrett flees, locking the barn door behind him. Booth and Herold are now trapped inside, with no idea how many men are out there. Then Herold says he wants out. He's sick of this life and wants to go home. He's done nothing wrong and wishes to proclaim his innocence.

"Captain," Booth calls out, not knowing the proper rank to use. "There is a man here who very much wants to surrender."

Then he turns to Herold in disgust: "Go away from me, damned coward."

Herold exits through the main door, wrists first. He is immediately taken away and arrested by the soldiers.

Lieutenant Baker calls to Booth, telling him that the barn will be set on fire within moments unless Booth surrenders. "Well, Captain," Booth cries out, his old sense of the dramatic now fully returned, "you may prepare a stretcher for me. Draw up your men. Throw open the door. Let's have a fair fight."

Then Booth hears the crackle of burning straw and smells the sickly sweet wood smoke of burning cedar. "One more stain on the old banner!" he yells, doing his best to sound fearless. No one quite knows what that statement means.

He looks across the barn and sees Lieutenant Baker opening the door. The actor hefts his loaded carbine, preparing to take aim.

Just as Abraham Lincoln felt a slight instant of pain and then nothing at all when Booth shot him, now Booth hears the crack of a rifle and feels a jolt in his neck, and then nothing. Sergeant Boston Corbett has fired a bullet and it slices through Booth's spinal cord and paralyzes him from the neck down. John Wilkes Booth collapses to the floor of the barn, the flames now climbing higher and higher all around him.

Boston Corbett, in his own way, is as much a zealot as Booth. Only his passion is religion. Incredibly, years before, Corbett cut off his own testicles with a pair of scissors after experiencing a moment of lust. Booth has now been shot by a man very much like himself: a rebellious fanatic. Corbett actually disobeyed orders when taking aim at the actor. Baker and Conger pull John Wilkes Booth from the barn moments before it is completely engulfed in flames. The actor is still alive.

As with Lincoln, the decision is made not to transport him, for any movement will surely kill the actor. But he is dead by morning anyway. His limp body is hurled into the back of a garbage wagon.

The flight—and life—of John Wilkes Booth has come to an end. He is just twenty-six years old.

THE MURDERERS DOOM. MISERABLE DEATH OF J. WILKES BOOTH, THE ASSASSIN OF PRESIDENT LINCOLN.
*Shot through the head by Sergeant Boston Corbett in a barn on Garrett's Farm, near Port Royal, near the Rappahannock, April 25, 1865.*

# CHAPTER SIXTY-TWO

FRIDAY, JULY 7, 1865
WASHINGTON, D.C.
DAWN

Two and a half months later, the rounding up of Lincoln's killers has become a national pastime. Secretary of War Stanton has personally taken charge of identifying the larger conspiracy that has grown out of Booth's single gunshot, pushing Lafayette Baker from the limelight. While some in the Confederate South now call Booth a martyr and hang pictures of him in their homes as they would for any family member, northerners are even more determined to see every last one of his co-conspirators found—and killed. The jails are full of men and women who have been trapped in the spider's web of the Stanton investigation. Some have absolutely nothing to do with Lincoln's death, like James Pumphrey, the Confederate-sympathizing owner of a stable, who spent a month behind bars. No one is immune from suspicion. Federal agents scour their list of suspects, making sure no one is overlooked. One missing suspect is twenty-one-year-old John Surratt, whose mother, Mary, provided Booth and his conspirators with weapons and lodging.

Mary herself sits inside the old Arsenal Penitentiary awaiting her fate. She's been locked up since her arrest on April 17. The trial of all the co-conspirators, including Mary, began on May 10, and some 366 witnesses were called before it was over, seven weeks later. From the beginning, the public viewed all the conspirators as clearly criminals. Certainly the drunken George Atzerodt and the brutish thug who attacked the Sewards, Lewis Powell, look the part. But Mary Surratt is different. Standing five foot six, with a buxom figure and a pretty smile that captivates some of the journalists in attendance, Mary has initially engendered some sympathy, and many Americans wonder if her life should be spared.

∽

But Mary's physical appearance, like that of her co-conspirators, began to change as the trial stretched into its sixth and seventh weeks. She suffered severe cramping, excessive menstruating and constant urinating from a disease known as endometriosis. She was barely tended to by her captors, or given the freedom to properly care for herself. Her cell was called "barely habitable" by one eyewitness, and court proceedings were stopped on more than one occasion due to her condition.

The other conspirators underwent physical change for a very different reason. Stanton insisted they wear a thick padded hood over the heads. Extra cotton padding was placed over the lids, pressing hard against the eyeballs. There was just one hole, but it didn't line up evenly with the mouth, making eating and breathing a challenge. Underneath the hoods the heat was intense, and the air stifling. All the sweating and the bloating of the skin from the heavy hoods conspired to make each conspirator look more and more swollen and rabid with each passing day. Over time they resembled not so much men, but crazed apparitions.

∽

After deliberating for three days, the nine-member jury finds Mary Surratt, Lewis Powell, George Atzerodt, and David Herold guilty. They will be hanged. As for Dr. Samuel Mudd, Michael O'Laughlen, Ned Spangler, and Samuel Arnold, their punishment will be the remote penitentiary of Fort Jefferson in the Gulf of Mexico.

There is no one willing to speak up for the men who will hang. But Mary Surratt's priest comes to her defense. So does her daughter,

*Guilty! Sentenced to hang (left column): Lewis Powell, David Herold, George Atzerodt, and Mary Surratt (not pictured). Sentenced to prison (right column): Samuel Arnold, Ned Spangler, Michael O'Laughlen, and Dr. Samuel Mudd (not pictured)*

Anna—though not her missing son, John. Mary Surratt's attorney frantically works to get an audience with President Andrew Johnson so that he might personally intervene on her behalf. Her supporters say she was just a lone woman trying to make ends meet by providing weapons for Booth and his conspiracy and point out that she didn't pull the trigger and was nowhere near Ford's Theatre.

There is hope. Not much, but a little. The other three sentenced to hang are all part of Booth's inner circle. Not so with Mary Surratt. Although Johnson will not speak to him, her attorney continues to argue to the fringe of President Johnson's outer circle, those who actively prevent him from speaking with the president, that her life should be spared.

∽

Mary Surratt spends the night of July 6 in prayer, asking God to spare her life.

In the morning, she refuses breakfast, and even at ten A.M., when her visitors are told to leave so that her body can be prepared, Mary is still hoping. She wears a black dress and veil. Her ankles and wrists are manacled. And then she is marched out into a blazing summer sun. She looks up at the ten-foot-high gallows, newly built for the execution of her and the other conspirators. She sees the freshly dug graves beneath the gallows—the spot where her body will rest for all eternity.

Mary Surratt, Lewis Powell, George Atzerodt, and David Herold climb the gallows staircase. They are seated in chairs on the platform at the top. Their hands and arms are tied to their bodies—the men's with ropes, Mary's with white cloth. Their legs are tied together at the ankles and knees so that they won't kick wildly after the hangman springs the door.

"Mrs. Surratt is innocent!" Powell cries out, just before a white cotton hood is placed over his head.

Outside the prison, Mary's supporters gather. Time is short. But there is still hope. Soldiers stand atop the penitentiary walls, just in case a last-minute rider approaches with a pardon. Inside the penitentiary, one hundred civilians have won the right to watch Lincoln's killers die. The muggy air is thick with anticipation.

All it takes is one word from President Johnson. Mary Surratt continues to pray.

"Please don't let me fall," she says to an executioner, getting vertigo as she looks down on the crowd from atop the tall, unstable gallows. He puts the white hood over her head, and then she stands alone, terrified that she might topple forward over the edge of the gallows before the pardon can arrive.

The death sentences are read in alphabetical order by General Winfield Scott Hancock, another old friend of Generals Grant and Lee from their days in Mexico.

Each trapdoor is held in place by a single post. At the bottom of the scaffold stand four hand-selected members of the armed forces. It is their job to kick away the posts on the signal from the hangman. Suddenly, that signal is given.

The trapdoors swing open. Mary Surratt, like the others, drops six feet in an instant. But unlike the others', her neck does not break, and

she does not die right away. The forty-two-year-old mother and widow, whose son would not come to her rescue out of fear for his own life, swings for five long minutes before her larynx is crushed and her body stops fighting for air.

Stanton lets the bodies dangle in the wind for twenty more minutes before pronouncing that he is satisfied. The corpses are buried in the hard prison yard.

Mary Surratt becomes the first and only woman ever hanged by the United States government.

# AFTERWORD

The saga of Lincoln's assassination went on long after he died. Indeed, it continues to this day, as historians and amateur sleuths alike debate a never-ending list of conspiracy theories. The full truth may never be known.

As for the other key figures in the dramatic events of April 1865, their fates are now part of the historical record.

The body of **John Wilkes Booth** was returned to Washington on the *John S. Ide*. Booth's dentist and his personal physician were both brought on board and testified that the body was that of Booth. It was photographed, and then the surgeon general, Joseph Barnes, who had tended to Lincoln in the president's final hours, performed an autopsy while the ship was sailing. The cause of death was determined to be a "gunshot wound in the neck," with the added notation that paralysis was immediate after Booth was shot, "and all the horrors of consciousness of suffering and death must have been present to the assassin during the two hours he lingered."

Dr. Barnes removed the third, fourth, and fifth cervical vertebrae from Booth's neck. These clearly showed the path of the bullet as it entered, then exited the body. The vertebrae are now housed at Walter Reed Army Medical Center, in the National Museum of Health and Medicine—although they are not on public display. Dr. Barnes then turned his completed autopsy over to Secretary of War Edwin

Stanton, who also took control of the photographs made of the corpse, and of Booth's diary, which was handed to him by Lafayette C. Baker.

Curiously, the photographs soon disappeared. And when Baker was later called upon to verify that Booth's diary actually belonged to the killer, he was astonished to see that "eighteen leaves," or pages, had been cut from the journal—allegedly by Secretary Stanton. Neither the photographs nor the missing pages have ever been found, casting more suspicion on Stanton's possible role in a conspiracy.

The secretary of war wished the Booth situation to be handled with as little public outcry as possible, and this meant forbidding a public funeral. On Stanton's orders, Lafayette Baker staged a mock burial, wrapping the body in a horse blanket and publicly hurling it into the Potomac. However, this was just a ruse to conceal the body's actual location. After the crowd on shore watched Baker dump a weighted object into the river, the ship traveled around a bend to the site of the old penitentiary, on the grounds of the Washington Arsenal. The assassin was buried in an anonymous grave beneath the prison's dirt floor, his body concealed inside the gun box that served as his casket. When, two years later, the penitentiary was shuttered and leveled, Booth's remains were moved to the family plot at Green Mount Cemetery in Baltimore, where they remain to this day.

Despite all evidence that Booth is actually dead and was buried in the grave bearing his name, various legends have maintained that he escaped into the South and lived a long life. In December 2010, Booth's descendants agreed to exhume the remains of Edwin Booth to see if DNA from his body is a match for the DNA in the vertebrae housed at Walter Reed. As the chief historian for the Navy Medical Department noted, "If it compares favorably, then that's the end of the controversy. If it doesn't match, you change American history." As of this writing, the outcome of that investigation is still pending.

∽

**Mary Lincoln** never recovered from Abraham Lincoln's assassination. She insisted on wearing only the color black for the rest of her life. Mary lingered in the White House for several weeks after the shooting, then returned home to Illinois, where she spent her time answering the many letters of condolence she had received from around the world, and also lobbying Congress for a pension. This was granted in 1870, for the sum of $3,000 per year. However, just when it appeared that Mary was recovering from her considerable grief, in 1871 her eighteen-year-old son, Tad, died of a mysterious heart condition. This brought on a downward spiral of mental instability, dramatized in spending sprees, paranoia, and delusions—once she almost jumped out of a building after wrongly believing she saw flames consuming the structure. Her only remaining son, Robert, had her committed to a mental institution in 1875. She spent a year there, during which she engaged in a letter-writing campaign to the *Chicago Tribune* that so embarrassed Robert he had her released. Mary moved to the south of France for four years, living in exile in the town of Pau before returning to Springfield. She died in 1882, at the age of sixty-three. She is buried alongside her husband.

∽

**Robert Todd Lincoln** went on to a stellar career as an attorney and then public official. He served as secretary of war from 1881 to 1885, during the James Garfield and Chester Arthur administrations, and served as U.S. minister to Great Britain from 1889 to 1893, under Benjamin Harrison. Although he was not present at Ford's Theatre when his father was assassinated, he was an eyewitness to Garfield's assassination in 1881 and nearby when President William McKinley was assassinated, in 1901.

John Wilkes Booth would have been enraged to know that Robert Lincoln and **Lucy Lambert Hale** spent the afternoon of Lincoln's assassination together, studying Spanish. It's possible that Lucy could have mentioned this upcoming appointment to the assassin during their final moments together that morning, fueling his jealousy. In the end, it doesn't matter, because Lucy Lambert Hale will forever be linked with John Wilkes Booth.

Secretary Stanton, out of respect for her father's position, refused to let her be called upon to testify at the trial. However, there were rumors that she was smuggled aboard the *Ides* to view Booth's body and wept openly at the sight. This has never been confirmed. Regardless, the intimacy of their relationship soon became widespread knowledge in Washington, D.C., and she was only too happy to escape to

Spain for the next five years while her father served as ambassador. Lucy and Robert Todd Lincoln continued to maintain a friendly relationship, but she chose to marry William Chandler in 1874. She bore one child, a son, at the age of forty-four. William Chandler went on to serve as secretary of the navy. Their grandson Theodore Chandler would become a highly decorated World War II navy admiral who was killed when kamikazes attacked his ship in the Pacific. Lucy Lambert Hale died of natural causes in 1915, at the age of seventy-four.

Robert Todd Lincoln died at his home in Vermont at the age of eighty-two, though not before being present for the dedication of the Lincoln Memorial in Washington, D.C., in 1922. He is buried in Arlington National Cemetery.

∽

**Laura Keene** would regret cradling Lincoln's head in her lap that night in Ford's Theatre. The assassination linked her troupe with the killing, and the attendant notoriety was hard on her already floundering career. The actress was eminently resourceful, however, and left America to barnstorm through England before returning in 1869 to manage the Chestnut Street Theatre in Philadelphia. She later took to lecturing on the fine arts and publishing a weekly art journal. Laura Keene died of tuberculosis on November 4, 1873, in Montclair, New Jersey. She was believed to be forty-seven, although she was often vague about her actual birthdate and may have been three years older.

∽

**Edwin Stanton** did not live long after the death of Abraham Lincoln, and those years he did live were fraught with controversy. Stanton clashed repeatedly with President Andrew Johnson over the process of Reconstruction. Johnson's vengeful policies toward the South were in direct contrast with what Lincoln had hoped for, and despite their earlier animosity toward each other, Stanton was keen to see Lincoln's wishes put in place. Tensions between Stanton and Johnson got so bad that in 1868 the president fired Stanton as secretary of war and replaced him with Ulysses S. Grant. Stanton refused to leave the office and was vindicated when the Senate voted that Johnson's actions were illegal. Johnson tried once again to replace Stanton, this time with General

Lorenzo Thomas. Stanton barricaded himself in his office to avoid being removed. The Senate, which had openly clashed with Johnson over other key issues, now began impeachment hearings, stating that Johnson did not have the authority to remove the secretary of war. Though Johnson escaped removal from office by one vote in the Senate, Stanton was the clear winner in the case. He retired soon after the vote, only to be nominated as a justice to the Supreme Court by the newly elected president, Ulysses S. Grant. Edwin Stanton died before he could take the oath. The end came on Christmas Eve 1869; at the age of fifty-five, Stanton died from a sudden and very severe asthma attack. Did he have any part in the assassination of Abraham Lincoln? To this day, there are those who believe he did. But nothing has ever been proved.

∽

Few men could have successfully followed Abraham Lincoln as president, but **Andrew Johnson** proved particularly inept. His Reconstruction policies were bitterly divisive, to the point that he warred openly with members of his own party. He dodged impeachment but was not reelected to office in 1868. Later in life, Johnson was reelected to the Senate, but soon afterward he died from a stroke, on July 31, 1875.

∽

**Lafayette Baker** became an instant celebrity for finding Lincoln's killer. The red-bearded detective wrote a best-selling memoir in 1867, *History of the United States Secret Service*. In the book, he detailed his role in finding John Wilkes Booth. Several of his claims, including that he'd handed Booth's diary to Edwin Stanton, led to a congressional investigation into his role in the disappearance of the diary. Soldiers had given Baker the diary upon returning to Washington with Booth's body. Baker then gave it to Stanton, who locked it in a safe for almost two years, never telling investigators that he had the crucial piece of evidence in his possession. The publication of Baker's memoir provoked a great public demand for Stanton to produce the diary. He did so reluctantly, but eighteen pages were missing. The secretary of war denied being responsible for excising the pages. The investigation ended without a formal placement of blame.

In 1960, a controversial amateur historian named Ray Neff came upon a description of the Lincoln assassination in a copy of *Colburn's United Service Magazine*, a British military journal. The article was dated February 5, 1868. Lafayette Baker was the author. Neff claims to have deciphered a coded message from Baker within the story. The substitution code revealed a message that reads thus: "It was on the 10th of April, 1865, when I first knew that the plan was in action. I did not know the identity of the assassin, but I knew most all else when I approached Edwin Stanton about it. He at once acted surprised and disbelieving. Later he said: 'You are a party to it, too.'"

Baker, decoded by Neff, goes on to add: "There were at least eleven members of Congress involved in the plot, no less than twenty Army officers, three Naval officers, and at least twenty-four civilians, of which one was a governor of a loyal state. Five were bankers of great repute, three were nationally known newspapermen, and eleven were industrialists of great repute and wealth. Eighty-five thousand dollars were contributed by the named persons to pay for the deed. Only eight persons knew the details of the plot and the identity of others. I fear for my life."

There is no consensus about whether Neff's hidden message is authentic. What we do know for sure is that Stanton did not hesitate to ask the previously disgraced Baker to lead the Booth investigation—this at a time when the secretary of war had every single detective in the nation at his disposal—and that Baker magically pinpointed Booth's actual location when the thousands of soldiers and detectives combing the woods and swamps could not.

It should be noted that Neff's hypothesis and his entire body of work have been repudiated and dismissed by the vast majority of trained historians and assassination scholars. *Civil War Times*, which originally published his findings about the cipher messages, later denounced him. Once Neff became involved with the movie *The Lincoln Conspiracy* and began promoting bizarre theories about Booth's escape and a later second life in India, he became even more ostracized from mainstream scholars.

The fact remains, however, that Stanton's withholding of Booth's diary was suspicious, as is the subject of the eighteen missing pages. No one has adequately explained this behavior, thus allowing some conspiracy theorists to continue to wonder if he had a larger role in Lincoln's assassination.

Baker became increasingly paranoid after the congressional investigation, certain that he would be murdered. And he was right! Just eighteen months after the investigation, he was found dead in his home in Philadelphia. While Baker was at first believed to have died from meningitis, evidence now points to a slow and systematic death by poisoning. Again, this evidence comes from Ray Neff. The Indiana State University professor used an atomic absorption spectrophotometer to analyze strands of Baker's hair. The results showed that arsenic had been slowly introduced into his system during the last months of his life. Comparing the rising levels of arsenic with diary entries made by Baker's wife, Neff noted a correlation with visits from Wally Pollack, Baker's brother-in-law, who was in the habit of bringing imported German beer to Baker's house whenever he came calling. Pollack, not incidentally, also worked under Secretary Stanton as a War Department employee. The suspicion is that Pollack poisoned Baker by mixing small amounts of arsenic into the beer. Whether or not he acted alone is a matter of conjecture.

∽

Abraham Lincoln's irresponsible bodyguard **John Parker** never presented himself for duty or tried to help in any way on the night of the assassination. Incredibly, Parker was not held accountable for shirking his duties. In fact, the first time he was seen after the assassination was when he showed up at a Washington police station the next morning in the company of a known prostitute. Formal police charges of dereliction of duty were pressed against Parker, but once again he was acquitted. Three years later, after many attempts to remove him from the police department, Parker was finally booted for "gross neglect of duty." He went on to work as a carpenter and machinist. He died of pneumonia on June 28, 1890, at the age of sixty.

∽

Lincoln's responsible bodyguard **William Crook** had a more esteemed career, working in the White House for more than fifty years—a time that spanned administrations from Abraham Lincoln's to Woodrow

Wilson's. However, it was his relationship with Lincoln that he trea-
sured most, and his 1910 memoirs provide a vivid insight into the journey to Richmond and the events of April 14. Critics have accused
Crook of padding his own part, but the book makes for compelling
reading. William Crook died in 1915 from pneumonia, at the age of
seventy-seven. He was buried in Arlington National Cemetery, in a
service attended by President Wilson.

∽

After the war, **Robert E. Lee** applied for a pardon for his acts against
the United States. Secretary of State William H. Seward did not file
the pardon but instead gave it to a friend as a souvenir. The document
wasn't discovered for more than one hundred years. President Gerald
R. Ford officially reinstated Lee as a U.S. citizen in 1975.

Marse Robert was buried not at his beloved Virginia home, Arlington, which was confiscated during the war and redesignated as a U.S.
military cemetery, but at Washington and Lee University, in Lexington, Virginia. He died on Columbus Day 1870, at the age of sixty-
three.

∽

Lee's counterpart on the Union side, **General Ulysses S. Grant,** had an
admirable career after the war ended. He remained in the army, helping to implement Reconstruction policies that guaranteed the black
vote. He saw his popularity soar in the North. Elected president in
1868, he served two terms in office. Grant's later years were filled with
travel and, later, financial upheaval. After losing his entire fortune to
bad investments in the early 1880s, he sat down to, with the help of
editor Mark Twain, write his memoirs. Considered by many to be one
of the best military autobiographies in history, Grant's life story was a
best seller. Royalties from the book guaranteed his family a comfortable life long after he died of throat cancer, on July 23, 1885.

The question "Who is buried in Grant's tomb?" seems an obvious
one, for Ulysses S. Grant is buried in this enormous mausoleum in
New York's Riverside Park. However, so is **Julia Grant**. She died on
December 14, 1902, at the age of seventy-six, and now lies alongside
her husband.

∽

After being discovered alive on the battlefield that day after the battle for High Bridge, **Colonel Francis Washburn** was immediately transported to a field hospital, then home to Massachusetts, where he died one week after Lincoln did. Coincidentally, he passed away on the exact same day as the Confederacy's **General James Dearing**, his opposite on the field of battle. They were the last two casualties of High Bridge.

∽

Two officers present at Sayler's Creek, **General James "Pete" Longstreet** and **General George Armstrong Custer**, followed remarkably different paths after the Civil War. Longstreet's longtime friendship with Grant figured prominently in his embrace of pro-Union Reconstruction efforts, much to the chagrin of diehard rebels, who soon began an active series of revisionist attacks on the great southern general, attempting somewhat successfully to impugn his reputation as a leader and paint him as a coward. By the time Longstreet died, in 1904, at the age of eighty-two, he had served as a diplomat, a civil servant, and a U.S. marshal. A house fire consumed all of his Civil War memorabilia, leaving almost no legacy other than his autobiography to set his wartime record straight.

General Custer continued to fight, using the same aggressive, impulsive tactics that served him so successfully at Sayler's Creek. In his time he would become far better known for his battles on America's western frontier and for his friendships with other larger-than-life figures, such as Buffalo Bill Cody. In June 1876, Custer and his Seventh Cavalry were sent to Montana to force Sioux and Cheyenne Indians back to their reservations. On the morning of June 25, his scouts reported that a small band of warriors were camped along the Little Bighorn River. Behaving in much the same fashion as he did at Sayler's Creek, Custer split his cavalry into three columns and attacked without making a preliminary study of the terrain.

The results were disastrous. Custer and his men were soon cut off, surrounded by a vastly superior force of Oglala Sioux under the legendary warrior Crazy Horse. Custer ordered his men to shoot their horses and stack the bodies to shield them from incoming rifle fire, but within an hour every last man was dead. When the Battle of the Little Bighorn was over, the bodies of the slain soldiers were stripped and mutilated, thanks to an Indian belief that the soul of a mutilated body would wander the earth without rest for eternity. Scalps were taken, stomachs slit open, eardrums punctured, and genitals dismembered. In the case of Custer's brother Tom, who had won his second of two congressional Medals of Honor at Sayler's Creek, his heart was cut out and eaten. Another brother, twenty-seven-year-old Boston, was also killed and scalped.

Strangely, the only body left unmutilated was that of George Armstrong Custer. When U.S. soldiers later came upon the battlefield, they described Custer's face as being a mask of calm. A round .45-caliber bullet hole in his left temple and another just below his heart were the only signs of violence—and point to the likelihood that he was killed by a long-range rifle shot.

Initially, Custer was buried in a shallow grave on the battlefield, next to his brother Tom. News of the devastating defeat was quickly conveyed to Fort McPherson, Nebraska, then on to Washington, D.C., by telegraph. Ironically, word of Custer's defeat arrived in the nation's capital on July 4, 1876—America's first centennial. In its own way, the death of Custer was as traumatizing as that of Lincoln, emboldening the United States Army to seek revenge against the Indians in the same way Lincoln's assassination had northerners seeking revenge against the South. Custer was just thirty-six when he died. His body was later relocated from the Little Bighorn and buried at the United States Military Academy at West Point.

∽

**William Seward** would live just seven more years after being attacked in his own bed on the night of Lincoln's assassination, but in that time he would undertake an activity that would leave an even longer-lasting legacy than the heinous attack. In 1867, while still serving as secretary of state and still bearing the disfiguring facial scars of the knife attack, he purchased Alaska for the United States. What soon became known as "Seward's Folly" would later be seen as a huge asset when silver and gold and oil were discovered in the new territory. Seward died on October 10, 1872. He was seventy-one.

∾

**Major Henry Reed Rathbone**, present in the box on the night Lincoln was shot, later married his date from that evening, **Clara Harris**. Unfortunately for Harris, Rathbone later went insane and killed her with a knife. He was institutionalized for the remainder of his life.

∾

**Boston Corbett**, the man who shot John Wilkes Booth, received a handsome reward for the killing, even though he'd disobeyed orders. He left the military soon afterward, first working as a hatter, then serving as assistant doorman for the Kansas state legislature. It appears that the mercury used in making hats, which was well known for causing insanity (giving rise to the term "mad as a hatter"), caused him to become mentally unstable. In 1887 he, too, was sent to an insane asylum, after brandishing a revolver in the legislature. He escaped, then moved north to Minnesota, where he died in the Great Hinckley Fire of 1894. He was sixty-two.

∾

**Dr. Samuel Mudd, Samuel Arnold,** and **Michael O'Laughlen** were all given life sentences for their roles in the assassination conspiracy. **Ned Spangler,** the besotted sceneshifter, received a six-year sentence. All were sent to the Dry Tortugas, a baking-hot group of islands west of the Florida Keys. Their jailers, black Union soldiers, had complete power over the daily movements of these white supremacists. O'Laughlen died of fever while in prison, at the age of twenty-seven. Spangler, Mudd, and Arnold were pardoned in 1869 by Andrew Johnson and lived out their days as law-abiding citizens.

The man who helped John Wilkes Booth and David Herold escape into Virginia, **Thomas Jones,** was circumspect about his role in the assassination for many years. He was taken into custody shortly after Booth was killed and spent seven weeks in the Old Capital Prison before being released. Even though he became a justice of the peace after the war, the tight-lipped former member of the Confederate Secret Service was ever after wary of persecution for aiding John Wilkes Booth and David Herold. That changed in 1893, when he wrote a 126-page book telling his side of the events. Jones died on March 5, 1895, at the age of seventy-four.

∞

Perhaps the most shadowy figure in the Lincoln conspiracy, **John Surratt,** Mary Surratt's son, could have been instrumental in reducing his mother's sentence by showing that her part in the assassination was that of passive support instead of active participation. But rather than give the testimony that might have spared her life, John Surratt fled to Montreal, Canada, immediately after the assassination, where he followed the news of his mother's trial and execution. Surratt then fled to England under an assumed name and later continued on to the Vatican, where he served in the Papal Zouaves. He was discovered and arrested but escaped. Another international search for Surratt soon found him in Alexandria, Egypt. Arrested again, he was brought back to the United States to appear before a judge. Amazingly, the jury deadlocked on his involvement. John Surratt was free to go. He died in 1916 at the age of seventy-two.

∞

**Mary Surratt's** body was reburied in the Catholic cemetery at Mount Olivet in Washington, D.C., where it remains to this day. The petition to spare Mary's life never got to President Andrew Johnson; his assistant Preston King kept the information away from Johnson. But apparently that action preyed on King's conscience. A few months later, King tied a bag of bullets around his neck and leapt from a ferryboat in New York's harbor; he was never seen again. He was fifty-nine years old.

# EPILOGUE

The last days of Abraham Lincoln's life included perhaps the most dramatic events in the nation's history. It is eerie that Abraham Lincoln found much solace in the play *Julius Caesar*, by William Shakespeare, given that the two great men met their ends in the same way. Caesar was betrayed by his countrymen, as was Lincoln. Both men died within months of their fifty-sixth birthday, before they could complete their life's work. Just as the story of Julius Caesar has been told and retold for centuries, the tragedy that befell Lincoln should be known by every American. His life and death continue to shape us as a people, even today. America is a great country, but like every other nation on earth it is influenced by evil. John Wilkes Booth epitomizes the evil that can harm us, even as President Abraham Lincoln represents the good that can make us stronger.

## Appendix

# RE-CREATION OF
# *HARPER'S WEEKLY*

The April 29, 1865, edition of *Harper's Weekly* was entirely devoted to the assassination and death of Abraham Lincoln. The edition went to the printers just hours after word reached Washington that John Wilkes Booth had been located and shot dead. This gives the writers' words an urgency and heartfelt emotion that allow modern readers to gain a very real sense of how the nation was reacting to Lincoln's death. On the day that it came out, Lincoln's funeral train was traveling from Cleveland to Columbus, Ohio, and the trial of the conspirators had not yet begun. The nation was still very much at a loss over how to deal with this national tragedy. Here we reprint the entire text of the article "The Murder of the President" as it appeared in that edition.

# HARPER'S WEEKLY.

### A JOURNAL OF CIVILIZATION

VOL. IX.—No. 435.]　　　NEW YORK, SATURDAY, APRIL 29, 1865.　　　[SINGLE COPIES TEN CENTS.
[$4.00 PER YEAR IN ADVANCE.

Entered according to Act of Congress, in the Year 1865, by Harper & Brothers, in the Clerk's Office of the District Court for the Southern District of New York.

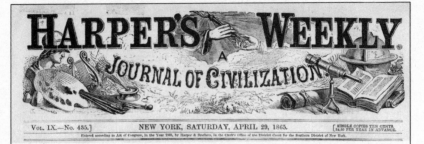

## THE MURDER OF THE PRESIDENT.

The Fourteenth of April is a dark day in our country's calendar. On that day four years ago the national flag was for the first time lowered at the bidding of traitors. Upon that day, after a desperate conflict with treason for four long, weary years—a conflict in which the nation had so far triumphed that she breathed again in the joyous prospect of coming peace—her chosen leader was stricken down by the foul hand of the cowardly assassin. Exultation that had known no bounds was exchanged for boundless grief. The record upon which had been inscribed all sorts of violence possible to the most malignant treason that ever sought to poison a nation's heart had been almost written full. But not quite full. Murder had run out its category of possible degrees against helpless loyalists in the South, against women and children whose houses had been burned down over their heads, and against our unfortunate prisoners, who had been tortured and literally starved to death. But there still remained one victim for its last rude stroke—one victim for whom, it was whispered in rebel journals South and North, there was still reserved the dagger of a BRUTUS. Beaten on every field of recognized warfare, treason outdid its very self, and killed our President.

The man who lent himself to traitors for this vile purpose was JOHN WILKES BOOTH, who sold himself, it may be, partly for the pieces of silver, but chiefly for the infamous notoriety attaching to such an act. There was an ancient vil-

lain who deliberately purposed to perpetuate the memory of his name among men by an act of awful sacrilege—a sacrilege so striking as never to be forgotten—and he burned the temple of the Ephesian Diana. EROSTRATUS gained his end, and has been remembered accordingly. A memory far more detestable is in store for JOHN WILKES BOOTH, who dared, by the commission of an infinitely greater sacrilege, to bring a whole people to tears.

He was the third son born in America of the eminent English tragedian JUNIUS BRUTUS BOOTH. There were three brothers, JUNIUS BRUTUS, Jun., EDWIN, and JOHN WILKES, all of whom inherited a predilection for the stage. EDWIN, however, is the only one of these who has attained a very eminent position as an actor, and he is probably surpassed by no living man. In justice to him it is proper here to state that he is true and loyal, and exacts our sincerest sympathy. The elder BOOTH, father of these three actors, died thirteen years ago. He passed the quieter portion of his life upon his farm, in Harford County, some thirty miles from Baltimore. JOHN WILKES BOOTH, the murderer, was born in 1839,

and is now only twenty-six years of age. He went upon the stage at the early age of seventeen, simply as JOHN WILKES. As stock actor he gained a fair reputation, and afterward assuming his full name, he began a more ambitious career. But, partly on account of his dissolute habits, he never achieved a marked success. He performed chiefly in the South and West. He has appeared but few times before a New York audience. In person he bears considerable resemblance to his father. His eyes are dark and large; his hair of the same color, inclined to curl; his features finely molded; his form tall, and his address pleasing. He abandoned his profession recently on account of a bronchial affection. It is said that he has frequently threatened to kill President LINCOLN. His companions have been violent Secessionists, and there are doubtless many others involved to a greater or less degree in his crime. The attempt to assassinate Secretary SEWARD was made probably by an accomplice. It is supposed that Secretary STANTON and ANDREW JOHNSON were to have been added to the list of victims. The latter, at least, received on Friday a card from BOOTH, but was not at home.

Those who were acquainted with BOOTH'S movements on the fatal Friday say that his manner was restless. He knew that the President and his party intended to be present at Ford's Theatre in the evening. He asked an acquaintance if he should attend the performance, remarking that if he did he would see some unusually fine acting. It was the general expectation that General GRANT would form one of the President's party, and there are many who suppose that a blow was intended for him as well as the President. The latter had passed the day in the usual manner. In the morning his son, Capt. ROBERT LINCOLN, breakfasted with him.— The Captain had just returned from the capitulation of ROBERT E. LEE, and the President listened with great interest to his narration of the detailed circumstances. After breakfast he conversed for an hour with Speaker COLFAX about his future policy as to the rebellion which he was about to submit to his Cabinet. At 11 o'clock the Cabinet met. Both the President and General GRANT were present. Having spent the afternoon with Governor OGLESBY, Senator YATES, and other leading citizens of his State, he went to the theatre in the evening with Mrs. LINCOLN, in order to unite in the general expression of popular joy for our late victories. The party consisted of Mrs. Senator HARRIS and daughter, and Major HENRY RATHBONE, Of Albany. They arrived at ten minutes before nine o'clock, and occupied a private box over-looking the stage. The play for the evening was The American Cousin.

BOOTH came upon his errand at about 10 o'clock. He left his horse in charge at the rear of the theatre, and made his way to the President's box. This box is a double one, in the second tier at the left of the stage. When occupied by the Presidential party the separating partition is removed, and the two boxes are thus thrown into one. We give an accurate plan of the box on page 259.—According to Major RATHBONE'S statement, the assassin must have made his preparations in the most deliberate manner beforehand. Of this fact there are at least four proofs, as we shall see: Stealthily approaching the dark passageway leading to the box, BOOTH, after having effected an entrance,

closed the hall door, and then, taking a piece of board which he had prepared for the occasion, placed one end of it in an indentation excavated in the wall, about four feet from the floor, and the other against the moulding of the door-panel a few inches higher. He thus made it impossible for any one to enter from without; and securing himself against intrusion in that direction, he proceeded to the doors of the box. There were two of those. Here also the villain had carefully provided before hand the means by which he might, unnoticed himself, observe the position of the parties inside. With a gimlet, or small bit, he had bored a hole in the door-panel, which he afterward reamed out with his knife, so as to leave it a little larger than a buck-shot on the inside, while on the other side it was sufficiently large to give his eye a wide range. To secure against the doors being locked (they both had spring-locks), he had loosened the screws with which the bolt-hasps were fastened. In regard to the next stage of BOOTH'S movements there is some degree of uncertainty. He had been noticed as he passed through the dress-circle by a Mr.

FERGUSON, who was sitting on the opposite side of the theatre. This man knew BOOTH, and recognized him. He had been talking with him a short time before. FERGUSON states that when BOOTH reached the door of the corridor leading from the dress-circle to the boxes he halted, "took off his hat, and, holding it in his left hand, leaned against the wall behind him." After remaining thus for the space of half a minute, "he stepped down one step, put his hand on the door of the little corridor leading to the box, bent his knee against it," when the door opened and BOOTH entered. After his entrance to the corridor he was of course invisible to FERGUSON, and, before the fatal shot, was probably seen by no one but the sentry at the door of the corridor. The latter he is said to have passed on the plea that the President had sent for him. What passed before the shot is only conjecturable. He made his observations, doubtless, through the aperture in the door provided for that purpose. And here we come upon another proof of a deliberately-prepared plan. The very seats in the box had been arranged to suit his purpose, either by himself or, as is more likely, by some attaché of the theatre in complicity with him. The President sat in the left-hand corner of the box, nearest the audience, in an easy arm-chair. Next to him, on the right, sat Mrs. LIN-COLN, Some distance to the right of both Miss HARRIS was seated, with Major RATHBONE at her left and a little in the rear of Mrs. LIN-COLN. BOOTH rapidly surveyed the situation. The play had reached the second scene of the third act. Mrs. LINCOLN, intent on the play, was leaning forward, with one hand resting on her husband's knee. The President was leaning upon one hand, and with the other was adjusting a portion of the drapery, his face wearing a pleasant smile as it was partially turned to the audience. As to the act of assassination, there are two conflicting statements. According to one, BOOTH fired through the door at the left, which was closed. But this seems to have been unnecessary; and it is far more probable that he entered rapidly through the door at the right, and the next moment fired. The ball entered just behind the President's left ear, and though not producing instantaneous death completely obliterated all consciousness.

Major RATHBONE hearing the report, saw the assassin about six feet distant from the President, and encountered him; but BOOTH shook off his grasp. The latter had dropped his weapon—an ordinary pocket-pistol—and had drawn a long glittering knife, with which he inflicted a wound upon the Major; and then, resting his left hand upon the railing, vaulted over easily to the stage, eight or nine feet below. As he passed between the folds of the flag decorating the box, his spur, which he wore on the right heel, caught the drapery and brought it down. He crouched as he fell, falling upon one knee, but quickly gained an up-right position, and staggered in a theatrical manner across the stage, brandishing his knife, and shouting, "Sic semper tyrannis!" He made his exit by the "tormentor" on the opposite side of the stage, passing MISS KEENE as he went out. The villain succeeded in making his escape without arrest. In this he was probably assisted by accomplices and by MOSBY'S guerillas.

The President was immediately removed to the house of Mr. PETER-SON, opposite the theatre, where he died at twenty-two minutes past seven the next morning, never having recovered his consciousness since the fatal shot. In his last hours he was attended by his wife and his son ROBERT, and prominent members of his Cabinet. His death has plunged the nation into deepest mourning, but his spirit still animates the people for whom he died.

## A DIRGE.

LOWER the starry flag
Amid a sovereign people's lamentation For him the honored ruler of the nation;

Lower the starry flag!

Let the great bells be toll'd

Slowly and mournfully in every steeple, Let them make known the sorrow of the people;

Let the great bells be toll'd!

Lower the starry flag, And let the solemn, sorrowing anthem, pealing, Sound from the carven choir to fretted ceiling; Lower the starry flag!

Let the great bells be toll'd,

And let the mournful organ music, rolling, Tune with the bells in every steeple tolling;

Let the great bells be toll'd!

Lower the starry flag;

The nation's honored chief in death is sleeping, And for our loss our eyes are wet with weeping; Lower the starry flag!

Let the great bells be toll'd;

His honest, manly heart has ceased its beating, His lips no more shall speak the kindly greeting;

Let the great bells be toll'd!

Lower the starry flag;

No more shall sound his voice 'in scorn of error, Filling the traitor's heart with fear and terror; Lower the starry flag!

Let the great bells be toll'd;

He reverenced the gift which God has given, Freedom to all, the priceless boon of Heaven, Let the great bells be toll'd!

Lower the starry flag;

Hit dearest hopes were wedded with' the nation, He valued more than all the land's salvation;

Lower the starry flag!

Let the great bells be toll'd;

His name shall live on History's brightest pages, His voice shall sound through Time's remotest ages; Let the great bells be toll'd!

### A NATION'S GRIEF.

AH! Grief doth follow fast on Victory! The vic-tors' shout is lost in silence, deep—Too deep for our poor human utter-ance. The jubilant flags that only yesterday Were the bright heralds of a nation's gain, Now droop at half-mast for her woe-ful loss. Our foremost Hero fallen, sore at heart we lie Prostrate, in tears, at our dear Lincoln's grave!

The dust of our great Leader, kissed to rest, And folded to our hearts, is there inurned, Beyond the breath of scandal, in sweet peace. Wounded with his wound, our hearts receive The mantle of his spirit as it flies.

His words remain to us our sacred Law: Do we not hear them from the Capitol?—

"Malice toward none, with charity for all!"

The blow at Sumter touched us not so much With grief, or awe of treason, as this last—This cruelest thrust of all at his dear head, Which with spent rage the baf-fled serpent aimed. It is the world's old story, told again,

That they who bruise the serpent's venomed head Must bear, even as Christ did, its last foul sting, Taking the Savior's Passion with His Crown!

With malice toward none, with charity for all, with firmness in the right, as God gives us to see the right, let us strive on to finish the work we are in, to bind up the nation's wounds, to care for him who shall have borne the battle, and for his widow and his orphans; to do all which may achieve and cherish a just and a lasting peace among ourselves and with all nations."—Last Words of President Lincoln's Second Inaugural.

### HARPER'S WEEKLY. SATURDAY, APRIL 29, 1865.
#### Abraham Lincoln.

GREATER love hath no man than this, that a man lay down his life for his friends. ABRAHAM LINCOLN has done that. He has sealed his service to his country by the last sacrifice. On the day that commemorates the great sorrow which Christen-dom reveres, the man who had no thought, no wish, no hope but the salvation of his country, laid down his life. Yet how many and many a heart that throbbed with inexpress-ible grief as the tragedy was told would gladly have been stilled forever if his might have beat on. So wise and good, so loved and trusted, his death is a personal blow to every faithful Ameri-can household; nor will any life be a more cher-ished tradition, nor any name be longer and more tenderly beloved by this nation, than those of ABRAHAM LINCOLN.

On the 22d of February, 1861, as he raised the American flag over Independence Hall, in Philadelphia, he spoke of the sentiment in the Declaration of Independence which gave liberty not only to this country, but, "I hope," he said, "to the world for all future time." Then, with a solemnity which the menacing future justified, and with a significance which subsequent events revealed, he added, "But if this country can not be saved without giving up that principle, I was about to say I would rather be assassinated upon this spot than surrender it." The country has been saved by cleaving to that principle, and he has been assassinated for not surrendering it.

Called to the chief conduct of public affairs at a time of the greatest peril, he came almost unknown, but he brought to his great office a finer comprehension of the condition of the country than the most noted statesmen of all parties, and that sure instinct of the wiser popular will which made him the best of all leaders for a people about to maintain their own government in a civil war. Himself a child of the people, he lived and died

their friend. His heart beat responsive to theirs. He knew their wants, their character, their powers, and knowing their will often better than they knew it themselves, he executed it with the certainty of their speedy approval. No American statesman ever believed more heartily than he the necessary truth of the fundamental American principle of absolute equality before the laws, or trusted with ampler confidence the American system of government. But he loved liberty too sincerely for passion or declamation. It was the strong, sturdy, Anglo-Saxon affection, not the Celtic frenzy.

With an infinite patience, and a dauntless tenacity, he was a man of profound principles but of no theories. This, with his insight and intuitive appreciation of the possibilities of every case, made him a consummate practical statesman. He saw farther and deeper than others because he saw that in the troubled time upon which he was cast little could be wholly seen. Experience so vindicated his patriotic sagacity that he acquired a curious ascendency in the public confidence; so that if good men differed from his opinion they were inclined to doubt their own. Principle was

fixed as a star, but policy must be swayed by the current. While many would have dared the fierce fury of the gale and have sunk the ship at once, he knew that there was a time to stretch every inch of canvas and a time to lay to. He was not afraid of "drifting." In statesmanship prudence counts for more than daring. Thus it happened that some who urged him at the beginning of the war to the boldest measures, and excused what they called his practical faithlessness by his probable weakness, lived to feel the marrow of their bones melt with fear, and to beg him to solicit terms that would have destroyed the nation. But wiser than passion, more faithful than fury, serene in his devotion to the equal rights of men without which he knew there could hence-forth be no peace in this country, he tranquilly persisted, enduring the impatience of what seemed to some his painful delays and to others his lawless haste; and so, trusting God and his own true heart, he fulfilled his great task so well that he died more tenderly lamented than any ruler in history.

His political career, from his entrance into the Illinois Legislature to his last speech upon the Louisiana plan of reconstruction, is calmly consistent both in the lofty humanity of its aim and the good sense of its method, and our condition is the justification of his life. For the most malignant party opposition in our history crumbled before his spotless fidelity; and in his death it is not a party that loses a head, but a country that deplores a father. The good sense, the good humor, the good heart of ABRAHAM LINCOLN gradually united the Democracy that despised the "sentimentality of abolitionism," and the abolitionism that abhorred the sneering inhumanity of "Democracy," in a practical patriotism that has saved the country.

No one who personally knew him but will now feel that the deep, furrowed sadness of his face seemed to forecast his fate. The genial gentleness of his manner, his homely simplicity, the cheerful humor that never failed are now seen to have been but the tender light that played around the rugged heights of his strong and noble nature. It is small consolation that he dies at the moment of the war when he could best be spared, for no nation is ever ready for the loss of such a friend. But it is something to remember that he lived to see the slow day breaking. Like Moses he had marched with us through the wilderness. From the height of patriotic vision he beheld the golden fields of the future waving in peace and plenty out of sight. He beheld and blessed God, but was not to enter in. And we with bowed heads and aching hearts move forward to the promised land.

## President Johnson.

No President has entered upon the duties of his office under circumstances so painful as those which surround ANDREW JOHNSON. The pause between the death of Mr. LINCOLN and the indication of the probable course of his successor is profoundly solemn. But there can be but one emotion in every true American heart, and that is, the most inflexible determination to support President JOHNSON, who is now the lawful head of a great nation emerging from terrible civil war, and entering upon the solemn duty of pacification.

ANDREW JOHNSON, like his predecessor, is emphatically a man of the people. He has been for many years in public life, and when the war began he was universally hailed as one of the truest and sturdiest of patriots. His former political association with the leaders of the Southern policy, his position as a Senator from a most important border State, indicated him to the conspirators as an invaluable ally, if he could be seduced to treason. If we are not misinformed, JOHN C. BRECKINRIDGE under-took this task; and how he failed—how ANDREW JOHNSON upon the floor of the Senate denounced treason and traitors—is already historical. From that moment he was one of the firmest friends of the Government, and most ardent supporters of the late Administration. His relations with Mr. LINCOLN were peculiarly friendly; and when the news of ROSECRANS's victory at Mill Spring reached the President at midnight, he immediately sent his secretary to tell the good news to Mr. JOHNSON.

He was appointed Military Governor of Tennessee upon the national occupation of that State, and for three years he has stood in that exposed point at the front, a faithful sentry. Formerly a slaveholder, and familiar with the public opinion of the border, he early saw the necessity of the emancipation war policy; and although in his addresses at the beginning of the war he spoke of it as still uncertain and prospective, his views ripened with those of the country, and when the policy was declared he supported it with the sincerity of earnest conviction.

His provisional administration of government in Tennessee, which was for some time debatable ground, was firm and faithful. By the necessity of the case he was the object of the envenomed hostility of the rebels and the bitterest opposition of the enemies of the Administration. The most serious charge of his exercise of arbitrary power was the severe oath as a qualification for voting which Governor JOHNSON approved before the Presidential election. When the remonstrants appealed to President LINCOLN, he replied that he was very sure Governor JOHNSON would do what was necessary and right. And while the opposition at the North was still loudly denouncing, JEFFERSON DAVIS, in one of his furious speeches in Georgia, after the fall of Atlanta, declared that there were thirty thousand men in Tennessee eager to take up arms the moment the rebel army appeared in the State. It was to prevent those thirty thousand from doing by their votes what they were ready to do by

their arms that the oath was imposed. JEFFERSON DAVIS furnished the amplest justification for the action of Governor JOHNSON. President LINCOLN was reproached for the too conciliatory character of his "Border State policy." Let it not be for-gotten that at the time when he was thought to be too much influenced by it he appointed Mr. JOHNSON Governor of Tennessee. That Governor JOHNSON'S course in the State was ape proved by the unconditional loyal men there is shown by the adoption of the new free constitution and the opening of the new era under the administration of Governor BROWNLOW.

Of a more ardent temperament than Mr. LINCOLN, whose passionless patience was sublime, Mr. JOHNSON has had a much sharper personal experience of the atrocious spirit of this rebellion. He has seen and felt the horrors of which we have only heard. The great guilt of treason is vividly present to his mind and memory, and his feeling toward the leaders who are morally responsible for this wasting war is one of stern hostility.

But the Governor of Tennessee in a most critical period of civil war is

now President of the United States at a time when the war in the field is ending and the peace of a whole country is to be secured. What is the great truth that confronts him at the opening of his new career? It is that the policy of his predecessor had been so approved by the mind and heart of the country, had so disarmed hostility and melted prejudice, that the spirit of that policy has almost the sanctity of prescription.

That President JOHNSON will so regard it we have the fullest confidence. That what every loyal man sees, so strong and devoted a patriot as he will fail to see, is not credible. That the successor of ABRAHAM LINCOLN will adopt a policy of vengeance is impossible. Of the leading traitors, as he said a fortnight since, he holds that the punishment should be that which the Constitution imposes. "And on the other hand," he added, "to the people who have been deluded and misled I would extend leniency and humanity, and an invitation to return to the allegiance they owe to the country." These are not the words of passion, but of humanity and justice. They express what is doubtless the conviction of the great multitude of loyal citizens of the country. With a modest appeal for the counsel and assistance of the gentlemen who were the advisers of Mr. LINCOLN, and with calm reliance upon God and the people, he addresses himself to his vast responsibilities amidst the hopes and prayers and confidence of his country.

## Mr. Seward.

THE bloody assault upon Secretary SEWARD, a "chivalric" blow struck at a man of sixty-five lying in his bed with a broken arm, has shown the country how precious to it is the life of a man who has been bitterly traduced by many of his former political friends since the war began. Before the shot was fired at Sumter, Mr SEWARD tried by some form of negotiation to prevent the outbreak of civil war. He was then— does Mr. HORACE GREELEY remember?— as-sailed with insinuations of treachery. Will Mr. HORACE GREE-LEY inform us how it was treacherous to try to prevent the war by negotiation with intending rebels, if, while the war was raging, it was patriotic to urge negotiation with rebels in arms? Will he also tell us whether it was more disloyal to the Union to recognize American citizens not yet in rebellion, or after they had slain thousands and

thousands of brave men in blood and torture to call them "eminent Confederates?" Will he teach us why Mr. SEWARD was to be held up to public suspicion because he communicated with Judge CAMPBELL and recommended Mr. HARVEY as Minister to Portugal, while Mr. GREELEY calls one of the basest panders to this scourging war, a man who does his fighting by sending criminals from Canada to burn down theatres and hotels in New York full of women and children, "a distinguished American" of the other party in our civil war?

For four years Mr. SEWARD, as Secretary of State, has defended this country from one of the most constantly threatening perils, that of foreign war. His name in England is not beloved. But seconded by his faithful lieutenant, Mr. ADAMS, he has maintained there the honor of the American name, and persistently asserted the undiminished sovereignty of the Government of the United States. In France, with the cool, clear, upright man who so fitly represented the simplicity and honesty of a popular Government, he has managed our relations with a skill that has protected us from most

serious complications in Mexico. Engaged with the most unscrupulous and secret of modern diplomatists, Louis NAPOLEON, he has with admirable delicacy of skill prevented his interference in our domestic affairs. His dispatches have been free from bluster or timidity. They all show, what his life illustrates, a perfect serenity of faith in the final success of free institutions and the strength of a popular Government.

Like every man in the country, Mr. SEWARD has been taught by the war. None of us are the same. The views of every man have been modified. The course of some organs of public opinion–of the New York Tribune, for instance—is wonderful and incredible to contemplate. There have been times when Mr. SEWARD was thought by some to be a positive hindrance to the war, a nightmare in the Cabinet. The Senate, with questionable friendship to the country, upon one occasion is understood to have asked his removal. But the President could ill spare so calm a counselor and so adroit a statesman. That they often differed is beyond dispute, but the President knew the sagacity and experience of the Secretary, and the Secretary said the

President was the best man he ever knew.

Such was the confidence and mutual respect of the relation between them that the country will regard Mr. SEWARD'S continuance in the Cabinet as a sign of the perpetuity of the spirit of President LINCOLN'S policy. Meanwhile, that he and his son, the able and courteous Assistant Secretary, lie grievously smitten by the blow that wrings the heart of the nation, a tender solicitude will wait upon their recovery. WILLIAM HENRY SEWARD has too faithfully and conspicuously served human liberty not to have earned a blow from the assassin hand of slavery. The younger generation of American citizens who, in their first manhood, followed his bugle-call into the ranks of those who strove against the infamous power whose dying throes have struck life from the President and joy from a triumphing nation, will not forget how valiant and beneficent his service has been, nor suffer the name so identified with the truest political instruction of this country to be long obscured by the clouds of calumny.

## GREAT PAN IS DEAD.

THE New York Tribune, in a late issue, after reprinting the infamous rebel offer of a reward of a million of dollars for the assassination of Mr. LINCOLN, Mr. JOHNSON, and Mr. SEWARD, says: "such facts and the corresponding editorials of the rebel journals countenance the popular presumption that the late murderous outrages in Washington were incidents of a comprehensive plot whereto the rebel leaders were privy. The burglarious raid on St. Albans, the attempts simultaneously to fire our great hotels, and other acts wholly out of the pale of civilized warfare, tend to strengthen this conviction."

In the next column the Editor speaks of the men who plotted the raid and the arson as "certain distinguished Americans" of the other "party to our civil war."

Does not the editor of the Tribune see that nothing can more profoundly demoralize the public mind than to call the men who plot arson and massacre "distinguished Americans?" ABRAHAM LINCOLN and GEORGE WASHINGTON were distinguished Americans. Has the editor no other epithets for GEORGE N. SANDERS and JACOB THOMPSON and CLEMENT C. CLAY? Is there no such thing as crime? Are there no criminals? Is the assassin of the President a man impelled by "the conflict of ideas" to a mistaken act? Is there no treason? Are there no traitors? Does the editor of the Tribune really suppose that because it is not the wish nor the duty of the American people to visit the penalty of treason upon every man at the South who has been in rebellion, it is therefore the duty of wise and honest men to invite JEFFERSON DAVIS and WIGFALL into the Senate of the United States, or ROBERT E. LEE, BEAUREGARD, and JOE JOHNSTON into the army?

The Editor of the Tribune may bow down to the ground and grovel before "eminent Confederates;" but it is not from them that the pacification of the South is to proceed. The first step in peace is to emancipate the people of the South from their servile dependence upon the class of "gentlemen" which has first deluded and then ruined them. How can it be done if we affect that respect which no honest man can feel? If there is one suffering Union man in Alabama who has been outlawed and hunted and starved, who has lain all day cowering in swamps and woods, and at night has stolen out and crept for food to the faithful slaves upon the plantations—who has seen his house destroyed, his children murdered, his wife dishonored—who has endured every extremity of suffering, and still believed in God and the flag of his country—and who now, following WILSON's liberating march, has come safely to our lines at Mobile—if there be one such man, who knows that his cruel agony and the waste and desolation of his land have come from "the leaders" of his section, and sees that when they are worsted in battle it is the Editor of the New York Tribune who hastens to fall prostrate before the meanest of them and salute them as "distinguished Americans" and "eminent Confederates," it is easy to believe that such a man should be overwhelmed with dismay as he contemplates the hopeless postponement of pacification which such a spectacle reveals.

Exactly that base subservience to the arrogance of a slaveholding class which has enabled that class to seduce and betray the people of their States is reproduced in the tone of the editor of the Tribune when speaking of it. Is JEFFERSON DAVIS a distinguished American?"

Is he any more so than AARON BURR and BENEDICT ARNOLD? No men despise such fawning more than those it is intended to propitiate. It is not by such men as JACOB THOMPSON and CLEMENT C. CLAY and HUNTER and BENJAMIN and SEMMES, it is by men unknown and poor, by men who have seen what comes of following the counsels of the "leaders," by men who have been tried by blood and fire in this sharp war that peace is to come out of the South. The men whom the editor of the Tribune calls by names that justly belong only to our best and dearest are the assassins of the nation and of human liberty. They would have wrought upon the nation the same crime that was done upon the President. They would have murdered the country in its own innocent blood. Not from them conies regeneration and peace. Let them fly.

But from the long-abused, the blinded, the down-trodden, the forgotten, the despised—from the real people of the South, whom riches and ease and luxury and cultivation and idleness and, all worldly gifts and graces sitting in high places, drugged with sophistries, and seduced with blandishments, and

threatened with terrors, and besotted with prejudice, and degraded with ignorance, and ground into slavery—these, all of them, white and black as God made them, are the seed of the new South, long pressed into the ground, and now about to sprout and grow and blossom jubilantly with peace and prosperity. Old things have passed away. The Editor of the Tribune is still flattering the priests whose power has gone. Great Pan is dead. Why should one of the earliest Christians swing incense before him?

## THE FLAG ON SUMTER.

THE old flag floats again on Sumter! Four years ago it was the hope, the prayer, the vow of the American people. Today the vow is fulfilled. The hand of him who defended it against the assault of treason, of him who saluted it sadly as he marched his little band away, now, with all the strength of an aroused and regenerated nation supporting him, raises it once more to its place, and the stars that have still shone on undimmed in our hearts now shine tranquilly in triumph, and salute the earth and sky with the benediction of peace.

To be called to be the orator of a nation upon

such a day was an honor which might have oppressed any man. To have spoken for the nation at such a moment, worthily, adequately, grandly, is the glory of one man. It will not be questioned that Mr. BEECHER did so. His oration is of the noblest spirit and the loftiest eloquence. It is in the highest degree picturesque and powerful. Certainly it was peculiarly fit that a man, fully inspired by the eternal truth that has achieved the victory, should hail, in the name of equal liberty, the opening of the era which is to secure it.

Even amidst the wail of our sorrow its voice will be heard and its tone will satisfy. Even in our heart's grief we can feel the solemn thrill of triumph that the flag which fell in weakness is raised in glory and power.

## THE FOLLY OF CRIME.

EVERY stupendous crime is an enormous blunder. The blow that has shocked the nation exasperates it, and in killing ABRA-HAM LINCOLN the rebels have murdered their best friend. His death can not change the event of the war. It has only united the loyal people of the country more closely than ever, and disposed them to a less lenient policy toward the rebellion. Whatever the intention or hope of the murder, whether it were the result of a matured plot or the act of a band of ruffians, whether it were dictated by the rebel chiefs or offered to their cause as a voluntary assistance by the hand that struck the blow, the effect is the same—a more intense and inflexible vow of the nation that the rebellion shall be suppressed and its cause exterminated.

There is no crime so abhorrent to the world as the assassination of a public man. Even when he is unworthy, the method of his death at once ameliorates the impression of his life. But when he is a good and wise man, when he is spotless and beloved, the infamy is too monstrous for words. There is but one assassin whom history mentions with toleration and even applause, and that is CHARLOTTE CORDAY. But her act was a mistake. It ended the life of a monster, but it did not help the people, and she who might have lived to succor and save some victim of MARAT, became, after his death, MARAT'S victim. All other assassins, too, have more harmed their cause than helped it. Their pleas of justification are always confounded by the event. That plea, where it has any dignity whatever, is the riddance of the world of a bad or dangerous man whose life can not be legally taken. It is to punish a despot—to bring low a tyrant. But the heart recoils whatever the excuse, the instinct of mankind curses the assassin.

In our own grievous affliction there is one lesson which those who directly address public opinion would do well to consider. Party malignity in the Free States during the war has not scrupled to defame the character of Mr. LINCOLN. He has been denounced as a despot, as a usurper, as a man who arbitrarily annulled the Constitution, as a magistrate under whose administration all the securities of liberty, property, and even life, were deliberately disregarded and imperiled. Political hostility has been inflamed into hate by the assertion that he was responsible for the war, and that he had opened all the yawning graves and tumbled the bloody victims in. This has been done directly and indirectly, openly and cunningly. In a time of necessarily profound and painful excitement, to carry a party point, the political opponents of Mr. LINCOLN have said or insinuated or implied that he had superseded the laws and had made himself an autocrat. If any dangerous plot has been exposed, these organs of public opinion had sneered at it as an invention of the Administration. If theatres and hotels full of men, women, and children were to be wantonly fired, the friends of the Administration were accused of cooking up an excitement. If bloody riots and massacres occurred, they were extenuated, and called "risings of the people," as if in justifiable vengeance, and as if the oppression of the Government had brought them upon itself.

This appeal has been made in various ways and in different degrees. A great convention intimated that there was danger that the elections would be overborne by Administration bayonets. Judge COMSTOCK, formerly of the Court of Appeals in this State, addressing a crowd in Union Square, declared that if a candidate for the Presidency should be defrauded of his election by military interference he would be borne into the White House by the hands of the people. Of the Administration thus accused of the basest conceivable crimes ABRAHAM LINCOLN was the head. If there were a military despotism in the country, as was declared, he was the despot. If there were a tyranny, he was the tyrant.

Is it surprising that somebody should have believed all this, that somebody should have said, if there is a tyranny it can not be very criminal to slay the tyrant, and that working himself up to the due frenzy he should strike the blow? When it was struck, when those kind eyes that never looked sternly upon a human being closed forever, and the assassin sprang forward and cried, Sic semper tyrannis, was it not a ghastly commentary upon those who had not scrupled to teach that he was a tyrant who had annulled the law?

The lesson is terrible. Let us hope that even party-spirit may be tempered by this result of its natural consequence.

## A SUGGESTION FOR A MONUMENT.

IT is very possible that the great affection of the people of the United States for their late President will lead to a general desire to erect some national monument to his memory. Should this be so, there is one suggestion which will doubtless occur to many besides ourselves. It is that no mere marble column or memorial pile shall be reared, but that the heart-offerings of the people shall be devoted to the erection of a military hospital, to be called the LINCOLN HOSPITAL, for soldiers and sailors—a retreat for the wounded and permanently invalid veterans of the war.

When, in the happier days that are coming, the wards shall be relieved of the lingering monuments of the contest, the foundation would remain for the public benefit. The soldiers and sailors had no more tender and faithful friend than ABRAHAM LINCOLN. He never forgot them; nor did he fail always to pay to them in his public addresses the homage which his heart constantly cherished. To a man of his broad and generous humanity no monument could be so appropriate as a Hospital.

## DOMESTIC INTELLIGENCE.
## OUR SUCCESSES IN NORTH CAROLINA.

GENERAL STONEMAN captured Salisbury, North Carolina, on the 12th inst., securing 1165 prisoners, 19 pieces of artillery, 1000 small-arms, and eight Stands of colors. The plunder found there was enormous, embracing 1,000,000 rounds of ammunition, 1000 shells, 60,000 pounds of powder, 75,000 suits of clothing, 35,000 army blankets, with large quantities of bacon, salt, sugar, rice, wheat, and 7000 bales of cotton. All that was not immediately available was destroyed. Stoneman's raid in East Tennessee and North Carolina has been one of the most important and des-

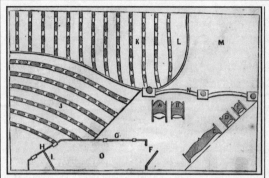

0. Dark Corridor leading from the Dress Circle to Box.—H. Entrance to Corridor. I. The bar used by Booth to prevent entrance from without.—J. Dress Circle.—K. The Parquette.—L. The Foot-lights.—M. The Stage.—F. Open door to the President's Box.—G. Closed door.—N. Place where Booth vaulted over to the Stage below

### PLAN OF THE BOX OCCUPIED BY PRESIDENT LINCOLN AT FORD'S THEATER, APRIL 14, 1865

tructive of the war. He has burned half a hundred important bridges, destroyed about 100 miles of track, captured trains, burned depots, and played the mischief generally with secesh property.

The next day after the capture of Salisbury, Sherman occupied Raleigh, with but little resistance. Governor Vance was taken by our cavalry on the same day. It is said that he was deputed by Johnston to surrender the State, but the power was afterward withdrawn. It is reported that Jeff Davis had joined Johnston at Hillsborough, and was still with him,

### CAPTURE OF MOBILE.

Mobile was captured by the national forces on the 12th of April.

On the 20th of March the Sixteenth Corps, under General A. J. Smith, left Dauphin on twenty transports, accompanied by gun-boats, and proceeded up an arm of Mobile Bay to the mouth of Fish River, where the troops were landed at Dauley's Mills. The Thirteenth Corps, under General Granger, left Fort Morgan, and on the 21st of March went into camp on the left of Smith, resting its left wing on Mobile Bay. Three days afterward this corps was followed by General Knipe with 6000 cavalry. On the 25th the Federal line was pushed forward so as to extend from Alabama City on the bay to Deer Park. The first point of attack was Spanish Fort, which is directly opposite

Mobile, and is the latest built and strongest of the defenses of that city. It guards the eastern channel of the bay. On the 27th the bombardment commenced. In the mean time the Monitors and gunboats were laboring hard to overcome the obstructions. They had succeeded so far that the Monitors Milwaukee, Winnebago, Kickapoo, and the Monitor ram Osage moved in line to attack at 3 P.M. An hour afterward a torpedo exploded. under the Milwaukee, and she immediately filled and sunk in eleven feet of water. There were no casualties. There was steady firing all night and the next day. At about 2 o'clock P.M. on the 29th a torpedo struck the port bow of the Osage and exploded, tearing away the plating and timbers, killing two men and wounding several others.

We give on page 268 an engraving illustrating the nature of the torpedoes found in the Bay. Those given in the sketch are those with the mushroom-shaped anchor. The slightest pressure causes explosion.

On the 8th of April an extraordinary force was brought to bear upon Spanish Fort. Twenty-two Parrott guns were got within half a mile of the work, while other powerful batteries were still nearer. Two gunboats joined in the tremendous cannonade. The result was that the fort surrendered a little after midnight. Fort Alexandria followed, and the guns of these two were turned against Forts Tracy and Huger, in the harbor, at the mouth of the Blakely and Appalachee rivers. But these had already been abandoned. The Monitors then went busily to work removing torpedoes, and ran up to within shelling distance of the city.

Shortly after the capture of Spanish Fort, intelligence of the capture and the fall of Richmond was read to the troops, in connection with orders to attack Fort Blakely. Several batteries of artillery, and large quantities of ammunition were taken with the fort, besides 2400 prisoners. Our loss in the whole affair was much less than 2000 killed and wounded, and none missing.

Seven hundred prisoners were taken with Spanish Fort. Mobile was occupied by the national forces on the 12th. In the mean time General Wilson, with a formidable force of cavalry, had swept through the State of Alabama. He left Eastport about the 20th of March, and advanced in two columns, each of

which, at about the same time, fought Forrest's cavalry, one at Marion and the other at Plantersville, which were respectively situated about 20 miles northwest and northeast of Selma. On the afternoon of April 2 Selma was captured, with 22 guns, and all the immense Government works, arsenals, rolling-mills, and foundries at that place were destroyed. It is probable that Montgomery was also captured, but later than the capture of Selma we have no details.

## MOURNING IN RICHMOND.

Roger A. Pryor stated in Petersburg that he believed Mr. Lincoln indispensable to the restoration of peace, and regretted his death more than any military mishap of the south. He and the Mayor placed themselves at the head of a movement for a town meeting to deplore the loss on both private and public grounds. General Robert E. Lee at first refused to hear the details of the murder. A Mr. Suite and another gentleman waited upon him on Sunday night with the particulars. He said that when he dispossessed himself of the command of the rebel forces he kept in mind President Lincoln's benignity, and surrendered as much to the latter's goodness as to Grant's artillery.

The General said that he regretted Mr. Lincoln's death as much as any man in the North, and believed him to be the epitome of magnanimity and good faith.

## ARREST OF SEWARD'S ASSASSIN.

A man was arrested on the 18th in Baltimore who is supposed to have been the assassin of Secretary Seward. He was recognized as such by the negro servant and Miss Fanny Seward.

## FOREIGN NEWS. THE REBEL RAM "STONEWALL."

The rebel ram Stonewall left Lisbon, Portugal, on the 28th of March, having been ordered away by the Portuguese authorities. The national steamers Niagara and Sacramento were forbidden to leave until twenty-four hours should have elapsed. These two vessels, about four hours after the Stonewall left, weighed anchor and moved toward the bar. The commander of the Belem Tower then fired upon them, considerably injuring the Niagara. The captains stated that they were only changing their anchorage-ground, and our consul at Lisbon has demanded that the Governor of Belem Tower should be removed, which demand has been conceded.

# NOTES

From a research standpoint, the events before, during, and after the Lincoln assassination were ideal. The many articles and eyewitness accounts were laden with an astounding amount of information. The following list of books, websites, and other archived information reflects the main research sources for this book. It bears mentioning that visits to the Sayler's Creek Battlefield, High Bridge, Appomattox Court House, Ford's Theatre, and the various historical sites along John Wilkes Booth's escape route will add immeasurably to the reader's understanding of all that came to pass in April 1865.

## Part One: TOTAL WAR

The siege of Petersburg and Lee's subsequent flight across the Virginia countryside are all very well documented. Some of the most fascinating insights came from the soldiers and generals who were there, many of whom wrote their memoirs and recollections years later. In reading them, one is transported back to that moment in time. The accounts of Sayler's Creek and the Battle of High Bridge, in particular, are vivid portrayals of courage under fire. What follows is a brief list of the books used in our research; thanks to the magic of Google's online books, many of the older titles can be easily accessed: *Red, White and Blue Badge: Pennsylvania Veteran Volunteers*, by Penrose G. Mark; *Confederate Veteran*, by S. A. Cunningham; *Battles and Leaders of the Civil War*, by Robert Underwood Johnson; *Pickett and His Men*, by La Salle Corbett Pickett; *Lee's Last Retreat: The Flight to Appomattox*, by William Marvel; *Four Years Under Marse Robert*, by Robert Stiles; *General Lee: A Biography of Robert E. Lee*, by Fitzhugh Lee; *Military Memoirs of a Confederate*, by Edward Porter Alexander; *Meade's*

*Headquarters, 1863–1865,* by Theodore Lyman; *Grant,* by Jean Edward Smith; *Lee,* by Douglas Southall Freeman; *Personal Memoirs of U. S. Grant,* by Ulysses S. Grant; *From Manassas to Appomattox: The Personal Memoirs of James Longstreet,* by James Longstreet; *Lee's Lieutenants: A Study in Command,* by Douglas Southall Freeman and Stephen W. Sears; *Tom Custer: Ride to Glory,* by Carl F. Day; *The Military Annals of Lancaster, Massachusetts,* by Henry Steadman Norse; *Biography of Francis P. Washburn,* by Michael K. Sorenson; and *The Memoirs of General P. H. Sheridan,* by General Philip Henry Sheridan. The Virginia Military Institute's online archive (http://www.vmi.edu/archives.aspx?id=3945) offers links to several more firsthand letters. In addition, the very excellent *Atlas of the Civil War,* by James M. McPherson, was always within arm's reach during the writing process; it shows in great detail the battle maps and movements of two great armies.

## Part Two: THE IDES OF DEATH

Writing about the chaotic final days of Lincoln's life meant accessing all manner of research, from online documents (such as the *New York Times'*s findings about Lincoln's Baptist upbringing) to websites devoted to the Lincoln White House (in particular, www.mrlincolnswhitehouse.org provided a treasure trove of information about everything from floor layouts to daily life, very often told in first-person accounts). The number of websites and easily accessed online articles is endless, and hundreds were scrutinized during the writing of this book.

The reader searching for an overview of April 1865 is encouraged to read the aptly named *April 1865,* by Jay Winik, which frames the events quite well. Other books of note: *"They Have Killed Papa Dead,"* by Anthony S. Pitch, and *American Brutus,* by Michael W. Kauffman; *Team of Rivals,* by Doris Kearns Goodwin; *Lincoln's Last Month,* by William C. Harris; *Lincoln's Body Guard: The Union Light Guard of Ohio,* by Robert McBride; and *Blood on the Moon: The Assassination of Abraham Lincoln,* by Edward Steers. For a compelling history of Washington, D.C., itself, the reader is encouraged to find a copy of *Washington Schlepped Here,* by Christopher Buckley.

## Part Three: THE LONG GOOD FRIDAY

For an hour-by-hour description of April 15, 1865, see the excellent *A. Lincoln: His Last 24 Hours,* by W. Emerson Reck; *The Day Lincoln Was*

*Shot*, by Jim Bishop; *Lincoln's Last Hours*, by Charles Augustus Leale; and *Abraham Lincoln*, by Carl Sandburg.

Of great interest are titles that offer conflicting viewpoints of the assassination, the motivations, and the people involved. Perhaps the most fascinating aspect of researching the Lincoln assassination was poring over the many very good books dedicated to this topic and the shock of discovering that many disagree completely with one another. *Dark Union*, by Leonard Guttridge and Ray Neff, and *Spies, Traitors, and Moles*, by Peter Kross are two of the more controversial titles.

For information on Mary Surratt, see *Assassin's Accomplice*, by Kate Clifford Larson.

## Part Four: THE CHASE

The search for Lincoln's killers and their subsequent trial was vividly portrayed in Kauffman's *American Brutus* and James L. Swanson's *Manhunt*. *Potomac Diary*, by Richtmyer Hubbell, provides fascinating insights into the mood in Washington. *History of the United States Secret Service*, by Lafayette Baker, is a rather verbose and self-aggrandizing account of Baker's exploits. Also of note: *Beware the People Weeping*, by Thomas Reed Turner; *Lincoln Legends*, by Edward Steers; *Right or Wrong, God Judge Me: The Writings of John Wilkes Booth*, by John Wilkes Booth; *The Life of Dr. Samuel A. Mudd*, by Samuel A. Mudd; and *Lincoln's Assassins*, by Roy Z. Chamlee

The arguments of Special Judge Advocate John A. Bingham can be found in *Trial of the Conspirators for the Assassination of President Abraham Lincoln*, by John Armor Bingham. Testimony can be found at http://www .surratt.org/documents/Bplact02.pdf.

# INDEX

Page numbers in *italics* refer to illustrations.

## About the Authors

**Bill O'Reilly** is the anchor of *The O'Reilly Factor*, the highest-rated cable news show in the country. He also writes a syndicated newspaper column and is the author of several number-one bestselling books. He is, perhaps, the most talked about political commentator in America.

**Martin Dugard** is the *New York Times* best-selling author of several books of history. His book *Into Africa: The Epic Adventures of Stanley and Livingstone* has been adapted into a History Channel special. He lives in Southern California with his wife and three sons.